MONTEVERDI

CLAUDIO MONTEVERDI

*[From the portrait reproduced in the " Fiori Poetici " (1644), in
the possession of the Biblioteca Ambrosiana in Milan.]*

MONTEVERDI

HIS LIFE AND WORK

BY

HENRY PRUNIÈRES

TRANSLATED FROM THE FRENCH BY

MARIE D. MACKIE

WITH NUMEROUS MUSIC EXAMPLES

DOVER PUBLICATIONS, INC.
NEW YORK

Published in Canada by General Publishing Company, Ltd., 30 Lesmill Road, Don Mills, Toronto, Ontario.
Published in the United Kingdom by Constable and Company, Ltd., 10 Orange Street, London WC 2.

This Dover edition, first published in 1972, is an unabridged republication of the work originally published by E. P. Dutton & Company, New York, in 1926. The present edition is published by special arrangement with J. M. Dent & Sons, Ltd., London.

International Standard Book Number: 0-486-22770-7
Library of Congress Catalog Card Number: 70-159686

Manufactured in the United States of America
Dover Publications, Inc.
180 Varick Street
New York, N. Y. 10014

FOREWORD

THE object of the present volume is to combine the story of Monteverdi's life with a critical study of his works. In spite of long and patient research in Italian archives, it has been possible to add here relatively little new material to the biography of the Master. On this subject, all that matters has been published long since. The investigations of Padre Caffi (1858), Padre Canal, S. Davari (1885), Angelo Solerti, Ademollo, Picenardi, and Emilio Vogel have provided documents which permit of a complete reconstitution of the life of the great musician, and it is in view of such a reconstitution that I have considered Monteverdi as far as possible in relation to the artistic circle in which he moved, among the composers contemporary to him, and that I have dwelt upon the life of the courts and cities in which his passionate life was lived, in which his talent was formed and matured.

The work of Monteverdi has, up to the present, been the subject of fragmentary and specialized studies only. The works of Goldschmidt, Alfred Heuss, Leichtentritt, Vogel, Riemann, Ambros, Kretschmar, and Cesari respectively, have borne upon particular aspects of a genius which, *ondoyant et divers*, is disconcerting in its multiplicity. In my opinion, it is Romain Rolland who, without embarking upon a technical study of the work of Monteverdi, has given us the profoundest judgments of it. With an intuition bordering upon genius, he has entered into Monteverdi's very soul, and defined synthetically the essential characteristics of his art. One can only regret that he should have confined himself to the dramatic works, and that he should have found no occasion to speak of the madrigals, of the sacred music, of the songs and cantatas, which are equally important. I have tried to throw light upon every aspect of Monteverdi's creative activity. I do not pretend, however, to have exhausted so vast a subject. Only a small part of his work has appeared as yet. Of the last collections of madrigals, of the *scherzi*, the *canzonette*, of all the religious compositions, only ancient editions in separate parts exist. Frequently these parts are scattered and the *tenor* has to be copied at Bologna, the *superius* at Breslau, and so on. I have tried to give an idea of the different styles practised successively or simultaneously by Monteverdi, and I believe that I am the first to make this attempt. Whilst the æsthetic ideal of the master varied little, yet his methods were continually modified in the course of time ; I have tried to mark the stages of this evolution.

Though Monteverdi was incontestably a great inventor of new forms, no one was more sensitive to surrounding influences. Certainly he saw clearly much that some of his contemporaries saw dimly, and achieved what others had scarcely dared to attempt ; but it seemed to me necessary, in order the better to explain the true significance of this master, who was without doubt the greatest of Italian musicians, to study his work in relation to that of his contemporaries and rivals.

I hope that those readers who find the critical study of his work too arduous will find some interest in the biography, rich in dramatic events, of a musician who knew the life of courts and camps, and whose great soul laboured under affliction for many years.

CONTENTS

PART I
MONTEVERDI AT CREMONA AND MANTUA (1567–1613)

PART II
THE DRAMATIC SPECTACLES AT THE COURT OF MANTUA

PART III
MONTEVERDI AT VENICE (1613–1643)

APPENDICES

PART I

*MONTEVERDI AT CREMONA AND
MANTUA (1567-1613)*

I

EARLY YEARS

1567–1605

On May 15th, 1567, Baldassare Monteverdi had his first-born child baptized in the church of SS. Nazari e Celso at Cremona, and gave him the names of Claudio Zuan Antonio.*

Baldassare, a doctor by profession, was in relatively easy circumstances, a worthy citizen, a man of culture and authority, devoted body and soul to the interests of his family, and gifted with a shrewd sense of the value of money. Such, at least, is the impression we get of him in his letters. There were many Monteverdis in Cremona, and it would be hazardous to try to establish bonds of family relationship between all whose names appear in the records of the town, yet it is evident that among his collateral relations and his ancestors, Claudio numbered doctors and musicians, or at least musical instrument makers.†

Cremona was celebrated, from the sixteenth century onward, for musical instrument workshops in which all kinds of stringed and wind instruments were skilfully manufactured. Charles IX of France sent to Cremona for violins for his musicians, and in 1585 the Duke of Mantua ordered wooden trumpets (*trombetti di legno*) from a maker whose name was no other than Domenico Monteverdi.‡

The inhabitants of Cremona were renowned for their industry and fine workmanship. They excelled as much in

---

* See Note 1. † See Note 2. ‡ See Note 3.

3

the weaving of delicate fabrics of silk and linen mixed as in the manufacture of violins of perfect shape. The Spanish rule, which weighed heavily upon the town, had not at this time succeeded in ruining its prosperity with taxes, *corvées* and levies. The severity of the foreign administration was tempered by the influence, temporal as well as spiritual, of Carlo Borromeo, a saint and a man of action, far-sighted and passionately devoted to his country. Attentive to his wise counsel, the Governor of Milan, to whose authority Cremona was subject, refrained from any systematic molestation of the Italians such as was later carried on by the Viceroy Fuentes, who, perturbed by Campanella's enterprise at Naples, and by the spirit of revolt which was manifesting itself among the peoples of Lombardy, turned the whole of Milan into an entrenched camp, ruining the citizens with crushing taxation, and the peasants with the enforced housing and feeding of his hordes of ruthless and greedy mercenaries.

Cremona was destined to suffer particularly from the Spanish exactions. The pride, the courage, the independent spirit of its inhabitants gave cause for anxiety. They gloried in their descent from ancient Roman families, and still looked back to the time when Signor Gabrino Fondulio, finding himself the object of the simultaneous adulation of Emperor Sigismund and Pope John XXIII, had, from the height of the gigantic Torrazo, displayed to these masters of the world the red city of Cremona girdled with high ramparts flanked with massive towers, with its palaces, its churches, its squares, its broad streets, and in the distance the fertile plain covered with rich crops, the vines hanging from the trunks of elm and poplar, the countless mills along the canal-banks, and the villages and castles with white walls gleaming through the verdure.

The inhabitants of Cremona, justifiably proud of their town, boasted of the Torrazo, " the wonder of Europe," the highest tower in Italy, and even, they said, in the world; of the cathedral in which were preserved the relics of more than one hundred and sixty saints; and finally of the very air they breathed, that *aria di Cremona*, so pure, so healthy, without its like in Italy. It would seem as though the temple, whose traces are to be seen near the gate of San Michele, erected, according to tradition, by the Romans to the Goddess Fever, had averted from the entire district the pestilence which ravaged the neighbouring provinces.*

The Emperor Sigismund had endowed Cremona with a university, the statutes and privileges of which were copied from those of the famous universities of Paris and Bologna. Though fallen from its ancient splendour, it maintained in the town a centre of culture. It was doubtless at this university that Claudio Monteverdi studied the humanities. It is certain that he received a sound education, thanks to which he was able subsequently to read the classics with profit, particularly Plato, whose doctrine was a constant subject of meditation with him. His correspondence shows evidence of a culture remarkable even at a time when musicians were on the whole more lettered than they usually are to-day.

He was certainly brought up in good middle-class surroundings, where art and letters were held in high esteem. His elder brother, Giulio Cesare, became, like himself, a musician, and this would lead us to believe that Baldassare Monteverdi was not hostile to his sons' vocation.† For that matter, music was so highly esteemed that there were at that time few professions in which it was possible to acquire so much honour and material benefit.

It is extremely likely that Monteverdi was at first a pupil of the choir-school of the cathedral. It was customary at that time for the *Maestro di Cappella* to teach his pupils not only church-singing, but also the rudiments of counterpoint and

* See Note 4.   † See Note 5.

composition. Monteverdi, moreover, refers to himself as a pupil of the *Maestro di Cappella* of the cathedral in the titles of his first works. As it happened, his master, Marc Antonio Ingegneri, was one of the foremost of Italian composers. Monteverdi could not have been in better hands, for fiery temperaments, naturally impatient of discipline, require to learn self-control in submission to the strict laws of art, before they can allow themselves by their own mastery to infringe those laws.

There was in Ingegneri something of the man of genius. His true value has gradually been acknowledged since his recognition as the author of twenty-seven responses, wrongly published under the name of Palestrina, which indeed would be worthy of that great musician if they were not written in a style absolutely different from that of the Maestro of Proeneste.* Ingegneri initiated his pupil into the secrets of counterpoint. He taught him to construct a motet and a mass in severe style, as well as to write *canzonette, villanelle* and madrigals with all the liberties permitted in these forms. At the same time he taught him singing and instrumental music. His reputation was equally great as organist and as violist, and under his direction Claudio soon attained a high degree of technical skill in playing several instruments.

At eighteen years of age, Monteverdi published his first works—spiritual madrigals for four voices—and had them published at Brescia with a dedication to Alessandro Franganesco, a rich citizen of Cremona. This work is dated July 31st, 1583. Unfortunately, only the bass part is extant, and it is not possible to form from it any idea of Monteverdi's talent at this time.

The following year, the *Canzonette a tre voci* appeared at Venice. In this graceful and popular genre, in which extreme

* See Note 6.

liberty of composition was not only tolerated, but to a certain extent consciously cultivated, Monteverdi already gave evidence of remarkable gifts. It was, however, in his first book of madrigals for five voices, published in 1587 by Gardano of Venice, that his budding genius first became manifest. In the title of this book, as in those of the preceding collections, he calls himself the pupil of Marc Antonio Ingegneri, but a perusal of the work soon shows how faithless the disciple was.

These madrigals are dedicated to a nobleman of Cremona, Count Marco Verità, who had patronised the author at his début, as Monteverdi shows in his preface. " I beseech my Lord, accept these madrigals as a simple testimony of my gratitude for the favours I have received at your hands. . . . And I can expect for compositions so youthful no other praise than that which is accorded to the flowers of Spring." *

Whilst this book is permeated with an exquisite atmosphere of youth, a study of the works which it contains reveals, as we shall see later, a command of technique, a boldness of composition extraordinary in an adolescent. Monteverdi's originality develops and becomes more striking in each of the succeeding books of madrigals.

He seems, however, to have been preoccupied with the problem of obtaining a settled situation. He went to Milan, and there won general praise for his talent as violist and composer.† In 1590 he dedicated his second book of madrigals to a Milanese amateur, Giacomo Ricardi. It is quite possible that it was during his stay at Milan that Monteverdi was brought to the notice of the Duke of Mantua, who was always on the watch for genuine talent. In any case, it was in the capacity of violist that he was engaged by Duke Vincenzo in the same year.

* See Note 7.   † See Note 8.

Mantua was at this time disputing with Venice and Ferrara the artistic hegemony of Northern Italy. For two centuries poets, painters, musicians, sculptors, architects had been flocking thither from every corner of Europe, in the certainty of finding honour and material advantage.

When Monteverdi entered the service of the Gonzaga family, Duke Vincenzo had been reigning for three years, and had spent much time on the reorganization and extension of his company of musicians. He had inherited from his father, Duke Guglielmo, a veritable passion for literature and the arts, and had become something of a connoisseur. He dabbled in poetry himself, and cultivated the society of artists and men of learning. He liberated Tasso, protected Galilei, attracted Pourbus and Rubens to his court, kept the most famous company of actors in Italy, and, as we shall see, contributed to enlightening Monteverdi upon the true direction of his genius by commissioning him to write musical dramas.

Vincenzo was the type incarnate of the princes of the Italian Renaissance, devoted to display, to fêtes, plays, balls, ballets, generous and cruel,* assassinating without hesitation any artist who failed them, overwhelming with gifts those who served them well. As a youth, he had been feared for his violence and cruelty. In 1582 his father had even banished him from his territory as the result of the cowardly assassination of the Scottish humanist, James Crichton—*l'ammirabile Critonio*. Meeting him one night, Vincenzo collided violently against him in the dark; Crichton drew his sword, and they fought. At Vincenzo's cry, " Hold, Scot, I am the Prince," Crichton knelt and delivered his sword. Vincenzo took it and plunged it in his heart. Ten years later, Vincenzo had settled down considerably; but not so much as to justify us in agreeing with the historian

* See Note 9.

who finds in his foppish face the mark of a magnanimous spirit.

Big and broad, fresh-coloured like a German, with blue eyes, thin hair curling on the temples, his face elongated by a short pointed beard, he was still handsome at nearly fifty years of age, and dressed sumptuously. There was much talk in Italy of his amorous adventures, and of the circumstances of his first marriage, which he had had annulled after some strange machinations. He got on well with his second wife, Eleanora de' Medici, who was indifferent to his manner of life.

He displayed extraordinary ardour in the pursuit of his pleasures. Love or music, the chase or the theatre, painting or alchemy, absorbed him successively. He brought as much diplomacy to bear on the purchase of Raphael's Madonna from the Canossa as on the acquisition of a province. Like his ancestors, who loved to have their portraits painted on the walls of their palaces with their favourite dogs and horses, he had a passion for these animals. His stables and kennels were famous. He was a great traveller, and visited Germany, France, Flanders, Hungary, Holland and Lorraine. He fought thrice against the Turks. Invariably accompanied by a splendid suite, he traversed Europe in search of pictures to buy, or artists to attach to his court.

There was at times something morbid in this perpetual agitation. Rubens' fine portrait gives him a strange expression. Vincenzo lacked his father's admirable mental balance. He was surrounded with astrologers and alchemists, to the despair of his wife, who knew that many a foreign court was chuckling over the prince who spent whole nights in breathless pursuit of the great secret.

From the moment of his accession, Vincenzo had busied himself in engaging the best musicians of Italy for his company. His *Maestro di Cappella* was the Dutch Giaches de

Wert, who had held the post since 1565. This remarkable composer of madrigals and motets was much appreciated by musicians and highly esteemed by the prince. Yet he had passed through difficult times. The singers under his direction had for years persecuted him outrageously. The most desperate of them all had even conceived the idea of wreaking vengeance on him by seducing his wife.* But time had passed, and the old composer was universally respected when Monteverdi settled in Mantua.

Towards 1581 Giaches de Wert had handed over the choir of the ducal chapel of Santa Barbara to his second-in-command, the excellent composer, Gian Giacomo Gastoldi, who, about the time that Monteverdi entered the service of the Gonzagas, was on the point of gaining an immense reputation throughout Europe by his charming *Balletti*, or *chansons à danser* for four or five voices, which could, however, easily be sung by a solo voice with lute accompaniment, or played by instruments for dancing. Few works, towards the end of the sixteenth century, had as great a success. Editions were published in various towns in Italy, France, Flanders and Germany.† Gastoldi was not only an elegant court musician ; he had written with equal success a large number of masses, motets, and canticles (*laude*).

At Mantua, Monteverdi was also in touch with the celebrated composer of sacred music, Viadana, *Maestro di Cappella* at the cathedral (San Pietro). The detail is important, for Viadana probably exercised some influence on Monteverdi's earliest religious compositions.

The organist of Santa Barbara at the same period was the composer Francesco Rovigo, who, having studied at Venice under Claudio Merulo, had returned to the court of Mantua after some years in Germany. He died on October 7th, 1597, one year later than Giaches de Wert.‡

* See Note 10.   † See Note 11.   ‡ See Note 12.

A Cremonese composer, Benedetto Pallavicini, who had been in the service of the Duke since 1582, then became *Maestro di Cappella.* He was an artist of some eminence who had given proof of his talent by the publication of a large number of sacred and secular compositions. He died on November 26th, 1601. Monteverdi, already *Maestro di Camera*, succeeded him.*

During the whole reign of Vincenzo there was so much coming and going among the musicians that it is very difficult to establish even approximately the membership either of the *Cappella* or of the *Camera.* We know that some dozen singers, who numbered among them composers of note, figured on the budget of the *Cappella* when Monteverdi entered the Duke's service. He must during some time have been a member of this company. He is called *cantore* by a functionary of the court, in a letter dated September 23rd, 1594.† We know, however, from the dedication of his third book of Madrigals that it was by virtue of his talent as violist that he was summoned to Mantua.‡

There was a very large number of instrumental performers at the court. Bertolotti quotes the name of seven violists in the pay of the Duke during the year 1597.§ Occasionally they formed a little orchestra for dancing, but generally they performed alone, or took part in madrigals. Indeed, after 1580 a madrigal was rarely sung *a cappella.* Most frequently, instruments and voices were combined, the instruments sometimes doubling the voices, sometimes replacing them. On the other hand, it was the exception for an orchestra to play compositions specially written for instruments, a fashion common in France. The Florentine company, the Francesini, formed and directed by a Frenchman, aroused the delighted wonder of the musicians, who confessed that they had never heard a concert given by a large number of different instruments playing together.*

Monteverdi, who was both an instrumentalist and a singer, must often have taken an active part in the performance of his own madrigals, and thus have found himself in continual relations with the Duke's singers, men and women. The latter formed a large and choice company. Vincenzo was very proud of them, and only permitted them to perform in public on solemn occasions, reserving to himself the pleasure of private performances.

The letters published by Ademollo † give us an idea of the extraordinary pains the Duke would take to attract to his court a woman-singer whose talent had been brought to his notice by his correspondents. A treaty with a neighbouring state gave him less trouble than the engagement of a *virtuosa* such as the famous Adriana Basile, who for many years graced his court. The engagement of the exquisite Caterinuccia Martinelli completely wore out all the Duke's secretaries. It was not enough to have the most satisfactory information about her voice; they must find out whether this child of thirteen years was virtuous and chaste; they had to decide whether Giulio Caccini at Florence, or Monteverdi at Mantua, should take her training in hand; and, when they had decided for Monteverdi, her itinerary from Rome, her native city, had to be drawn up in the most minute detail. We shall have elsewhere occasion to speak of the principal women-singers of the court in discussing the performances of the *Orfeo* and the *Arianna*.

Among those who belonged to what Ademollo irreverently calls the musical harem of the Duke was the daughter of one of the violists of the Court, Claudia Cataneo. Monteverdi appears to have fallen in love with her only a few months after his arrival at Mantua, and married her with Vincenzo's

consent. By her he had two sons, Francesco and Massimiliano, to whose future he later devoted himself with
passionate attention.*

A short time after his marriage, Monteverdi received
orders to prepare for a long journey. Vincenzo had decided
to conduct in person the troops he had raised to the assistance of the Emperor Rodolph, who was being threatened
by the new Sultan, Mohammed III. Magnificent as ever,
the Duke of Mantua was accompanied on this warlike expedition by a large troop of courtiers and servants necessary to
his habits or his pleasures. Among them were several of
his favourite singers. Claudio Monteverdi numbered among
his travelling companions the eunuch Feodoro Bacchino,
and the bass-singers Serafino Terzo and G. B. Marinoni.†
The latter seems to have been his particular friend. At
the evening halt, in the Duke's tent, Monteverdi and his
companions would frequently receive orders to perform
madrigals, singing and playing their parts on various
instruments.

We do not know what were the musician's impressions
during the unfortunate campaign of 1596. Rodolph's
army arrived too late to prevent the Turks from taking the
fortress of Erlau on the Transylvanian frontier, and finally
suffered the heavy defeat of Keresztes, by which the Sultan
became master of almost the whole of Hungary. Was
Monteverdi present at these battles? Did he hear the
groans of the dying on the battlefields, the distant thunder
of the cavalry attack? It seems probable. In any case,
the fact that he knew camp-life at first hand, that he had
shared the fatigue of armed men riding through distant

* See Note 19.   † See Note 20.

countries, helps one to understand the heroic and martial spirit which animates certain of his works.   On the Hungarian battlefields, he certainly garnered a rich store of impressions, which served him well in the composition of the *Combattimento* and the warrior madrigals.

Before setting out, Monteverdi had taken his wife to Cremona, and left her with his father, Baldassare Monteverdi. The financial situation of the young couple was not brilliant. The musician had a certain position to keep up at Mantua, and was obliged to have a carriage and horses, and men and women servants.   His monthly salary was only twelve and a half Mantuan crowns, that of his wife, ninety-four Mantuan lire.   During his absence his wife received only half of this meagre salary, and the business of supplying her needs devolved upon the old doctor.   The composer himself had had considerable expenses to meet in the course of his travels, and came home heavily in debt.   He had, moreover, suffered disappointment in another direction.   The old choirmaster Giaches de Wert had died on May 6th, 1596, while Monteverdi was camping in the Hungarian plains, and the Duke had not considered him for the vacancy, but had immediately given it to his countryman, Benedetto Pallavicini.   All that Monteverdi gained from this painful expedition, therefore, was a series of mortifications, so that it was without enthusiasm that he received orders from the Duke, three years later, to accompany him to Flanders.

This was no warlike expedition, but a pleasure trip to those wealthy cities from which so many excellent painters and musicians came to Mantua.   Monteverdi once more confided his wife to the safe keeping of his father, and set out in the Duke's train on June 7th, 1599.*

Vincenzo and his large escort passed through the high Tyrolean passes to Trent, and thence to Innsbruck.   At

* See Note 21.

Innsbruck he turned towards Lorraine by way of Basle, and arrived at Spa after a month's hard travelling. The baths of Spa were famous at the time, and people came from all over Europe to take the waters. Travelling musicians flocked round the springs, singing in all conceivable languages, or playing various instruments. As in our own time, life in certain fashionable watering-places was very gay, and music was one of the favourite amusements of the bathers. According to the testimony of the traveller Bergeson, who passed through the town some years later, there were continual concerts, dances, ballets and serenades.*

The Duke stayed a good month at Spa, then left for Liége, where he was the guest of the Prince Bishop Ernst of Bavaria, brother of Duke Guglielmo, and like him a great lover of music. On August 21st, Vincenzo reached Antwerp and hastened to visit the studios of well-known painters—in particular those of Rubens and Pourbus—as well as the shops of dealers in curiosities and *objets d'art*, while the Duke's secretaries tried discreetly to negotiate the Crown jewels, so as to keep pace with the prodigalities of their sovereign.

Only a few days were spent at Antwerp, for the Duke was expected at Brussels, where he was received with ceremony on August 26th. He remained there until September 21st, in the midst of continual fêtes given in his honour.

It was probably at Spa and at Brussels that Monteverdi came into contact with the new productions of the French school. Giulio Cesare Monteverdi, in the manifesto which prefaces the edition of the *Scherzi Musicali*, which we shall consider later, emphasises the importance of the Flemish journey in the development of his brother's talent. Claudio Monteverdi was, he asserts, the first in Italy to practise " the French manner of vocal writing in the new style which

* See Note 22.

has been much admired during the last three or four years, whether as the accompaniment of the words of motets or madrigals, of songs or arias." *

This passage has always been falsely interpreted. It cannot be assumed that it relates to the French *chanson* as written by Jannequin or Orlando di Lasso, whose works were well known in Italy. This was a narrative, descriptive and picturesque genre with which the Italians were quite familiar, and they had themselves created vast tone-pictures on this model.

What Monteverdi discovered in Flanders was that music " *mesurée à l'Antique* " which the members of Baïf's Academy in Paris, Claude le Jeune, Thibault de Courville, Jacques Mauduit, Du Caurroy, vied with each other in composing. This new type of music was beginning to be known outside Parisian musical circles. The Flemings were interested in it, and publishers included compositions by Le Jeune and Du Caurroy in their song-books.†

Monteverdi was doubtless little interested in Baïf's classical researches, and in his French verse regulated by syllabic quantity, but he was certainly struck by the elegant rhythmic formulæ of certain *chansonnettes mesurées* and was inspired by them in his *Scherzi Musicali*.

He probably also heard *airs de cour* and *vaudevilles* which attracted his attention. These compositions, in which musicians such as Claude Tessier or Pierre Cerveau excelled, were sometimes rendered by a solo-voice accompanied by the lute,‡ sometimes performed in the same way as madrigals or *chansons* by several voices and instruments. Generally a melodic phrase was given out by the soprano, and repeated by the other voices in chorus. These airs, which were written in syllabic counterpoint, must have delighted Monteverdi, in spite of the poverty of their harmony, by their rhythmic freedom, and by the beauty of their melodic form. It was a music all in half-tints, of touching simplicity, of supreme elegance. The influence of the *airs de cour* appears in certain madrigals *alla francese* of Monteverdi's last period, but I think it is possible to perceive it in certain accents, in certain turns of the melodic phrases of the *Scherzi Musicali* and of the madrigals forming Books IV and V.

The Duke of Mantua also appreciated French music. As early as 1596 he directed M. de la Clielle, one of his Parisian correspondents, to procure him new verses and arias.* He was in communication with Jacques Davy du Perron, Bishop of Evreux, a friend of Ronsard and of Baïf, and a member of the *Académie du Palais*, and asked him to contribute verse of his own composition.† It is not astonishing, therefore, that Monteverdi should, in the course of his visit to Spa, have heard the most recent compositions of the French school, and should have been influenced by them, as his brother testifies.

The very technique of French singing could not fail to attract his attention. It was full-voiced; its abrupt powerful rhythms seemed to him particularly appropriate to express certain effects of terror or anger. He made use of it both in his motets and in his secular work.

During the same journey, Monteverdi also had his first experience of the *ballet de cour* which had been created in Paris in 1581 and was by way of subjugating Europe. The poet Ottavio Rinuccini was the first to introduce it into Italy, and Monteverdi subsequently composed one of the most perfect types of dramatic ballet. He was attracted by the rhythms resulting from the use of dotted notes, so much in favour among the French instrumentalists.

* See Note 26.   † See Note 27.

Monteverdi was endowed with an extraordinary faculty of assimilation. He profited by all he had heard on the French borders; his brother tells us that he turned it to marvellous use in his own works. It may seem paradoxical that Monteverdi should have been influenced by French music at the very moment of its decadence. It is comprehensible that Palestrina should have followed the example of the illustrious Franco-Flemish polyphonists who were his masters, but it might reasonably appear odd that Monteverdi should owe anything to men such as Du Caurroy, Mauduit, Tessier, who, in spite of their talent, are so vastly inferior to him.

Such reasoning, however, implies a misapprehension of the true state of music at the end of the sixteenth century. The art of polyphony, having reached its full development in France and Flanders, had there exhausted itself at the time when in Italy it was in the blaze of glory which preceded its extinction. The problem of the renovation of musical forms had therefore presented itself to French musicians some twenty years before far-sighted minds had conceived it in Italy. Baïf and the musicians of his Academy, as steeped in classical antiquity as were later the members of Bardi's *Camerata*, wished to subject French vocal music to the strict metrical laws of Greek versification. They studied the effect of complicated rhythmic combinations, and attempted to apply classical metres to music. Assuming, for example, that the minim and the crotchet correspond to long and short syllables in poetry, it is perfectly simple to create dactyls, spondees, or anapæsts by the combination of a minim and two crochets, of two minims, or of two crotchets and a minim. From these experiments there resulted new and strange rhythms which were entirely independent of the current triple or quadruple time.

They also conceived the idea, in common with the Florentine

musicians, of reviving antique drama; but, instead of rendering the whole drama musically, as the Florentines did, they composed it of declamatory scenes alternating with songs and dances performed by the chorus. The dramatic ballet owes its origin to the performance of these classical fantasies at a court fête.* As far as music is concerned, all this ardent research resulted in curious monodies decorated with long expressive *melismata*, exquisite *chansonettes*, subtle and incisive of rhythm, *airs de cour*, and *narrations de ballet* in which the melody tends rather to comply with the suggestions of prosody than to fulfil the exigencies of lyrical declamation.

Monteverdi would doubtless have been unable to tolerate the domination of any single personality; on the other hand, he was profoundly interested in these curious experiments. Though they could, and did, lead to nothing, he was able to gather some useful material from them.

Monteverdi was the more interested in Baïf's reform in view of the fact that it was carried out in a direction quite new to him. In common with Luca Marenzio, Gesualdo di Venosa, and Gagliano, he had sought the salvation of music in an enrichment of the language of harmony, in the reinforcement of its expressive power. Like them, he doubtless hoped to recapture the spirit of classical antiquity by employing chromatic and enharmonic modes, the beauty of which had been praised by Nicola Vicentino, the theorist of the young school, and shown in practice by Ciprian de Rore and Orlando di Lasso. Claude Lejeune and Mauduit, on the other hand, did not attack the question of harmony. Their counterpoint is very free of dissonances, even when by chance they write in chromatic style, and they concentrated entirely on the relations between poetry and music, which they desired to combine indissolubly. As we have pointed out, a new

* See Note 28.

form of lyrical monody had been the indirect result of these experiments in rhythm.

Some ten years after the experiments of Baïf and his friends, the poets, men of learning and artists, who met in Florence at the home of Giovanni Bardi, had conceived the idea of restoring solo-singing to its primitive splendour, as it had been known and practised by the ancients.* Their researches were carried out from a different standpoint from that of the Parisian academicians, who had had no regard to declamation and to tonic accent, but had been solely preoccupied with moulding music on the rhythms of verse; such men as Galilei, Emilio del Cavalieri, Peri, Caccini conceived the problem differently. Their object was to imitate the Greek " spoken song " with the accompaniment of the lyre or of its modern counterpart, the lute.

From about 1585 to 1600, Florence was entirely preoccupied with efforts to restore the antique *melopeia*. But the Florentines, who were principally singers and amateurs, were chiefly concerned with melody and contour, while Gesualdo and Monteverdi, who were pure musicians, sought principally effects of harmony and colour.

In 1590, Emilio del Cavalieri, in collaboration with Laura Guidiccioni the poetess, produced two little musical pastorals, *Il Satiro* and *La Disperazio de Fileno*, which caused profound perturbation in the artistic world of Florence. The object of the authors was to prove that a solo-voice could, without the assistance of harmony, express the most diverse emotions and could lead the spectator from sadness to gaiety, from tears to laughter, as the ancients had done, without the help of polyphony; they wished also to demonstrate a new type of solo-singing. Now, the principal part of a madrigal or a *chanson* had for long past been undertaken by a solo-voice. The point here was to maintain a clear enunciation

* See Note 29.

while singing, a thing quite new at the time, save for certain experiments which had been made within the Florentine group, by Vincenzo Galilei, Jacopo Corsi, Giulio Caccini and Jacopo Peri. The latter, whose reputation as a violist had spread throughout Italy, played a most important part in the reform which was being brought about. He set to music *Dafne*, a lyric drama by the poet Ottavio Rinuccini, which was successfully performed every year from 1594 onwards at the house of a wealthy amateur, Jacopo Corsi, who had replaced Giovanni Bardi after the latter's departure for Rome.

Monteverdi, who between the years 1595 and 1600 was continually moving about Europe, can only have known of the experiments of the Camerata by hearsay, but they must have aroused his curiosity.

The efforts of these poets, singers and amateurs to realize a purely literary ideal, even though it should involve the sacrifice of the rich possibilities of polyphonic music, could not have found much favour in his eyes. He was at this time occupied with the composition of the admirable madrigals of Book IV, and, master as he was in the expression of the profoundest human emotions, the most delicate natural impressions, through the medium of five-part music, he must, in common with the majority of the great madrigalists of the time, and particularly Orazio Vecchi, have regarded with something like pity the dreary psalmody of the Florentine musicians. But he was too intelligent not to see the expressive effects that could be attained by lyrical declamation moulded upon the spoken word.

It is highly probable that Monteverdi was present at the performance of Jacopo Peri's *Euridice* with a libretto by Rinuccini on October 6th, 1600. We know that the Grand Duke of Tuscany had this piece ceremonially performed to celebrate the marriage of his daughter Maria de' Medici with the King of France. Among the many princes who came from all parts of Italy to take part in the celebrations was the Duke of Mantua, brother-in-law of the new queen.* Whether Monteverdi was in his suite is not known, but it is highly probable. In any case, he must have soon been in possession of all the details he required about the performance, and, while there is no authorization for believing that he, like Marco Gagliano, at once made common cause with the Florentine musicians, yet a study of the madrigals of Book V, which were composed about this time, shows that he had been profoundly impressed with the *stile recitativo*, and had tried to put it to original use in his polyphonic work.

Recitatives were certainly sung at Mantua during the ensuing years. The famous Francesco Rasi, who had given a superb performance in the *Euridice*, was a member of Vincenzo's musical company and had been lent by him for the ceremony.† It is clear that he continued to sing works composed in the new style.

Monteverdi was at the time completely absorbed in the composition of the madrigals of Book V. The remarkable audacity of these works caused their performance to create something like a sensation in musical circles and provoked the fury of the purists and conservatives. Copies, more or less faithful, were circulated, and produced a kind of stupefaction. It must be confessed that the liberties which the author had taken with traditional rules were of a nature to justify the excitement.

In 1600 there appeared at Venice a work entitled *L'Artusi overo delle imperfettioni della Musica moderna*. As the title shows, this work was a protest against modernism in music. Its author, Canon Artusi, a talented musician who had a considerable reputation as contrapuntist, posed as the champion of tradition, and lamented the degeneration of the art of

* See Note 30.   † See Note 31.

music. From his point of view, he was perfectly justified. Yet, all the same, he was in error, as are the critics of to-day who believe that music will perish because the rules on which it has been based hitherto are no longer respected. He complains quite justifiably that the new composers—he implies Gesualdo and Monteverdi—are solely preoccupied with delighting " sense " and not with satisfying " reason." It is the eternal quarrel of the intellect and the senses. He deprecates the pride of artists who desire to call everything in question instead of following in the path of the masters— in short, he leaves unsaid none of the commonplaces uttered at all times and in all places by conservative critics. Monteverdi is not mentioned in this book, but quotations from his madrigals show that he was the main object of Artusi's attack.

Three years later, in 1603, the theorist returned to the charge, and, while repeating his arguments, criticised with singular obtuseness the madrigals of Books IV and V which were being circulated in manuscript.

Monteverdi, who had at first taken no notice of these attacks, makes a scornful allusion to them in the preface to Book V. He states that he will publish his reply under the title of *Seconda prattica overo perfettione della Musica moderna* —a parody of Artusi's title—and that his object is to show publicly that the composition of his works is no mere question of hazard, but that there exists another system of harmony than that of which Zarlino codified the laws, and that in the matter of harmony and discord the modern composer takes account of other considerations than those which directed the practice of the old masters. They were exclusively preoccupied with structure, with the adjustment of the different parts in accordance with the possibilities of music. Monteverdi might have said that they wrote " pure music." The moderns seek above all to translate into living expression

the emotions suggested by poetry. The former sacrificed
the poetic text to harmony. The latter desire that harmony
should be the attentive handmaid of verse. Monteverdi
himself knows the rules of the old style, and if he infringes
them, it is of set purpose.

On November 26th, 1601, the *Maestro di Cappella* Benedetto Pallavicini, who had been ailing for a month past, died
of a malignant fever. Monteverdi immediately wrote to the
Duke to solicit the appointment. Recalling Giaches de
Wert, who had formerly combined the functions of *Maestro
di Camera* and *Maestro di Cappella*, he prayed the Duke to
grant him the same privilege.* His wish appears to have
been granted without delay. A short time afterwards,
Vincenzo Gonzaga, who wished to see him permanently
established at the court of Mantua, granted him letters of
naturalization dated April 10th, 1602, by which the musician
and his descendants were entitled to the privileges conferred
by the title of citizen of Mantua.†

Monteverdi was now in charge of the intractable company
of singers and players. He had to supervise everything,
conduct the rehearsals and the private performances in which
Vincenzo took especial delight. He had also to compose
madrigals at breakneck speed to the words of some favourite
poet, or devise music for *entrées de ballet* of which a brief
scenario was given him. Finally, he taught music to the
children and young singers. The charming Caterinuccia
Martinelli was confided to his care, with instructions to
make of her a perfect *virtuosa*.

The salary Monteverdi received for all this work was small,
and, forced to keep up a certain appearance at the court,

with a wife, two children, and an expensive house, he was frequently in financial straits. He had to invoke his father's help, and was involved in continual discussions with the treasurers, to obtain the regular payment even of what was due to him.* As long as he lived at Mantua his letters are full of complaints on this score, and they were certainly made with good cause, since in his subsequent life at Venice he makes no allusion to any difficulties of the kind with the Serene Republic.

He lived in Mantua in a perpetual state of agitation and fatigue. Accustomed as he was to the bracing air of Cremona, he found the impure and fever-laden air of the lagoon exceedingly trying. The whims of the Duke meant crushing work for him. He worked slowly, and to be forced to carry out in a few days a sudden commission for madrigals or *divertissements* was torture to him. On several occasions he fell ill from pure exhaustion, and was obliged to go to his father's house at Cremona to rest. He was there in the month of December, 1604, in a state of profound depression, accompanied by his wife, who had just borne him a second child.† Medicine, diet, rest—nothing had succeeded in improving his condition. " I do most heartily pray your most Serene Highness," he writes to the Duke, " for the love of God, no longer to put so much work upon me ; and to give me more time, for my great desire to serve you, and the excess of my fatigue will not fail to shorten my life ; and if I live longer, I may yet be of service to Your Serene Highness, and of use to my poor children."

It is doubtful whether at this time he was thinking of leaving Mantua, yet his fame was spreading, and he would have had no difficulty in finding generous patrons ; but it was not without hesitation that he could leave the service of a prince to whom he had pledged himself. The latter had

* See Note 34.   † See Note 35.

to give his consent to the termination of the engagement, otherwise the insult shown to the patron was certain to be avenged by death at the hands of some assassin.

Monteverdi was in cordial relations with the court of Ferrara. Book IV of the Madrigals is dedicated to the academy of the *Intrepidi* of that town. The musician also expresses his gratitude for marks of esteem received from them. He alludes in his letter of dedication to the desire he had in 1597 to have these madrigals performed from the manuscript before Duke Alfonso II. The death of this splendid prince prevented the realization of his project.

It will be noticed that Monteverdi was not given to hasty publication. This explains how Artusi could quote in 1600 madrigals which were only printed in Venice five years later. Moreover, Monteverdi says himself that the position of Master of the Musicians was given him by the Duke of Mantua after the performance of Book V of the madrigals, which was only printed in 1605.

Monteverdi rightly attached a special importance to this fifth Book. He wished to dedicate it to the Duke of Mantua as his most perfect work; and indeed it is a masterpiece. Polyphonic music here appears in unwonted forms of almost monstrous beauty. The art of the madrigal reaches its supreme expression. The way is closed. Monteverdi was not long in issuing from the *impasse* in which a man like Orazio Vecchi obstinately remained. Making a complete *volte-face*, he laid hands on the aristocratic spectacle invented and laboriously carried out by the Florentines, and turned this humanistic plaything into modern music-drama.

II

THE FIVE BOOKS OF MADRIGALS AND THE SCHERZI

WITH the publication of Book V of the *Madrigali a cinque voci* in 1605, the first phase of Claudio Monteverdi's musical activity comes to a close. Before considering the conditions in which he began the composition of the music-dramas, and the way in which he readopted the form of the madrigal whilst transforming it into a cantata for solo voice with thorough-bass, it is essential to consider rapidly the first books of madrigals. These pieces, with their perennial poetry and youthfulness, lend themselves particularly to literary commentary, but detailed examination of their structure and technique is necessary in order to appreciate the part played by Monteverdi in the evolution of musical expression.

The madrigal originated in Italy about 1530. It was the product of the combination of the traditional motet of the Netherlands with the Italian *frottola*, but the product bore little resemblance to its constituent elements. The *frottola*, popular in spirit, written in homophonic and syllabic counterpoint, represented at the beginning of the sixteenth century the reaction of the Italian masters against the excess of science and technical complication favoured by the Northern school. To a certain degree, the *frottola* symbolized the revolt of melody which had been sacrificed to the cult of counterpoint. Famous French and Flemish musicians established in Italy had soon fallen under the spell of this rustic genre, of which the masters were Bartolommeo Tromboncino and Marco Carra; they were glad to abandon the pedantic complications, the infinite subtleties rendered necessary by the composition of a mass for five voices on a single given theme, which they had to develop and vary by augmentation and diminution, by every imaginable process until it became absolutely unrecognizable. After the composition of a mass on the theme of *L'Homme Armé* or *Douce Mémoire* which had already served as *canto fermo* to an incalculable number of different masses, these *frottole* must have come as a delightful relaxation. The simple harmony, of set purpose rudimentary, and more instrumental than vocal in its nature, accompanied the brief rhythmic melody which was most frequently sung by a solo-voice, the other parts being played on the lute or harpsichord.

Musicians such as Adrian Willaert, Arcadelt, and Verdelot, who felt the naïve charm of the *frottole*, were, however, too practised in their art not to conceive more delicate combinations. In their search for a new genre which would allow them to throw off the strict obligations involved by the composition of a mass or a motet, they discovered the madrigal, which was, at the time of the Renaissance, the principal channel of the evolution of musical technique, and an admirable medium of musical expression.

From the beginning the madrigal was characterised by the extreme liberty of its structure. The musician took verses of any metre he chose (generally a five- or six-lined stanza taken from a poem) and treated it either in homophonic counterpoint or in a polyphonic style of curious workmanship. The music of the madrigal is much less an end in itself than that of the masses or motets; the poetic text is its *raison d'être*, and the music reflects all the suggestions of that text. The composer does not aim only at transposing into appropriate melody and harmony the prevailing atmosphere of the short poem; he endeavours to paraphrase minutely its ideas and its very language. Long festoons of thirds weave themselves about the " chains of love " ; sighs are translated by pauses and breaks in the melody; the idea of duration, of immobility, is expressed by the holding of a single voice, the others carrying on their parts relentlessly. The voices rise on the words " heaven," " heights," " ascension "; they fall on the words " earth," " sea," " abyss," " hell." The notes scatter in silvery groups round the words " laughter," " joyous," " gay." Finally " martyrdom," " sadness," " pain," " cruelty," " tears " are expressed by audacious discords and unexpected modulations. This preoccupation with literal translation, with the exact rendering of detail, is peculiar to the madrigal style, and the influence of the new genre on the old forms such as the motet, the *chanson française*, the mass, can be seen in the use of " madrigalisms " which finally created a vast repertory of musical commonplaces on which composers drew unsparingly.

The madrigal, as created by Adrian Willaert and Arcadelt, was written in the traditional modes, but, profiting by the liberty peculiar to the genre and desiring to enhance descriptive effects, certain musicians introduced the use of accidentals which produced modulations then unknown, and prepared the way for the tonalities of modern music and harmonic cadences. Monteverdi was destined to play a decisive part in this transformation of musical language.

Monteverdi regarded Ciprian de Rore as his master. This musician was, with Nicola Vicentino, the first to use the chromatic style in his madrigals about 1550. These experiments had created a profound impression. At a time when minds were permeated with the memory of ancient music, the innovators justified their experiments by claiming to restore the chromatic and enharmonic modes described in Greek and Latin treatises which had recently been discovered. Zarlino, the champion of tradition, was opposed by Vicentino, whose treatise, *L'Antica Musica ridotta alla moderna pratica* (1555), was the breviary of the musicians of the vanguard. Orlando di Lasso practised the new style for some time, and composed some fine chromatic madrigals, but he did not continue in this direction, and seems later to have regarded with distaste the works of his youth.

The chromatic style as practised by musicians such as Ciprian de Rore and Ingegneri bears little resemblance to the style now called by that name. Its essential characteristic consisted in the use of accidentals, which were foreign to the mode in which the madrigal was sung. They did not, properly speaking, involve modulation. Monteverdi's great achievement was to transform the somewhat incoherent use of these accidentals into a clear method of transition from one key into another.

The disciples of Ciprian de Rore were grateful to him for having thus become the pioneer of chromatic music, and hailed him as the father of modern musical language. They spoke much of the harmonic boldness of the celebrated madrigal *Calami sonum ferentes*, and hailed his reaction against the excessive complications of polyphonic writing. Ciprian, indeed, had concentrated upon preventing the melodic theme from being lost in the inextricable interweaving of the parts. In his music, as in that of Orlando di Lasso, a definite melody is clearly heard through the polyphony. It can easily be isolated and sung by a solo voice, the other parts being played as an instrumental accompaniment. The idea of revealing the melodic line and of allowing the words to be heard was quite new. Adrian Willaert, heir of the Franco-Flemish tradition, had never considered the point, and like his masters had aimed at "the perfection of harmony," to use Monteverdi's own words. This was the ideal of a large number of musicians, and Palestrina himself was on the side of tradition rather than on that of the reformers. On the other hand, round Ciprian de Rore rallied themselves the majority of the Venetian and Neapolitan madrigalists who, about the time of the publication of Monteverdi's first book, were seeking to make music more melodious and more expressive without, however, sacrificing the rich resources of polyphony. The most brilliant of these musicians were Luca Marenzio, Giovanni Gabrieli, Luzzascho Luzzaschi, Ingegneri, and Don Gesualdo, Prince of Venosa.

Ingegneri who, as we have seen, was Monteverdi's master at Cremona, was, like Ciprian de Rore, striving towards an ideal of melodic beauty and simplicity. Charles Bordes (in his analysis of the Responses of Ingegneri which he attributes to Palestrina) has brought out very clearly the novelty of the style of these works.* Everything, he notes, is subservient to declamation. The interweaving of contrapuntal patterns is replaced by vertical harmonies, clear chords which permit the words of the dying Christ to be heard by the whole congregation. The master's regard for declamation is such that he returns to a kind of free diaphony, moulded upon the accents of the spoken word. Monteverdi subsequently expressed his approval of his master's attention to declamation in singing. Although less bold than Ciprian de Rore, Ingegneri was also one of the first to adopt the chromatic style which Palestrina and his rivals had neglected. We shall see the part which chromatic dissonances were to play in the madrigals of Monteverdi. Yet Ingegneri was by no means a revolutionary. All his works, masses, motets and madrigals, betray a great preoccupation with purity of style.

Monteverdi, in his youth at least, does not seem to have come under the influence of Giovanni Gabrieli, his contemporary. He makes no reference to him in the preface of the *Scherzi Musicali*. The similarities of style to be observed in these works can very well be explained by a common cult for Ciprian de Rore and his direct disciples. Monteverdi was certainly much struck by the audacities of Don Gesualdo, who, however, only accumulated dissonances with the avowed

* See Note 36.

intention of causing astonishment (*far stupire*). This is the epoch in which extravagance (*stravaganza*) is regarded as the finest quality in drama. The desire to leave the beaten track, to discover something new, was manifesting itself powerfully then as now. It is possible that Gesualdo contributed to eliminating from Monteverdi's mind the last trace of the respect in which he had at first held the rules of his art, but he served no other purpose. There is to be perceived in Gesualdo no sense of modern tonality. His innovations are an end in themselves; they lead to nothing.

Luca Marenzio, on the other hand, being some ten years Monteverdi's senior, may very well have pointed out to him the way he was to take. This marvellous musician shows a very modern sense of harmonic modulation. The style of his madrigals is very similar to that of Monteverdi's first works, though it is more precious, less haphazard. The preoccupation with the expression of personal emotion is clearly to be seen, and one can even say that the madrigals of Luca Marenzio are already animated by that dramatic sense which is the essential characteristic of the madrigals of Monteverdi.

We can say nothing of Monteverdi's earliest work, published in 1583, for only an uninteresting fragment has survived. The *Canzonette a tre voci* published the following year are of the purest classical type. They are divided into two unequal sections, each of which is twice repeated. The melody is clearly defined, the rhythm lively and graceful. The last one in the book is delightful. The first phrase is as follows:

EXAMPLE I

Hor ca-re can - zo - net-te   Si - cu - - ramente an-dre - te

The affected *naïveté* of the verse is not without charm. "Now, dear songs, you will go peacefully, singing joyously, kissing in gratitude the hands of him who shall listen to you."

Monteverdi published these delicious songs at the age of seventeen. His work long bore traces of the fascination he had felt as a young man for this popular form, in which extreme liberty of composition was general. The most severe contrapuntists permitted fifths and octaves in writing *villanelle* and *canzonette* for three voices, and obtained new effects by the violation of scholastic rules. Monteverdi took advantage of these liberties in writing his madrigals.

In 1587, Gardano of Venice published the first book of madrigals for five voices, a work destined to make Monteverdi celebrated throughout Europe. On the title-page, as on those of the two earlier collections, the author calls himself the " disciple of Marc Antonio Ingegneri," but a glance at these compositions is enough to show all that divides the disciple from the master. Ingegneri had always shown profound respect for the rules of his art. Extremely liberal in his ideas, he had not concealed his sympathy with the new tendencies, but had himself succeeded in combining a varied and expressive style with great correctness. Monteverdi felt none of these scruples. Even in his earliest compositions he cast aside all scholastic prejudice. Ingegneri's music was like some carefully tended garden ; under Monteverdi's rule, weeds invaded the flower-beds and wild flowers raised their perfumed blooms insolently above the complicated designs of the box-wood.

The concision of style and the frequent use of a refrain in the madrigals of the first book recall the style of the *canzonette*, but the harmony is much richer and more elaborate. The use of the chromatic style is more timid than in Gesualdo's or even in Luca Marenzio's work ; the form recalls rather

that of Ciprian de Rore, who, however, never went as far as
Monteverdi in the multiplication of dissonances.   They arise
most frequently from a very peculiar use of retardation in the
various parts and of their simultaneous or deferred resolution.*

EXAMPLE 2

Monteverdi also makes frequent use of augmented fifths,
which produce effects of voluptuousness and melancholy.†

EXAMPLE 3

Thus Monteverdi's technique has already a personal colour
in these melodies which proceed by large intervals, with
fearless leaps of ninths or elevenths, in his modern sense of
tonality, and in his contempt for the rules prohibiting the use
of consecutive fifths and octaves, and false relations.   On the
contrary, he gets effects of extraordinarily expressive power
from the violation of these rules.

But what is more striking in this first collection than any
technical detail is the bubbling life, the youthful vigour which
permeates them, the intelligent paraphrase of the text by the
music, which discreetly emphasizes all the important details
yet preserves a marvellous coherence.   There is in this book
no trace as yet of the dramatic feeling which inspires the
subsequent collections.   The three last madrigals, which form
a trilogy, *Ardo si, ma non t'amo ; Ardi o gela ; Arsi e alsi,* would
have lent themselves to dramatic treatment ; they are, in point

* See Note 37.   † See Note 38.

of fact, the weakest in the book, and Monteverdi maintains throughout the lyric style.

The second book, published at Venice in the following year (1590), shows considerable progress on the first. The twenty-one madrigals it contains are perceptibly more developed, and have lost that resemblance to the *chansonnette* which character-ized such pieces as *Se pur non mi consenti, Filli cara et amata, Fu mia la pastorella.* There is indeed, only one piece, *S'andasse Amor a caccia*, which, in its swift grace, recalls the manner of Jannequin and Lasso. The whole collection is astonishing in its variety. By the side of madrigals conceived along tradi-tional lines such as *Donna nel mio ritorno*, there are others perfectly original in style such as the delightful *Non son in queste rive* with its bold modulation from C to E major and its consecutive descending fifths,

EXAMPLE 4

or such as *Non si levava l'alba*, which ends with the repetition of the original melody adapted to different words, and thus anticipates the *aria da capo*. Certain of the madrigals are markedly polyphonic in form; others, on the contrary, are written in homophonic style, with vertical harmonies. We feel that the composer is no slave to theory, but a musician guided by inspiration or fantasy, reserving to himself the right of observing or violating rules according to his desire and the object he aims at. For him the end justifies the means, and the essential is to suggest powerfully to the hearer feelings and impressions.

Like all the contemporary madrigalists, even like Bach and

Rameau, who came a century later, Monteverdi interprets
the metaphors of the text by appropriate melodic figures.
The rising sun which gilds the mountain-tops inspires him
thus :

EXAMPLE 5

e gl'al - ti mon-ti en - - do - - - - - - - - - - - - - - - ra

The *dolci legami* are translated by chains of thirds, and the
line *Facendo mille scherzi e milli giri* is sung to a phrase in
which a rapid succession of notes brings to the mind the swift
movements expressed in the text. This literal interpretation
of ideas and words seems puerile to us to-day, but it was the
idiom of the epoch, and, without wishing to attach particular
importance to Monteverdi's use of the current vocabulary, it
would be idle to attack him on that ground. Such literal
interpretations, moreover, did not prevent Monteverdi from
trying to render the spirit and the atmosphere of the poem.
The finest madrigal in the book, *Ecco mormorar l'onde*, is
characteristic from this point of view. It is permeated with
a pastoral atmosphere of delicious coolness. The brook is
babbling, birds are twittering, the air is exquisitely clear. This
is no rough objective description ; it is the delicate suggestion
of a mood. Scenes similar in inspiration are to be found later
in the operas of Cavalli and Lulli, but there the orchestra plays
the part here confided to the voices. In this madrigal, the
supple thirds unrolling above the voices recall those phrases
for muted strings which, in Lulli's work, enchant the sleeping
hero on the bank of the murmuring brook.

EXAMPLE 6

l'au - - - - - - - - ra e   tua   mes - - - - - - - -

And how profound is the impression of mystery, of awakening nature, which is given by the opening of this madrigal, when tenors and basses murmur *Ecco mormorar l'onde* while the other voices repeat the phrase in echo !

EXAMPLE 7

Ec-co mor-morar l'on - de

In the admirable *Non m'è grave il morire* the tragic chords which support the melodic phrase *Lagrimar per pietà* already anticipate the dramatic style of the *Orfeo*.

The third book, published in 1592, contributed considerably to Monteverdi's reputation, and eight reprints are known to have been made between 1592 and 1622. As far as harmony is concerned, there is nothing specially new in the book, and historians who have noted as an innovation the use of suspensions in the beautiful madrigal *Stracciami il core* show that they have not taken the trouble to read his two first books. It is true that Monteverdi has accumulated in this madrigal, which is in very free fugal style, all possible harmonic innovations, so that Padre Martini was able to quote it as a peculiarly typical example of his madrigal writing.

In this madrigal Fétis has noted with dismay " the double dissonances produced by the suspension of the ninth and fourth, of the ninth, seventh and fourth, and of the fourth and sixth resolved on the fifth " at the words *Non può morir d'Amor*.

EXAMPLE 8

non   può   mo - rir   d'A - - mor   al - - ma fe - de - - le

In this book there are as yet no chords of the seventh or ninth taken without preparation, and yet as Fétis, the first to throw light on Monteverdi's part in the modal revolution, has pointed out, the characteristic quality of modern tonality is already defined in it by the frequent use of the harmonic relation of the fourth and seventh, which thus acts as leading note, finding its resolution on the tonic. " Now it is precisely this relation of the fourth degree and the leading-note, *i.e.* of these cadences which distinguishes modern tonality from plainsong, in which no other resolutions were necessary than those of the optional dissonances produced by suspension."

While the harmonic structure of the third book differs little from that of the preceding collection, the same is not true of the way in which the parts are disposed. Progressions by consecutive thirds and sixths, which were the exception, are frequent. The author tends to lay increasing emphasis on one part—soprano or alto—as though it had been written for a solo voice, the others accompanying it in the same way as instruments. This distribution is very remarkable in the two magnificent madrigals *O Primavera, gioventù de l'anno* and *Perfidissimo volto*, which are animated by a concentrated and profound passion.

There is obvious attention to clarity of enunciation. Whilst the *Plainte d'Armide abandonnée* presents characteristics of liturgical psalmody rather than of dramatic declamation, recalling thereby Orlando di Lasso's *Plainte de Didon*, yet in

several madrigals there are melodic phrases almost recitative
in character. This would lead one to suppose that, whilst
following a different direction, Monteverdi was nevertheless
in close touch with the experiments of the Camerata Bardi.

EXAMPLE 9

Vatte — ne pur cru – del conquel-la pa - ce che lascia me

We are obliged to lay special emphasis upon the technique
of Monteverdi's madrigals, but it must be noticed that he
never stands out as a stylist. He never appears to have
attempted, as Gesualdo did, to astonish his hearers with inventions, with freaks in the matter of harmony. His only object
is to express as intensely as possible the passions which agitate
the human soul. From this time onwards he is a master in the
art of interpreting in music the most complex, the most
varied emotions.

The fourth book appeared in March 1603, but the madrigals
which it contains had been composed some time before, since
several of them were criticized by Artusi in 1600. Artusi's
attack has given rise to some astonishment. It has been
remarked that there are to be found in the work of Luca
Marenzio, whose authority he invokes, the same bold dissonances resulting from retardations, the same chromatic
passages, the same modulations. That is quite true, but what
revolted Artusi was doubtless not so much the violation of
traditional rules—false relations, augmented fifths, and ninths
—as the absolute novelty of Monteverdi's very conception of
the madrigal. Up to that time the genre had been essentially
vocal in character. The most revolutionary madrigals of

Gesualdo or Marenzio are obviously written for voices.
Monteverdi, on the contrary, from the fourth book onwards,
seems to have composed his madrigals for instrumental
performance.   It must be confessed that it would be extremely
difficult to sing certain madrigals of Book IV.   It is no easy
matter to find three voices capable of singing in perfect tune
passages such as the following, which are chosen from a host
of similar passages:

EXAMPLE 10

Io mo - - - - - - - - ro   Io va - do

Madrigals such as *Sfogava con le stelle*, or *A un giro sol*, look
far more like fantasies for viols (such as Frescobaldi might
have written) than madrigals intended to be sung by human
voices.   Indeed, in the first, there is a strange effect of
vocalization in which the voices are treated as instruments.
The lilt of the dotted notes recalls the French *airs de ballet*
which Monteverdi had heard in the course of his journey in
Flanders.

EXAMPLE 11

O -

    In the second, vocal passages, in broad undulations in thirds,
represent the waves of the sea exactly in the same way as
operatic composers, half a century later, did in writing for the
orchestra.   The form of the madrigal can be seen breaking

up in all directions. It already contains the orchestra, anticipates the cantata for solo-voice, and foreshadows the great dramatic narrations of the Opera. We, who know the result of these intuitions of genius, cannot sufficiently admire such prophetic compositions, but we can understand the stupefaction of Monteverdi's contemporaries. These madrigals are magnificent works, but they are simply not madrigals.

It would be idle to examine individually the twenty madrigals of Book IV, in view of the profound technical analysis made by Dr. Leichtentritt. The impression of splendid barbarity given by the first books is reinforced. Emotions are expressed with vehement power, instincts run wild. Nothing could be stranger than the contrast between the insipid text, in which the dying flames, the sweet bonds of Love, are celebrated in choice language, and the brutality of the musical expression. In *Si ch' io vorrei morire*, the poetic text expresses an impudent gallantry, the music is permeated with a sensuous ecstasy which would be disconcerting if one did not have in mind the atmosphere of voluptuous passion in which Monteverdi lived at the court of Mantua.

The fifth book of the madrigals (1605) is one of the first works of the kind published with the addition of a *basso continuo*, optional in the case of the first thirteen, obligatory in the last six. Thus we can see how the new genre was definitely developing in the direction of the new forms, the aria and cantata.

From the harmonic point of view, this book contains an innovation which was destined to revolutionize music. For the first time, chords of the seventh and the ninth are taken without preparation and determine a tonal cadence. We can feel Monteverdi's delight in his discovery, for he multiplies such cadences.

EXAMPLE 12

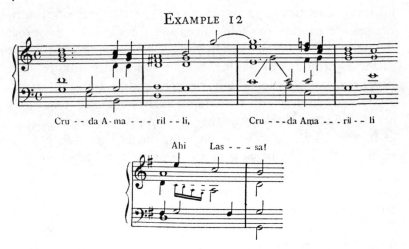

"In taking without preparation the dominant seventh and ninth, the *tritone*, the diminished fifth and the minor sixth," observes Fétis, "Monteverdi completes the transformation of tonality and not only gives music expressive and dramatic power, but creates a new system of harmony." This new use of the seventh caused considerable surprise to his contemporaries. "Our ancient masters," writes Artusi, "never taught that sevenths could be employed so systematically and without preparation." It is doubtful whether Monteverdi realized the significance of his discoveries, for his prefaces and letters contain no allusion to his very original conception of harmony. He seems to have been directed by pure intuition in this renovation of musical language.

Throughout this book, Monteverdi appears obsessed with the question of dramatic style. We noticed in Book III some examples of lyric declamation. Recitative is frequently to be found in Book IV; it dominates the whole of Book V. It is a curious situation. Monteverdi refuses to reject deliberately an antiquated genre by following the example of such men as Emilio del Cavalieri, Peri, Caccini,

Sigismondo d'India in composing arias for a solo-voice with *basso continuo*, yet profits by their creations in the style of the Florentine monody when writing madrigals for five voices.

Monteverdi was profoundly interested in the experiments of the Camerata, but he was too essentially a musician to resign himself to an impoverishment of music. The Florentines meant to clear the ground entirely before creating their new style. On the pretext that polyphonic writing prevented the poetic text from being distinctly heard, and thus annihilated poetry, they wished to replace an art of incomparable richness by a new art, pure in line certainly, but despoiled of everything which had once made the beauty of music. Monteverdi, with a Venetian passion for colour, could not adapt himself to the linear style of the Florentines. In this he was certainly of the same opinion as Orazio Vecchi, Banchieri and a host of other eminent composers of the time. Moreover, the use he makes of the *stile recitativo* in his madrigals for five voices must have seemed like sacrilege to the Florentine purists who were preaching a return to ancient simplicity with the faith of sectarian iconoclasts. In short, he remained faithful to the ideas of his master Ingegneri as regards the necessity of preserving the intelligibility of the words, but took advantage in setting them to music of the style, intermediary between speaking and singing, which was being practised by the innovators.

The madrigal *O Mirtillo* was certainly conceived by Monteverdi in view of execution by a solo-voice. This becomes obvious if the madrigal is arranged as shown in Example 13, no change being made in the motion of the parts.

One obtains thus an aria for solo-voice such as those which Caccini and Sigismondo d'India were then popularizing, in which the Florentine recitative softens, becomes melodious and tuneful.

EXAMPLE 13

Monteverdi's dramatic style, which later made the *Orfeo*, can be perceived throughout this collection. Here and there can be found those passionate exclamations, those melodic intervals of the diminished seventh which he uses so frequently in his opera. The drama is obviously becoming an obsession with him. The general impression of the first four books of madrigals is distinctly lyrical, the fifth, on the contrary, is entirely dramatic. The madrigals *Ecco Silvio, Ma se con la pietà, Dorinda, Ecco pieghando le ginocchie a terra, Ferrir quel petto Silvio* are taken from Guarini's *Pastor Fido* and are connected so as to form a dramatic action to madrigalesque music. There was nothing particularly daring about this attempt. The general preoccupation with drama was so powerful at that time that there was a large number of musicians, hostile to the Florentine reform, who treated scenes from pastorals and comedies in polyphonic style. In 1600 a pastoral set to music in four parts by Guasparre Torelli had been published at Venice under the title *I Fidi Amanti*,* and the inveterate fidelity to this system, maintained by Orazio Vecchi and his disciple Adriano Banchieri, long after the triumph of the monody was assured, is well known.† Indeed, why Monteverdi continued to write in the madrigal style remains somewhat obscure. Narrations and dialogues are all important, the other parts being reduced to the rôle of accompaniment. Why, therefore, did he not simply write solos with orchestral accompaniment? The scene in which Dorinda throws herself at Silvio's feet and implores him to strike her with the arrow she offers him (No. 7) belongs to drama, not to the madrigal. The very fact that he wrote a thorough-bass part intended for instrumental accompaniment proves sufficiently that Monteverdi was no longer at his ease in the madrigal *a cappella*. The madrigal *Ahi come un vago sol* is the prototype of those two-part cantatas with thorough-bass which were to be so frequent in seventeenth-century music. The two tenor voices sing accompanied by the *basso continuo*, and the soprano voices intervene only at infrequent intervals to execute melodic figures which could very well be played by the violins. The principal voices are treated as solos, as later in the operas and cantatas.

The last piece of the collection forms a contrast with those which precede it. It is a vast composition in nine parts, written in the purest Venetian style as popularized by Giovanni Gabrieli. The voices are divided into two choruses supported by the bass. These choruses answer each other in canonical imitations and are united in a powerful finale. The style and the broad well-marked rhythm of the madrigal *Questi vaghi concenti* reappear in the choruses which open and conclude the operas of the Roman school.

In the fifth book of the madrigals, taking it all in all, music

* See Note 39.   † See Note 40.

reaches its highest levels, but I do not think that one can assume, as has often been assumed, that the genre here finds its perfect and definite expression. The true models of the madrigal style are to be found rather in the work of Luca Marenzio. Monteverdi never considered the madrigal as an end in itself, but as a means of reaching a new ideal, which he but dimly perceived, and which defined itself more and more clearly, namely, dramatic expression. But the madrigal, which is essentially a lyric form, could not resist such efforts. In the hands of the maestro of Cremona, it broke up; but from its ruins were created new musical forms, arias, duos, cantatas, which Monteverdi later incorporated in the lyrical drama.

It was about 1606 that Monteverdi composed the *Scherzi Musicali*, a work destined to contribute more than any other to his popularity, at least during his lifetime. According to his brother, who prefaced the Venetian edition of this collection, published in 1607, with an interesting manifesto, he made use in it of that *canto alla francese* which he had heard in Flanders and which was destined to become popular throughout Italy. The term is vague. Whilst it is quite true that the name was generally applied to a certain manner of singing with the full voice, powerful and abrupt, and to a certain rhythmic process consisting essentially, as M. André Pirro * observes, of a binary grouping of the notes in the cadences, yet it is also clear that Monteverdi brought from his Flemish voyage, with other foreign habits, a truly original manner of composition peculiar to the Parisian school. If, indeed, one takes the pains to score the *Scherzi Musicali* without dividing the melody into bars, placing the verses one below the other, it will be recognized that these songs were composed on metric plans in the

* See Note 41.

same way as the *chansonnettes* of Baïf set to music by Claude
Le Jeune, Du Caurroy or Mauduit.

Monteverdi, who was most profoundly influenced by
humanistic ideas, and who was at the time seeking in Plato and
the Greek philosophers a solution to the problems which he
could not solve with the sole assistance of the theorists of
musical art, could not fail to be interested in the French researches. Plato had taught him that rhythm, together with
melody, was the very essence of music. Up to that time he
had concentrated his efforts principally upon melody, and
upon harmony considered as a powerful means of expression.
He had somewhat neglected rhythm, the marvellous effects
of which had been praised by the ancients. In Flanders, he
found himself suddenly in the presence of artists who, while
they were no less in love with antiquity than himself, were
attempting to combine closely poetry, melody and rhythm, so
that, from the strictly musical point of view, there was much
to interest him permanently in these perfectly new rhythmical
formulæ, so arresting and original, which arose from the
application of verse-metres to music.

EXAMPLE 13A

qu'est de-ve-nu ce bel œil qui mon â - me éclairoit jà de ses rays

C'est un a-mant, ouvrez la por - - te, Il est plein d'amour et de íoy

que fai-tes-vous, estes vous mor - te? Non vous ne l'es - tes que pour moy.

It was as musician much more than as poet that he appreciated this French *musique mesurée*. He did not attempt to
compose airs to Italian poetry written in antique metres,

although a good deal of it existed. In common with a large
number of French musicians,* he preferred to take rhymed
stanzas and to deduce from the general rhythm of the verse a
metrical formula to which he adapted the melody.

Monteverdi, who had always affirmed his predilection for
symmetrical repetitions, for the strict development of sequences,
for the *basso ostinato*, felt a lively pleasure in composing instrumental *chansons* and *ritornelli* on constantly recurring rhythmic
formulæ of great simplicity. Sometimes, however, he
delighted in more subtle metrical combinations, but it is rare for
him to compose the music of each verse according to a different
metrical plan, as Claude Le Jeune or Mauduit did.   With the
exception of a single piece, *La Violetta*, which is a *canzonetta*
of classical form, all the three-part *Scherzi* are constructed on
preconceived rhythmic plans, and Monteverdi scarcely ever
allows himself any liberties with the rhythm.

It would be vain to seek his models elsewhere than in
France.   On the contrary, one has but to glance at the *airs
mesurés* of Mauduit, of Caurroy, Le Jeune, Courville and their
companions to recognize the affinity.†

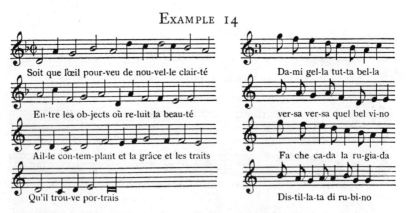

EXAMPLE 14

Soit que l'œil pour-veu de nou-vel-le clair-té

Da-mi gel-la tut-ta bel-la

En-tre les ob-jects où re-luit la beau-té

ver-sa ver-sa quel bel vi-no

Ail-le con-tem-plant et la grâce et les traits

Fa che ca-da la ru-gia-da

Qu'il trou-ve por-trais

Dis-til-la-ta di ru-bi-no

French influence is also evident in the harmonic structure

* See Note 42.   † See Note 43.

of these three-part songs: the counterpoint is syllabic and dissonances rarely appear. There is not a shadow of an imitation. Monteverdi rejects the dissonances, the false relations, the chromatics, from which he obtained such powerful effects in his other works, particularly in his madrigals. He seems principally concerned with rhythmic precision and grace.

It must, however, be recognized that the melodic inspiration of these charming pieces owes nothing to France. Their form is entirely Italian.

As in the French *airs de cour*, the form of the *Scherzi* is strophic, the same melody serving for several stanzas. Each repetition is preceded by an instrumental *ritornello* in three parts, about equal in length to the *chanson* which it precedes. It is constructed on the melodic theme of the *Scherzo*, and follows, although freely, a preconceived rhythmic scheme. Monteverdi shows here his love of the sequence which he uses in a kind of thematic development. The bass marks the rhythm to which the other parts conform more freely. Occasionally the bass repeats the same figure several times in succession, and only indulges in some liberties towards the end. A note printed as an introduction to the work states that each *ritornello* was to be played twice before the entry of the voices, and once between each verse by two violins, and a chitarrone or harpsichord. The first stanza was to be sung in three parts to the accompaniment of violins which doubled the voices. The second stanza could be sung by a solo voice, and the last stanza was to be sung, like the first, in three parts.

The collection of the *Scherzi Musicali* concludes with a *Balletto*, a suite of songs in dance-rhythms preceded by an instrumental introduction. It is an interesting example of the *Suite*, and there seems to be little doubt that the author was inspired in this composition by the suites of dances of varied rhythms which composed the French *ballet*. The instrumental piece which opens the *divertissement* is entitled *Entrata*. It is the classical *entrée* of the French ballet, and is followed by danced *chansons* which differ in key and in rhythm. There are to be seen successively a *Pavane*, a *Galliarde*, a *Coranto*, a *Volte à* 3, *Allemande*, and a *Gigue à* 3. But the question arises as to whether these dances are actually Monteverdi's own work, or that of his brother, Giulio Cesare. Their rather meagre structure tends to confirm the latter assumption.

It appears that, in spite of the great success of the *Scherzi Musicali*, proved by the number of published editions, Monteverdi's intentions remained obscure for a large number of his auditors, who were disconcerted by these pieces *sans mesure réglée*, which were sung according to syllabic quantity in the French manner. The pedant Artusi returned to the charge, and under the pseudonym of Antonio Braccino da Todi published at Venice in 1608 a pamphlet entitled *Discorso secondo musicale* * which was intended to confound his adversary. " What is there to say of these *Scherzi Musicali*," he cries, " save that their author knows nothing about time nor about the signs he employs to indicate it ? The three songs, *O Rosetta*, *Damigella* and *Clori Amorosa*, in particular, have, on paper, the same time, the same signature, but the melodies obey different rhythms. If the time noted for the two first is correct, then it is false for the third. Whatever Monteverdi may do, or claim to do, he has proved that he knows nothing of musical proportion." Further on, he notes that Monteverdi, having used the " C " time-signature, has not hesitated to put three minims in a bar. If Artusi had consulted the *musique mesurée* of the French masters, he would have seen that they also used time-signatures to indicate nothing more than the *prevailing* rhythm of the piece. For

* See Note 44.

want of this knowledge, Artusi was astounded by these successions of crotchets and quavers which cannot be reduced to simple time, save by constant alteration of the time-signature, and wondered by what aberration people could hail as a man of genius a musician who was incapable of distinguishing triple from quadruple time.

PART II

THE DRAMATIC SPECTACLES AT THE
COURT OF MANTUA

I

THE ORFEO

THE Duke of Mantua, Vincenzo Gonzaga, had, as we have seen, been present at the celebrations in Florence in 1600 on the occasion of the marriage of Maria de' Medici and Henry IV. Giulio Caccini's *Rapimento di Cefalo*, with a libretto by Chiabrera, and Jacopo Peri's music to Rinuccini's poem *Euridice*, had won him over to the cause of musical drama. His sons shared his feeling. The hereditary prince, Francesco, was passionately fond of the new style, and Ferdinando Gonzago, the future Cardinal, then a student at the University of Pisa, himself composed libretti which he set to music. We know from the correspondence between the two brothers with what interest they followed the evolution of the new dramatic genre. While Emilio del Cavaliere was having his oratorio *La Rappresentazione di Anima e di Corpo* performed in Rome, while, following his example, Agazzari, Quagliati, Landi, Kapsberger and other eminent Roman musicians were attempting to put the *stile recitativo* into practice, there had been successfully performed in Florence a musical comedy, *E morti et i vivi*, a revival of the *Dafne* and, on December 5th, 1603, Caccini's *Euridice* composed to the libretto which had already been set to music by Jacopo Peri.* The new style seemed already to be congealing into formulæ. It was in vain for Caccini to adorn his frigid *melopeia* with *melismata* and embellishments

* See Note 45.

55

moulded upon the accentuation of the words, it but rarely
offered organized melodic periods, profound dramatic feeling.*
The few expressive songs to be found here and there in the
musical dramas of Caccini, of Peri, of Cavaliere only accentuate their general meagreness and the monotony of the
melopeia which drags its slow length along above the thorough-
bass.　The enthusiasm of the public can only be explained
by the novelty of the undertaking and the incomparable
talent of the performers.

As early as 1603 the Duke of Mantua was preoccupied
with the introduction of musical drama at his court.　He
engaged a large number of artists, the youthful Roman
Caterinuccia Martinelli, whom he handed over to Monteverdi, and the Neapolitan harpist Lucrezia Urbana.　He
already had in his service excellent women-singers capable
of performing the new music, in particular the famous Jewess
surnamed Madama Europa, sister of the composer Salomone
de Rossi, himself in the service of the Duke in the capacity
of violist, and Sabina, pupil of the great singer Francesco
Rasi, who had played the principal rôle in Peri's *Euridice*
in Florence in 1600.　In January 1607, Vincenzo besought
the Grand Duke of Tuscany to lend him Giov. Gualberto
Magli for a fortnight.　This famous *castrato* had been trained
by Giulio Caccini and excelled in recitative.

On February 23rd, 1607,† Prince Francesco hastened to
communicate to his brother, who was retained at Pisa by
his studies, the following important piece of news : " There
will be a performance to-morrow of the piece which was sung
in our Academy.　This is thanks to Giov. Gualberto, who
has behaved very well, having not only learnt the whole of
his part by heart, but performed it in the most graceful and
touching fashion, so that I am entirely satisfied with him.
As the libretto has been printed, in order that each spectator

* See Note 46.　　　　　　　　† See Note 47.

may have it in his hands while the piece is being sung, I am sending you a copy of it." This was the libretto which Monteverdi had just set to music—the *Orfeo*.

We do not know in what circumstances Monteverdi composed the score of the *Orfeo* to a libretto by the poet Alessandrio Striggio, secretary to the Duke and son of the famous madrigalist. Prince Francesco seems to have played an important part in the affair.* Indeed, it is to him that the printed score was dedicated.

The *Orfeo* was performed under his auspices, during one of the meetings of the *Accademia degli Invaghiti* which were held in the Royal Palace. It was quite a private, experimental performance, to which were invited only the intimate friends of the sovereigns. The success was decisive. The hereditary prince announced it to his brother in the following terms : " The piece was performed to the satisfaction of all who heard it. And indeed, My Lord the Duke, not satisfied with having been present at the performance, and with having heard numerous rehearsals, has ordered another performance, which will be given to-day in the presence of all the ladies of the town, and it is for this reason that Giov. Gualberto is still here. He has done very well, and given great pleasure to all by his singing, and especially to My Lady the Duchess."

This letter, with another addressed to the Duke by the poet Dom Cherubino Ferrari, who writes, after reading the score, that no better rendering of human emotion could be conceived than that given by the poet and the musician, constitute all the strictly contemporary records of the success of the *Orfeo* which have been preserved. Yet that success was considerable. Monteverdi's work was, at the instigation of the Duke of Mantua, performed two years later in Turin, and perhaps in Florence. A concert performance was given

* See Note 48.

at Cremona, and doubtless in other towns. The score printed at Venice in 1609 was reprinted in 1615.

The *Orfeo* is incontestably the masterpiece of the *Riforma Melodrammatica*. Monteverdi masters the Florentine system, penetrates its defects, realizes its possibilities. Like Vecchi, he sees that it is unnecessary to enslave music to poetry, that music can be itself a kind of true poetry, capable of expressing emotion as truly as words.

The great achievement of the ancients had been to awaken emotion, and Monteverdi, having often tried to reach this end in his madrigals, attains it magnificently in the *Orfeo*. He adopts the form of musical drama invented by the Florentine *Camerata*, but enriches it with a host of technical details borrowed from the Italian madrigalists and organists, and from the French composers of *airs de cour* and *ballets*. In point of fact, the Florentines fought shy of music. They concentrated on sequestrating it, on preventing it from " destroying poetry." Monteverdi does not fear it, because he is its master. He thinks that it should play an important part in drama. While Marco da Gagliano, himself a thoroughbred musician, inspired rather by the experiments of Caccini, seeks to render the drama more musical by multiplying *canzonette* and choruses in madrigal style, Monteverdi follows rather the example of Jacopo Peri and of Sigismondo d'India, and gets to grips with the recitative itself, rather than with accessory details. At the same time, by an inspiration of genius, and influenced by the prestige of the French ballets in which instrumental music played an important part, he brings into play all the resources of the orchestra in order to express emotion. One cannot say that Monteverdi was an inventor of musical forms to the same degree as Jacopo Peri, Emilio del Cavaliere, or Caccini, but he was able to turn all their discoveries to advantage and to create the masterpiece they had vaguely conceived, but which their own genius was powerless to create.

Striggio's tragedy is closely akin to the pastoral genre illustrated by Rinuccini and Chiabrera, and, in common with the latter, the author lays himself open to criticism by his *stile gonfiato*, by the conventional majesty of his verse, and by the insipidity of his mythological intrigue. But Monteverdi was capable of so making this poem his own, of so " warming it with the flame of his music " that it becomes as living, as moving as the music itself. There are, moreover, moments of pathos in the libretto, and the tragic scenes are treated with vigorous sobriety.

The piece comprises a short prologue and five acts. The first act is occupied with the songs of nymphs and shepherds who joyously celebrate the nuptials of Orpheus and Eurydice, while the spouses sing their mutual love.

In Act II, Orpheus has returned to his own country, and greets the places familiar to his youth. The shepherds welcome him joyously, but Silvia, the messenger of doom, arrives to announce the death of Eurydice from the sting of a serpent. Orpheus utters a single cry, then remains plunged in grief, while the shepherds pour forth lamentations. Soon he returns to himself, and, rebelling against Fate, swears to snatch the prey of Hell from its jaws. In the third act, Orpheus arrives on the banks of the river of Hades, and having lulled the savage pilot asleep by his melodious song, enters into the fatal bark alone. In the fourth act, Orpheus, the conqueror of death, returns towards the light of day, leading Eurydice; furious spirits pursue them; fearing to lose her, he breaks his compact and turns back. Eurydice, already a fleeting shade, bewails her fate for a moment, and disappears while the infernal chorus sings its victory. The

fifth act is weak.   The poet avoids the horrible *dénouement* of
the legend, the rending of Orpheus by the Bacchantes.   He
prefers, after a scene in which Echo replies to the despair of
Orpheus, to introduce Apollo, who, as " Deus ex machina,"
offers to his son that he shall enter living into immortality.
Orpheus and Apollo ascend to heaven in a chariot, while
the chorus celebrate in song and dance the apotheosis of the
lyre-bearer.

Among the Florentines, dramatic expression was confided
to the voices only.   The meagre *ritornelli* of Cavaliere are
purely decorative.   But with Monteverdi it is quite another
matter;   the instruments are almost as important as the
voices.

The basis of the drama is certainly declamation, but we
are a long way here from the lifeless recitative of the Florentine innovators.   Monteverdi's recitative is rich in melodic
accents.   There are arias and songs in the *Orfeo*, but the
striking point is that all the principal scenes are treated in
free recitative style.   In the admirable narration of the
Messenger, so moving in its simplicity, a few chromatics
and a sudden modulation from E into E flat major are sufficient
to give an impression of anguish and horror.   Silvia's narration is accompanied by a small positive organ (*organo di
legno*) and a chitarrone.   The plaintive, veiled tones of
these instruments, which succeed abruptly to the brilliant
and ringing high notes of the treble viols and harpsichord
which accompanied the voices of the shepherds, must have
further accentuated the impression of gloom.

Orpheus' despair, when he has cast off the stupor into
which the fatal message has thrown him, is again expressed
in the recitative style.   It is difficult to say, in this celebrated

passage, what is most admirable, whether its dramatic intensity or the intelligence with which its least details are worked out. *" Tu sei morta,"* murmurs Orpheus, scarcely conscious as yet of the possibility of such horror. " Thou art dead, and I live," and gradually the tone rises. His whole being rebels against destiny. Now he cries aloud; he will go and claim Eurydice from the King of Darkness, and will bring her back to the light. Then great peace descends upon his soul, and he utters the exquisite phrase, " I shall bring thee back; thou shalt once more see the light."

EXAMPLE 15

Doubt assails him. Yet no matter; if he fails, he will remain with her among the dead, and he bids a solemn farewell to the earth and to the sun.

EXAMPLE 16

The way in which the phrases of this song, while exactly moulded on the poetic text, maintain a perfect balance is a marvel. This is truly melody unbound.

In the first act, Orpheus' love-song, *Rosa del ciel*, is a magnificent example of an aria recitative. The recitative is perfectly free in form, but, while reflecting intimately all the suggestions of the text, it is so tuneful that it can be regarded as a true melody. It is a far cry from this to the hollow narrations of Peri and Cavaliere.

Monteverdi, in the same way as Lulli did later, excels

in extracting from the very sound of a word the melody
latent within it.   For him, there are no two ways of expressing
the same words in music.   When a group of words recurs
in the course of the drama, it invariably reintroduces the
same melodic figure.   The Messenger cries, " *Ahi ! caso
acerbo !   Ahi fat' empio e crudele !   Ahi, stelle ingiuriose,
Ahi, Ciel avaro !* "

EXAMPLE 17

A little later on, the shepherd utters the same imprecations,
and the chorus takes them up in its turn at the end of the
act.*   The melody undergoes some slight changes in respect
of the value of the notes, but the intervals are unchanged.

Monteverdi's recitative tends to become an *arioso*.   Generally the first and the last phrases are more pronouncedly
melodic in character than the rest of the piece.   The recitative
which is terminated by Orpheus' ardent prayer, *Rendete mi
il mio bene, Tartarei Numi,* is a model of this aria-recitative
style.†   Frequently the extremely melodious opening phrase
is repeated at the end of the passage, thus forming a kind of
rudimentary *aria da capo*.   The shepherd's song in the first
act, *In questo lieto e fortunato giorno,* is a curious example of
this.   The opening phrase and its repetition occupy three-
quarters of the entire passage.‡

In addition to these aria-recitatives, in which the recitative
is enclosed by the repetition of the initial phrase, Monteverdi
makes frequent use of the strophic aria, in which different
stanzas are sung, if not to the same melody, at any rate on

---

* See Note 49.   † See Note 50.   ‡ See Note 51.

the same bass. This is the case in the air of *Music* in
the Prologue. The recitative changes with each stanza, but
the bass, in its general outline at least, remains the same, and
gives a profound coherence to the whole. In Act IV, Orpheus,
while leading Eurydice back to earth, sings on the same bass
(ascending and descending runs repeated in sequences) three
stanzas, the melodies of which, whilst offering considerable
points of resemblance, are not identical.*

The aria in which Orpheus pleads with the infernal deities
in the third act is one of the oldest examples known of an
air in concerted style. The figured bass is performed by a
small positive organ doubled by a chitarrone, while two violins
contend with the voice throughout the first stanza. Two
cornetti, succeeded by two harps (*arpe doppie*), replace the
violins in the succeeding stanzas, thus modifying the tone
atmosphere of the passage. The violins, cornetti, or harps
are heard as soon as the voice ceases, and play brief *ritornelli*
at the end of each stanza.

EXAMPLE 18

* See Note 52.

The vocal part is ornamented. Following the example given some years earlier by Caccini in his *Nuove Musiche*. Monteverdi himself composes the expressive *vocalises* and *melismata* with which the voice-part should be decorated, but publishes simultaneously a perfectly unadorned version of the melody, as though he wished to leave the choice open.

EXAMPLE 19

The melodic contour is only slightly defined, and the whole passage is rather a highly ornate recitative than an aria in the sense in which we understand the term now. Whilst in the dramatic narrations Monteverdi seems to have drawn his inspiration from Peri, in Orpheus' strophic aria he takes Caccini as his model. It is an exercise in virtuosity, with trills, and reiterated notes which show off to the full the technical skill of the singer, but it maintains at the same time a highly expressive quality. At one time the voice seems to sob :

EXAMPLE 20

A beautiful melodic phrase, twice repeated, serves as conclusion.

EXAMPLE 21

Ahi' chi nie - ga il con - for - to al - le   mie   pe - - ne ⌒

By the side of these arias in recitative style, we find others in rhythmic form after the fashion of the *Scherzi Musicali* and the French *airs mesurés*, such as the two airs which Orpheus sings in Act II,* *Ecco pur ch'a voi ritorno* and *Vi ricorda o boschi ombrosi*. The first is constructed upon the following metrical scheme ∪∪—∪—∪——; the scheme of the second is more complete, but, as in the French *airs de cour*, remains unchanged in the various succeeding stanzas.

EXAMPLE 22

Vi ri-cor-da o bosch' om-bro - - si   Vi ri-cor-da o bosch' om-bro - si

De miei lun -ghi aspri tormen - ti   Quando i sas - si à miei la- men - ti

The bass keeps to this rhythm, and the *ritornelli* are constructed, in the same way as those of the *Scherzi Musicali*, upon a motive repeated in strict sequences in the bass. The dreamy, melancholy atmosphere of these airs corresponds pretty well to the atmosphere of the *airs de cour*, though the melodic contour is entirely Italian.

There are few scenes in which Monteverdi introduces two or three solo-voices simultaneously. There is still no intermediary between the monody and the madrigal. The only passage which already offers something like a genuine

* Note See 53.

duet is that which Apollo and Orpheus sing together in ascending to heaven.* The two voices following each other in canonic imitations, or uniting in long chains of thirds the runs and *fiorituri* with which the parts are decorated, make of this passage one of the most ancient examples of the classical operatic duet.

The choruses, which are numerous and important, are extremely varied. Monteverdi here displays his astonishing mastery of the madrigal form, and, indeed, several of these choruses are pure madrigals, bringing into play all the possibilities of the most audacious polyphony. This is so in the chorus of spirits: *Nulla impresa per uom si tenta in vano*, which celebrates Orpheus' victory, and which, as M. Romain Rolland points out, " is resplendent with all the pride of the Renaissance." This five-part chorus is supported by the regals, the small positive organ (*di legno*), five trombones, two *bassi da gamba*, and a *contrabasso*. Its splendour recalls certain motets of the school of Gabrieli.†

In addition to the choruses in imitations, Monteverdi introduces frequent homophonic choruses in syllabic diction in precise and well-marked rhythms. In Act I the chorus of shepherds, *Vieni Imeneo*, supported by the orchestra, bears to heaven the ardent and joyous prayer of a whole people.‡ Elsewhere, the two genres are felicitously combined, but the madrigal style predominates, and Monteverdi frequently renders exactly the images suggested by the poem. The voices ascend on the words *cielo* (heaven) or *salita* (ascent), they scatter rapidly on *fugge* (flight), and *il precipizio* (precipice), is the occasion for an impressive descending sixth. These details in no way diminish the general expressive value of the passage. Terror, grief, revolt are powerfully rendered in this chorus, which expresses the lamentations of the shepherds after the death of Eurydice.§

* See Note 54.   † See Note 55.   ‡ See Note 56.   § See Note 57.

Sometimes, to make a contrast, Monteverdi inserts a duet
or a trio between two choruses. This happens in the pastoral
scenes of the first act; and these passages are treated in very
simple homophonic style, in the same way as the *canzonette*
and *villanelle* for two or three voices which were so popular
two or three years earlier.

Frequently the voices combine with the instruments in
choruses with dancing in the French fashion. Some are
treated, partially at least, in imitation, but this is the exception, and most frequently the diction is syllabic, and the
harmonies are vertical. These ballets, which were played,
sung and danced, comprise several alterations of time. That
in Act I is very characteristic from this point of view. *Lasciate
i monti* is sung by the voices entering successively in canon
in common time. This first part forms the *entrée* proper of
the ballet. Having taken up their positions, the nymphs
begin the dance in lively well-marked rhythm in 3/2 time:
qui miri il sole. An instrumental *ritornello* in 6/4 time inter-
rupts the voices for a moment, but the dance proceeds, and
the voices re-enter to conclude the chorus with further stanzas
in 3/2 time. Quite a little orchestra composed of five *viole
da braccio*, three chitarroni, two harpsichords, a double harp,
a *contrabasso di viola* and a small *flûte-à-bec* (*flautino alla
vigesima*) accompanies the voices and plays the *ritornello.*

The whole score shows considerable attention to variety
of effect. The *Euridice* of Peri and Caccini are both tedious
by reason of their lack of colour. The lines are delicately,
or even occasionally vigorously drawn, but there is little
play of light and shade. Everything is on the one plane,
joy or sadness. On the contrary, contrast abounds in the
Orfeo of Monteverdi. The powerful Venetian colourist is
at work. The first act is a luminous tone-picture in clear
tints. It is almost entirely given up to joyous shepherd
choruses with dancing. There is no action, properly speak-

ing, but only the evocation of a rural landscape in an atmosphere of serene joy.   The atmosphere of the second act is sombre throughout.   The songs in which Orpheus hails his country are inspired with a grave sadness, as though the hero were under the spell of foreboding, and when the grief-stricken exclamations of the messenger reach his ears from far off, he immediately grasps what has befallen him.   Overwhelmed, he can do no more than murmur " Alas ! " when the fatal tidings are announced.   An abrupt modulation from C into A major on Silvia's arrival gives the effect of a cloud brooding over the scene, and, till the end of the scene, the music maintains its gloomy character.   In Act III, by the substitution of brass for the strings, Monteverdi produces a dark and truly malevolent effect.   The fourth act is all in half-tints, suited to the pale light which reigns in the infernal regions, and in Act V there is a progression from the dark despair of Orpheus to the golden glow of the musical apotheosis.   Later, Monteverdi obtained these colour effects by harmony and rhythm only, but here he principally employs the orchestra to that end.   In this, he shows an astonishing sensitiveness to the expressive value of each instrument, and to what we call instrumental colour, but in this he is no innovator, as has often been stated.

In the course of the sixteenth century the marvellous effectiveness of trombones, cornetti, and trumpets in infernal scenes, of trumpets and drums in warlike action, of flutes and oboes in pastoral intermezzi, of viols in scenes of love or sadness, of harps, lutes or regals in apotheosis scenes, had gradually been recognized.   This is the way in which instruments were employed in families in the mysteries, the *sacre rappresentazioni*, as well as in court interludes.   There was nothing revolutionary in Monteverdi's making use of all the instrumental performers of the Duke of Mantua ; * on

* See Note 58.

the contrary, this was strictly traditional. Progress was to
consist in simplifying the orchestra, in readjusting its balance,
in giving it a sounder basis, to the detriment of its brilliance
and variety.

What is quite peculiar to Monteverdi is the use of symphonic
fragments as genuine " leading motives " to ensure the unity
of the drama, and to express certain definite feelings. The
piece entitled *Ritornello*, which is not a *ritornello* in the ordinary
sense of the word (since it is not associated with a song from
which it takes its melodic themes), seems to be as it were
the " leading motive " of Orpheus. It is heard during the
prologue between the verses sung by *Music* to announce
the subject of the play, it reappears with slight modifications
at the end of Act II and of Act IV. In the same way, the
symphony for seven instruments which bursts out like an
imperious supplication at the end of Act II reappears modified,
and is played *pianissimo* by the viols and the small positive
organ at the moment when Orpheus prepares to enter the
bark of the sleeping Charon while invoking the powers of
Hades. It is again played by seven instruments after Orpheus'
prayer, *Rendete mi il mio bene, Tartarei Numi*, and concludes
Act III, following on the chorus of spirits, *Nulla impresa per
uom si tenta in vana*. It expresses the amorous daring of
Orpheus, who does not so much implore the Gods as command
them. Finally, the infernal symphony which opens Act III,
which is confided to the drums, cornetti and regals, reappears
in Act V after the scene of Orpheus' despair, expressing the
ghastly enchantment of the region in which Eurydice lives.

The Prologue opens with a Toccata, a magnificent movement in four parts, abrupt and powerful in rhythm. It was
played three times by an orchestra in which the brass
predominates (*clarino, vulgano, trombe con sordine*). With its
runs in sequences, its joyous clamours, it is very characteristic
of Monteverdi's orchestration.

The *ritornello* which follows, and which we can regard as the " leading motive " of Orpheus, is constructed upon the rhythmic plan of the bass repeated four times in strict sequence. This process recalls that of the *ritornelli* of the *Scherzi Musicali*, and the opening *ritornello* of Orpheus' Air in Act II, *Ecco pur ch'a voi ritorno*. Here the bass repeats four times in sequence the same melodic and rhythmic theme which the two *violini piccoli alla francese* embellish with figures in thirds of an elegant simplicity. We have seen that the air of Orpheus conforms to a strict metrical plan. The same arrangement reappears in the five-part *ritornello* of Orpheus' second air, *Vi ricorda, o bosch' ombrosi*, which is also metrical. Monteverdi therefore seems to have had in mind, in composing these *ritornelli*, the rhythmic formulæ so much in favour among the French masters. Its style, like that of the French ballets, is only very slightly polyphonic; single chords support a melodic theme played in thirds by the violins.

The *sinfonie* are never dominated by a rhythmic figure frequently repeated. The style is free and varied. Whilst the five-part *sinfonia* which concludes Act I recalls somewhat the style of the French ballets, the symphony on the banks of the Styx, with its heavy homophonic chords interrupted by silences, is Monteverdi's own, and there is nothing in contemporary music with which it can be compared.

Other symphonic passages are polyphonic in character; for example, the passage in seven parts, which celebrates the victory of Hades over Orpheus, played by cornetti, trombones and regals. This superb *sinfonia* recalls the sumptuous sonatas of Gabrieli.

In Act I the curious *ritornello* which precedes the shepherds' trio is nothing less than a *ricercare* for organ in five parts on a bass theme obstinately repeated in sequences. Two themes are ingeniously elaborated in canon.

EXAMPLE 23

What, we might ask, is this piece of church music, which might be the work of a Giov. Gabrieli or a Claudio Merulo, doing in this opera? The explanation is that it embodies the impression of rude strength and harsh gravity which best befits true shepherds. We are among the mountains of Greece, and not in the artificial Arcadia of the Italian academicians.

Monteverdi is not a man of formulæ. He takes advantage of all the formulæ current in his day, of all those which he himself invented or brought to perfection. By the side of *ritornelli* on strict metrical plans we find *sinfonie* in homophonic or polyphonic style, *toccate, ricercari, morisques*. By the side of dramatic recitatives we find aria-recitatives, strophic airs, *airs mesurés*, choruses in homophonic style or in counterpoint, and ballets played, sung, and danced. Monteverdi brought to the development of the new form of tragedy in recitative all the technical resources of which his genius disposed. He turned the aristocratic spectacle of Florence into modern musical drama, overflowing with life and bearing in its mighty waves of sound the passions which make up the human soul.

II

THE "ARIANNA" AND THE FÊTES OF 1608

IN July 1607, while the Duke, accompanied by his favourite musicians, was resting at the baths of Sampierdarena, Monteverdi went to Cremona. His wife Claudia had been in failing health for some time past, and Monteverdi doubtless wished to confide her to the care of his father, who, as we have seen, was a doctor. He was in great need of rest himself. He complains of his health in a letter written on July 28th to excuse his delay in setting to music a sonnet which the Duke had sent him. His compatriots gave him an enthusiastic welcome; the *Accademia degli Animosi* gave in his honour, on August 10th, a concert during which fragments of the *Orfeo* were performed. Leaving his wife and two children at Cremona, Monteverdi left some days after the ceremony for Milan to confer with the poet Dom Cherubino Ferrari.

In going to Milan he was not actuated solely by the desire of showing the score of the *Orfeo* to a friend in a friendly way. The Carmelite monk, Dom Ferrari, was famous for his talent in the invention of interludes, spectacles, ballets, tournaments. He was at the moment much occupied with the creation of something new and singular for the fêtes which were to be given at Turin and Mantua on the occasion of the marriage of Francesco Gonzaga and Princess Margaret of Savoy. In a letter addressed to the Duke of Modena, he recalls that he has employed his talent in the service of the Dukes of Savoy and Mantua, and has provided them with poetic texts and all kinds of inventions. "I am well practised," he writes on

March 8th, 1608, " in this kind of dramatic composition, as
can testify Claudio Monteverdi, *Maestro di Cappella* of the Duke
of Mantua, who consults me about his compositions." *
Monteverdi, therefore, had gone to Milan to submit the *Orfeo*
to the professional judgment of this monk, who was an expert
in all matters relating to the theatre.

Whilst Monteverdi was in Milan, the *Scherzi Musicali*
were being published at Venice. Monteverdi, who was too
busy to supervise this publication, had entrusted it to the care
of his brother Giulio Cesare. Giulio Cesare, who was six
years younger than his brother, was also a musician. He seems
to have had little talent as a composer, to judge from pieces of
his composition published in the collection of the *Scherzi
Musicali*, but he rendered signal service to his brother. At the
court of Mantua, he seems to have acted as his factotum, and
was continually occupied in supervising rehearsals, in copying
music, in practising with the singers.

On his return to Cremona, Monteverdi found his wife
in a desperate state. She died on September 10th and was
buried in the church of SS. Nazaro e Celso. His grief was
profound. He was left with two young children, and was
deprived of his helpmeet, herself an excellent musician,
capable of understanding him and standing by him in the
struggle he had to go through in the cause of his art. Nor
was the privacy of his grief respected. Claudia was hardly
buried when the Duke sent for him, and Monteverdi had
to return to Mantua to prepare the marriage festivities.
Federigo Follino wrote him an affectionate letter persuading
him to return, condoling with him upon the loss of a noble
wife of outstanding talent, but exhorting him to return to
Mantua. " The moment has come," he writes, " to attain
to the greatest glory that man can hope for on earth." With
an effort to control his grief, Monteverdi set out for Mantua.

* See Note 59.

His sorrow-stricken soul found consolation in his work, and his own despair found utterance in the laments of the forsaken Ariadne.

For the libretto of the tragedy which Monteverdi was to set to music the Duke of Mantua had commissioned the most famous poet in Italy in the genre, Ottavio Rinuccini.

Himself of noble birth, this poet was accustomed to the society of the greatest princes. It was said of him that he had been in love with Maria de' Medici, and that this was the sole reason for his continual journeys to France.* A violent cabal had recently been formed against him in Florence, and had forced him to hold aloof from the preparation of the fêtes to celebrate the marriage of the hereditary prince of Tuscany. In the state of wounded pride in which he was, Rinuccini had enthusiastically accepted the proposal of the Duke of Mantua, and had set to work, taking as subject of his tragedy the pathetic story of the misfortunes of Ariadne.

Meanwhile, Ferdinando Gonzaga had somewhat heedlessly accepted a libretto from the Florentine poet Cini. The recitatives and soli of this opera, *Teti*, were set to music by Jacopo Peri, the *ensembles* being reserved for Monteverdi and the composers of the Mantuan court. Cini and Peri had almost finished their work when the order was countermanded from Mantua by Ferdinando, who had been advised of his father's agreement with Rinuccini and Monteverdi.† The *Teti* was therefore put aside. The text has disappeared,‡ but we can deduce from one of Jacopo Peri's letters that it contained nothing strikingly original.

Peri continued to neglect instrumental accompaniments, and for his thorough-bass only used harmonic instruments, a harpsichord, a great lyre and a harp. He desired doubtless to imitate the sound of the lyres which had accompanied the voices in ancient music.

* See Note 60.   † See Note 61.   ‡ See Note 62.

Monteverdi returned to Mantua on October 10th, and showed some impatience to obtain Rinuccini's libretto, for the Duke intended to celebrate the marriage in January, and the musician was dismayed at the brief time allowed him. As soon as the poet arrived in Mantua, Monteverdi set to work. But unfavourable circumstances caused the postponement of the date fixed for the marriage ceremonies. Seeing that the *Arianna* could not be ready for carnival-time, the Duke decided to have another spectacle, less difficult of execution, performed in January. Rinuccini offered the Duke his *Dafne*, which had once been set to music by Jacopo Peri, and subsequently by the Florentine musician Marco da Gagliano. The Prince Ferdinando had been ordained Cardinal on Christmas Day ; it was decided that this preliminary spectacle should be performed in his honour.*

We have information relating to the performances of the *Dafne* in Marco da Gagliano's celebrated preface to the printed score.† Monteverdi's pupil, Caterinuccia, achieved a signal triumph on this occasion, as did a singer of the Tuscan court, Antonio Brandi, called Il Brandino. We know that Rinuccini had considerably modified the original libretto, and that the musician had adroitly interpolated in the score several airs and madrigals composed by the cardinal Ferdinando di Gonzaga. The score of *Dafne* is of great interest, in that it shows the tendency of drama in recitative to become tuneful.

Marco da Gagliano,‡ himself the pupil of one of the last Florentine defenders of the contrapuntal tradition, had already composed numerous masses and motets when the performance of *Dafne* opened up new horizons before him. He had been attracted to the ideal of emotional expression which Monteverdi and Gesualdo, Prince of Venosa, were striving to attain, and adopted at once the creed of the Florentines. The pleasure of the spectator must arise from

* See Note 63.　　　† See Note 64.　　　‡ See Note 65.

his comprehension of the words.   Now this theory is certainly
more literary than musical.   But Da Gagliano was a far better
musician than Peri or Emilio del Cavaliere.   Without perhaps
being conscious of doing so, he reintroduced music into sung
tragedy.

In glancing through the score of the *Dafne*, one notices
that the melodic phrase falls into harmonious periods, that
the *melopeia* no longer drifts vaguely along, finding a precarious support in the accentuation of the words : it has a
more definite contour.   Marco da Gagliano makes no attempt
to express passion in music, as Monteverdi or Sigismondo
d'India had done ; he is preoccupied mainly with form.
The *Orfeo* and the *Dafne* therefore symbolize the two channels
by which the *melodramma* was approaching dramatic expressiveness and formal beauty.   The tendencies are conflicting ; they
converged in the last works of Monteverdi and in the works
of such men as Cavalli, Luigi Rossi, Cesti, of all those creators
of expressive beauty to whom history is only now beginning
to pay homage.

The *Arianna* was due to succeed the *Dafne*.   Monteverdi
was working at it in a positive fever.   He had almost finished
the score on February 2nd and several of the singers who
were to perform in it had already arrived from Florence
when a catastrophe occurred.   The charming Caterinuccia
Martinelli, the pupil of Monteverdi, who was to have taken
the part of Ariadne, fell ill of smallpox and died in a few weeks.
She was mourned by all.   The Duke commanded that she
should be interred in a splendid tomb, and the poets vied with
each other in writing verses to celebrate the rare attainments
of the youthful singer, but seventeen years old.

The sovereigns of Mantua went to Turin for the marriage
ceremony.   The celebrations were of long duration, and the
Duke prolonged his absence until May.

Meanwhile, Rinuccini had returned from Florence to

Mantua, and was, with Monteverdi, putting the finishing touches to the preparations for the *Arianna*. On February 26th, a meeting was held at the Palace at which were present Rinuccini, Monteverdi, the architect Vianini, and Federigo Follino, the historian of the court fêtes. It was decided at this meeting to enliven the *Arianna* with a *divertissement* to please the Duchess. Caterinuccia had then seemed better, and there was no talk of replacing her. It was decided that Chiabrera's interludes for Guarini's comedy, *l'Idropica*, should be composed by the principal musicians of the court. Monteverdi took charge of the prologue, Salomone de Rossi, D. Giov. Giacomo Gastoldi, Marco da Gagliano, Giulio Cesare Monteverdi and Paolo Birt divided the interludes between them. It was perhaps at the same meeting that Rinuccini, to comply with a wish expressed by the Duchess, came to an agreement with Monteverdi respecting the composition of a third spectacle. This spectacle was the *Ballo delle Ingrate*.

Later, Monteverdi told how the excessive fatigue caused by this business very nearly killed him. He had none of the extraordinary facility of certain of his rivals; he worked relatively slowly, left nothing to chance, and never wrote a bar which had not its *raison d'être*. The composition of a lyrical drama such as the *Arianna*, of an important prologue, and a ballet all in less than six months was a task above the strength of a man in a state of physical and mental exhaustion. The death of Caterinuccia on March 8th aggravated the difficulties with which he was struggling; it was moreover a terrible blow to him personally, for he had had the entire training of the young artiste.

Monteverdi advised the Duchess to engage a singer from Bergamo to replace Caterinuccia, but this singer refused to come to Mantua when approached. No one else had been found, when the Duchess heard that the actress Virginia

Andreini, also called *La Florinda*, who had just arrived at Mantua with the company of the *Fedeli* to play Guarini's pastoral, had been heard to sing admirably fragments of the *Arianna*. She was sent for, and, to everybody's delighted astonishment, sang to perfection " the most difficult passage " —doubtless the famous *Lamento*. It is quite comprehensible, indeed, that a tragic actress, gifted with a fine voice, should be able to interpret far better than any concert-singer music such as Monteverdi's, which requires above all highly emotional and very dramatic rendering.

While Monteverdi and Rinuccini were composing the *Ballo delle Ingrate*, Marco da Gagliano and Striggio were working on another ballet, *Il Sagrificio di Ifigenia*, by order of the hereditary prince. The consequence was that there were incessant intrigues and mutual accusations of plagiarism. The preparations were finished in this stormy atmosphere, and not before time, for the ducal couple were about to enter Mantua, followed by a host of princes, lords, cardinals and gentlemen from all parts of Italy.

It was in the presence of an assembly which Follino estimates at six thousand, and the resident of Modena at four thousand, that the *Arianna* was performed, on May 28th, 1608, in an immense theatre constructed by the architect Vianini in the interior of the castle. The performance of a *melodramma* had never been witnessed by so large a gathering. The guards were powerless and the authority of Carlo Rossi, commander in chief of the Mantuan army, was insufficient to maintain order. The Duke was obliged to intervene several times in person. Yet in order to keep down the numbers, he had forbidden the officers and servants of his household to be present at the spectacle.

The best singers of Mantua and Florence took part in the performance. In the rôle of Ariadne, Virginia Andreini drew tears from the whole assembly. Later, the poet Marino recalled how " Florinda had sung the cruel torments of Ariadne, and drawn a thousand sighs from a thousand breasts."* Francesco Rasi also did wonders.   Brandino, Orlandi, Settimia Caccini, all three lent by the Grand Duke of Tuscany for the occasion, passed almost unnoticed.

Of the *Arianna* we possess only the text of Rinuccini's drama, so classical in its beauty that it has been called Racinian,† some contemporary descriptions of the performance published by Solerti, and finally, the music of Scene VI, in which Ariadne, forsaken by Theseus, laments her fate.   It was, moreover, this lament of Ariadne which ensured the success of the work.   Monteverdi, perhaps because he had put his whole soul into it, attached peculiar importance to it.   He frequently quotes it in his letters.   He had a separate edition of it published,‡ and later arranged it as a madrigal for five voices, to the great regret of Doni, who reproached him with " thus having disfigured the pearl of his compositions."   He even adapted it to a sacred text.   Copies of the Lament spread throughout Italy.   The famous Adriana Basile sang it at Naples, and Severo Bonini tells us that there was not a house in Italy possessing a harpsichord or theorbo which did not have the music.

This is incontestably Monteverdi's finest dramatic passage. Grief is expressed with a majesty which recalls the masterpieces of ancient Greece.   Heart-rending as it is, this grief is without grimace or convulsion.   It is the grief of Niobe, who sees her children perish, so that it is possible, on reflection, to understand the letter—at first sight enigmatic—in which Monteverdi states that he was inspired by Plato in composing this passage.   " When I was about to compose the lament of Ariadne, I could find no book which could enlighten me on natural methods of imitation, nor which would even authorize me to imitate, save Plato, and he in a manner so obscure, that,

* See Note 66.   † See Note 67.   ‡ See Note 68.

with my feeble comprehension, I could scarcely comprehend the little which he revealed."* While pedants were laboriously discussing the modes and metres of ancient music, Monteverdi, by the intuition of genius, had rediscovered the imitation of nature as Greek artists had understood it.

In the light of contemporary descriptions, we can realize that the score of the *Arianna* was composed on the same principles as that of the *Orfeo*. A very large number of instruments was engaged in the performance. Each scene was accompanied by the instruments which corresponded best to its dramatic character. In the prologue, during the gradual descent of the cloud bearing Apollo, a symphony of various instruments was heard, first alone, then as an accompaniment to the voice of the god.

The orchestra was placed behind the stage, so as to be hidden from the spectators.† The lament of Ariadne was accompanied by viols. Monteverdi, in common with Mersenne, seems to have thought that the viol, which " imitates the voice in all its modulations," is better suited to the accompaniment of voices than the violin, and is specially suited to " sad and grave " passages in " broad, slow rhythm." ‡

Rinuccini's tragedy was modelled upon the plan of ancient drama. There is a somewhat conventional prologue, followed by the main action divided into five acts separated by choruses. Theseus' disembarkment in the first act is full of heroic grandeur. Alone at nightfall, Theseus and Ariadne recount their love. Ariadne, in spite of her lover's promises and protestations, her soul troubled by sinister presentiments, is invaded by melancholy. Act II shows Theseus' hesitations ; tortured by ambition, love, remorse, he resolves finally (like Titus in Racine's *Berenice*) to yield to reasons of state and abandon Ariadne. In Act III, Ariadne awakens, and is anxious at Theseus' absence. Reassured by her confidante,

* See Note 69　　　† See Note 70　　　‡ See Note 71.

she reproaches herself for having doubted her lover, and sets off to seek him.

Act IV opens with the narration of a messenger, who has seen the departure of the fleet. Ariadne, scarcely able to support herself, enters and utters her complaint, which is interrupted from time to time by the exclamations of the chorus and the exhortations of her confidante. Every shade of grief is magnificently expressed by the poet—desire for death, dejection, anguish, self-pity, revolt, despair. One can imagine the comfort Monteverdi must have derived from the composition of this scene, in which he gives expression to the grief which had tortured him since the death of his own beloved Claudia. Indeed, the great power of this Lament resides less in its plastic beauty than in the variety and intensity of its dramatic feeling.

EXAMPLE 24

Las-cia - te mi mo - ri - re   Las-cia - te mi   mo - ri - re

This is no mere recitative : words have become song, and this passage remained unparalleled in its intensity until the advent of Gluck.

Though the melodic intervals of the diminished seventh and fifth were then new, Monteverdi knew their expressive power. He uses them with felicitous audacity.

EXAMPLE 25

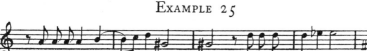

Se tu sa-pes - si ——— Oh Di-- - - - o   Se tu sa - - pes-si oi - - - me!

In Act V a messenger announces the arrival of Bacchus, and the marriage of the liberator God with the blushing Cretan. The piece terminates in rejoicings celebrating simultaneously in song and dance the nuptials of Ariadne and of Marguerite of Savoy. This *dénouement* somewhat impairs an admirable tragedy. It appears to have been commanded by the Duchess of Mantua, who found the subject a little gloomy for performance at a wedding.*

Other splendours followed the representation of the *Arianna*. On June 2nd there was a performance of Guarini's comedy, the *Idropica*, interspersed, in the old fashion, with musical interludes which were simply the pretext for a display of sumptuous scenery. Monteverdi had only composed the prologue, which Follino describes thus : †

" After the guests were seated, a signal was sounded by trumpets at the back of the theatre. At the third blast the curtain disappeared as if by magic, revealing three clouds so skilfully made that they seemed natural. Below them, waves rolled and broke. A woman's head slowly emerged. With measured movements, she arose, and, as the trumpet blasts died away, she landed on the banks of a small island. Then, accompanied by the orchestra, she sang a melody so touching, that all present were moved."

Follino's account also tells us of another touching piece of music written by Monteverdi for this occasion. The *Ballo delle Ingrate* expresses the same sadness. Doubtless, in this year of sorrow, his genius could express no other emotion but grief.

The *Ballo delle Ingrate*, performed on June 4th, 1608, is a highly important work, and it is astonishing that it should never have been the subject of attentive study by historians of music. It is, in fact, the only ballet *alla francese* that we possess in its entirety. There is no question that it was

* See Note 72.   † See Note 73.

produced under the influence of the new type of spectacle invented in France ; moreover, Rinuccini's son, in the preface to the complete works of his father, has credited him with having been the first to introduce into Italy the *ballet de cour.** Before writing the *Ballo delle Ingrate*, Monteverdi had on several occasions composed ballets of this type. In a letter of December 1604 he is much occupied with a choreographic *divertissement* on the subject of Diana and Endymion. The Duke had restricted his commission to one *entrée de ballet* for the Stars which accompany the Moon, one *entrée* for the Shepherds, Endymion's friends, and an *ensemble* of Stars and Shepherds. For the moment, he is occupied with the ballet of the Stars only, and has just devised a scheme which seems to him ingenious and original. The *ensembles*, executed to a brief lively tune played by all the instruments, are to alternate with *pas de deux* danced to an air played by five *viole da braccio*. Thus all the Stars are to dance in pairs successively, and the resumption of the *ensemble* between the figures will avoid monotony.

The plan of the *Ballo delle Ingrate* is different. For that matter, it bears a close resemblance to the principal ballets which were being performed at the court of Henry IV—the *Ballet d'Alcine*, for example, given in 1609.† But in the *Ballo delle Ingrate* the opening *Récit* is replaced by a long scene in recitative which outlines the subject of the ballet, and the scenery bears witness to the high degree of perfection to which Italian scenic artists had attained for some years past. When the curtain rose, the formidable jaws of Hell were revealed, lighted from within by glowing vapours. In the foreground of the stage, which was connected with the auditorium by inclined platforms, were Venus, Eros and Pluto, who carried on a dialogue in recitative. Pluto agreed to allow the *Ingrate* to come back to Earth for a few moments, so that the

* See Note 74.　　　　　　† See Note 75.

ladies of the company, who might be guilty of like cruelty, might be warned by their example.

Then the unhappy souls advanced through the flames of Hell in pairs, keeping time to the music. They were represented by eight women-dancers, and eight men dressed as women wearing frightful masks. They descended into the auditorium and began to dance a ballet which comprised various figures, all of which were performed in the French way to a single melodic theme.

The *Entrée*, properly speaking, was composed of a very simple theme in common time.

EXAMPLE 26

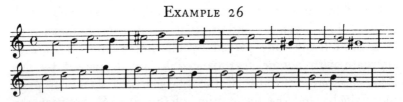

The souls of the unfortunate entered to this theme frequently repeated, " advancing with slow and natural steps." Having arrived in the auditorium, they began to dance to the same air. When the first figure was terminated the violins changed the rhythm.

EXAMPLE 27

The third figure was danced to common time, and the fourth in 6/4.

EXAMPLE 28

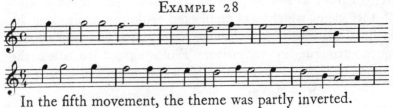

In the fifth movement, the theme was partly inverted.

EXAMPLE 29

The sixth and last consisted in a repetition of the original theme slightly modified.

EXAMPLE 30

This was the French manner of dancing a ballet; it explains why the music of a ballet, the performance of which, according to contemporary records, took up several hours, occupies only a few pages in Philidor's copies. Only the theme of the *Entrée* was set down, but no account was taken of the many rhythmic variations which were introduced at great length by the twenty-four violins.

Plastically speaking, this ballet, in conformity with the French style, belonged as much to pantomime as to the dance properly speaking. The *Ingrate*, by mimicry and attitude, continually expressed the idea of profound despair.

After the ballet, Pluto sang a long narration divided into five stanzas by the repetition of a *ritornello* in three parts on the theme of the dance. He exhorted the ladies to show compassion, threatening them with Hell if they continued to show themselves *ingrate*. To depict this gloomy region, his voice took on a sinister tone, with a descending *glissando* of an eleventh on the words *là giù* (beneath the earth).

EXAMPLE 31

An - - tro è   là   giù   di   lu-ce e d'aer   pri - - - vo

Then he commanded the *Ingrate* to return to their sombre dwelling. They then danced the second part of the Ballet to the same air as before, and, returning to the stage, disappeared with gestures of distress into the flaming jaws of Hell.

The procession was closed by a single *Ingrata*. Just as she was about to disappear, she turned, and bade a touching farewell to the light; for a moment her voice was heard with that of her companions, exhorting ladies, young and old, to compassion. This lament, sung by Virginia Andreini, who had previously interpreted the rôle of Ariadne, contributed greatly to Monteverdi's renown. It is the most interesting passage of the work. It is poignantly expressive, and, for dramatic intensity, may be compared with Ariadne's lament, or the scene of Orpheus' despair. The preceding dialogues and narrations bear traces of haste. Monteverdi was exhausted and cannot have been profoundly inspired by all this conventional court language, devoid as it is of any human feeling. Certain imitative passages are to be noted, for they anticipate the *Combattimento*; for example, this fragment which represents the battle.

EXAMPLE 32

It is equally interesting to note the attention to thematic uniformity which leads Monteverdi to compose all the *ritornelli* and *sinfonie* of his score on the same theme as the ballet itself.

This preoccupation with thematic unity is still more pronounced in his religious compositions.

Faithful to the system which he had adopted in the *Orfeo*, Monteverdi employed for the accompaniment of each of the *dramatis personæ* the instruments corresponding best to the character. Venus sang " to the sounds of very sweet instruments," and Pluto must certainly have been accompanied here, as in the *Orfeo*, by the brass. The curtain rose to a long roll of " discordant drums." In the French fashion, the orchestra accompanying the voices was separate from the dance orchestra, and was hidden behind the stage, whilst the latter was on a platform in the auditorium.

The strangers, who had flocked·to Mantua from all parts of Italy, returned to their homes celebrating the magnificence of the Duke and the rare talent of his servants. In the autumn of the same year, 1608, the Grand Duke of Tuscany, in spite of his desire to eclipse the glory of Mantua, had to content himself with tournaments, ballets and naumachias. He was not able to produce a tragedy like the *Arianna*, of which the music was being sung everywhere. The *melodramma* was no longer confined to Florence ; it spread throughout the Peninsula. First Florence, then Mantua had played their part, Rome and Venice were to come, but the spectacles performed in Florence in 1600 and in Mantua in 1608 lived long in the public memory.

MONTEVERDI AND THE GONZAGA FAMILY

HENCEFORTH, Monteverdi's genius for dramatic music was universally recognized. The preface of one of his works recalls that Ariadne drew tears from thousands of spectators, and that Monteverdi thus revived the great marvels of ancient music.* His rivals pay him homage. Jacopo Peri, with the disinterestedness of the great artist, exalts his dramatic style, and Marco da Gagliano speaks with enthusiasm of the *Arianna* in the preface to *Dafne*. Yet Da Gagliano had had his triumph at Mantua. It is even possible that Monteverdi may have resented his success, and it would be quite comprehensible that he should do so, for, while the whole of Italy was hailing the composer of the *Lamento*, the court of Mantua seems to have slightly neglected him. Perhaps his own sadness and gloom were partly responsible for this. After having worked night and day to crowd into five months the composition of the *Arianna*, the prologue of the *Idropica* and the *Ballo delle Ingrate*, after having conducted the rehearsals and supervised the execution down to its smallest details, he had received a ridiculously small remuneration, while Marco da Gagliano, who, beyond two pastorals which he had composed before his arrival at Mantua, had only written a single interlude for the *Idropica*, had received an honorarium of 200 crowns. Monteverdi was hurt, and was perhaps, moreover, astonished at the increasingly close connection between the rulers of Mantua and the representatives

* See Note 76.

of the Florentine school. This was in point of fact the time when Marco da Gagliano was collaborating with the Cardinal Gonzaga and retouching his musical compositions, and when advances were being made to attract to Mantua Francesca, the daughter of Giulio Caccini, who was already celebrated as a composer. Monteverdi must have felt the court of Mantua guilty of base ingratitude towards him. Once the celebrations were over, he felt completely exhausted. He was a martyr to headache. After this effort, he felt himself in a state of complete moral and physical depression.

He started for Cremona with his two young children, and, once at home, he declared to his father that he would not return to Mantua. The old doctor, much troubled by his son's condition, and realizing that he was acquiring under the Gonzaga much honour but little wealth, approved his decision, and undertook to write to the Duke to beg him either to release Claudio, or to restrict his functions to those of *Maestro di Cappella* only. The Duke did not reply, but Chieppio, the Secretary of State, wrote a friendly letter to persuade the musician to resume his duties. This letter crossed the one which Baldassare Monteverdi wrote to the Duchess begging her to use her influence. His son, he says, is ill, he cannot stand the air of Mantua; old man as he is, he does not know what would become of him if his son were to die leaving him two little children to bring up. The Duke's service is too onerous; he himself has often had to come to his son's assistance, more particularly during the journeys in Hungary and Flanders, during which he spent more than 500 ducats to provide for the needs of Claudia and the children.

Chieppio's kind letter seems to have exasperated the musician, who must have been at this time in a state of morbid irritability. The long letter in which he replied, on November 30th, has often been reproduced from Davari.* One can feel

* See Note 77.

that it has been written straight off at a sitting. He will not
return to Mantua, he says, it would be the death of him.   He
is suffering from continual headache and from an inflammation
which medicine is powerless to cure.   Drugs are of no avail.
The Duke did him the honour to take him to Hungary ; he
still feels financially the effect of the journey, as of that to
Flanders.   The Duke has decided to raise his salary to
2 5 crowns a month, but as he is to be obliged to provide for
Campagnola the page, who has been entrusted to his care,
that really only amounts to 20 crowns.   The Duke did
him the honour to invite his collaboration in the wedding
celebrations ; his only reward was fifteen hundred lines to
set to music and a serious illness.   He did not receive even
a public expression of gratitude.   The Duke promised him
a pension of 100 crowns, but, after the wedding, only
70 crowns were spoken of, and various deductions were
made over and above.   He enumerates all the great musicians
who, before him, had made their fortune at the court : Orazio
della Viola, Luca Marenzio, Filippo de Monte, Palestrina,
Luzzaschi, Fiorini, Rovigo.   He himself earns hardly
enough to keep him with a single servant, and he has two
children to provide for !

" To give two hundred crowns to Marco da Gagliano," he
exclaims, " who has done next to nothing, and nothing to me,
who have done what I have done ! "   No, it is much better
that he should not return to Mantua, where his fortune is as
bad as his health, and he relies upon Chieppio to arrange
matters and obtain his release.   He concludes, of course, by
a protestation of eternal gratitude to the house of Gonzaga.

The nervous condition in which he was naturally led him
to exaggerate somewhat.   Of a highly susceptible temperament, he could not adapt himself to the thousand servilities of
court life.   In 1604, because some rascally treasurer had
made him wait for payment of his salary, he had addressed

to the Duke a violent letter, which had, however, the satisfactory result that he thenceforth received payment of his due
with as much regularity as the disorderly service of the
treasury permitted.

In his letter he made no mention of several acts of liberality
which the Duke had performed towards him, more particularly
of the grant in 1604 of 1197 Mantuan lire to purchase an
estate or a house. His complaints had their effect ; the Duke
ordered his return, but recognized the justice of his complaints
by raising his salary to 300 crowns, and granting to him and
his heirs a pension of 100 crowns of 6 Mantuan lire.

1609 and 1610 were, for Monteverdi, years of comparative
repose. He returned to the madrigal, wrote *Le Lagrime
d'Amante al sepolcro dell' Amata* to the memory of poor Caterinuccia, composed various motets for the chapel, arranged the
lament of Ariadne for five voices, and set to music Marini's
Complaint of Leander. He excelled in the composition of
Laments, and continually received commissions for them. In the
same year, the *Orfeo* was published at Venice, the publication
having been supervised by his brother, Giulio Cesare. Monteverdi passed the summer of 1609 at Cremona. Two letters
dated August 24th and September 10th show that he is busy
writing madrigals for the Duke, and there is no more talk of
leaving his service. He is even troubled because one of his
compatriots, Galeazzo Sirena,* requires the title of *Maestro di
Cappella* as a condition of entering the service of the hereditary
prince. " If God," he writes, " wills that I should survive
the Duke, the Prince would thus have his *Maestro di Cappella*,
and what could I do then but quit Mantua immediately. " †

The post of *Maestro di Cappella* which Monteverdi had
received after the death of Benedetto Pallavicini in 1601,
carried with it a kind of superintendence of the Chamber and
Chapel music. Illustrious composers had held it with honour

* See Note 78.   † See Note 79.

in the past, and in one of his letters Monteverdi recalls with pleasure the names of his predecessors, Striggio, De Wert, Rovigo.

The post was very absorbing. Monteverdi was ceaselessly occupied with rehearsals, and with the audition of singers who were offering their services to the Duke of Mantua. Before engaging them, he had to refer the matter to the Duke, giving him the most precise information respecting their qualities and defects. It is well worth while to note the minute details into which Monteverdi goes when giving his opinion upon the voice of a contralto to whom he has given a hearing. The letter of June 9th, 1610, for example, is a most precious document for the history of the technique of singing. When absent from Mantua, he received orders to bring back singers or instrumental performers. He found many recruits among his compatriots of Cremona, more particularly players of wind instruments.*

Monteverdi was at the head of the Duke's company of musicians, but he was seconded both in the Chamber and in the Chapel by eminent musicians such as G. Gastoldi, who since 1582 had been choir-master of the ducal chapel of Santa Barbara.

Enclosed by the enormous mass of the Palace buildings, Santa Barbara presented to the admiration of the courtiers its elegant Renaissance façade and its sumptuous marble facings which glittered when the light of the candles caught them. Two large galleries were erected facing each other for the musicians, so that the choruses could sing in dialogue in the way introduced to Venice by the Gabrieli.

It seems that as long as Gastoldi was *Maestro di Cappella* at Santa Barbara, Monteverdi spent little time on the composition of masses and motets for the religious ceremonies, and devoted himself particularly to secular music; but after

* See Note 80.

Gastoldi's departure in 1609 he eagerly took up this type of composition, which was new to him.   In the spring of 1610 he finished a mass to the Virgin * for six voices in strict polyphonic style which marks an extraordinary contrast with the style of his madrigals of the same period.

In the autumn of 1610 he went to Rome, with the intention of having his compositions published there, and of soliciting for his eldest son Francesco, then aged ten years, an entrance to the Roman seminary with a scholarship.   Passing through Florence, he must have been interested in the serious disputes which divided the Academicians of the *Elevati* into two irreconcilable camps.   The poets Buonarotti and Cini had declared open warfare on the pompous (*gonfiato*) style of Chiabrera and Rinuccini, and were successful in keeping the latter out of the court fêtes.   Rinuccini, seeing that Jacopo Peri was not finishing the *Narcisso* which he had written for him, handed over a copy to Monteverdi.†   He soon gave another copy to Loreto Vittori, however.   Monteverdi was perhaps accompanied by Rinuccini when he resumed his journey to Rome.   The letters he had with him for the Cardinal Borghese and the Cardinal di Montalto, and the protection of the Cardinal Gonzaga, opened every door to him, but did not succeed in obtaining for him the modest favours he had come to request.   His mass and various motets were published in Venice, and he continued to petition the Papal court in vain through the intermediary of the Cardinal Gonzaga and the resident of Mantua.   He had, however, the satisfaction of hearing some good music and some excellent singers.   At the Palazzo della Cancelleria, the home of the Cardinal di Montalto, he heard the famous Ippolita Marotta, whose fame had spread throughout Italy.   Monteverdi, though he admired her voice, preferred to her both Francesca Caccini, whom he had just heard in Florence, and who was

* See Note 81.   † See Note 82.

able to accompany herself on various instruments, and still more the renowned Adriana Basile, " because she sings, plays, and speaks to perfection, and even when she is silent gives cause for admiration and well-deserved praise." *

Adriana Basile had arrived in Mantua after long and difficult negotiations on June 26th, 1610.† She was considered to be the finest singer and actress in Italy, and had been able, by the dignity of her life and by her intelligence, to awaken respect as well as admiration. She was treated as a lady of quality and the greatest princesses admitted her to their intimacy. Monteverdi had been enchanted with her the first time he had heard her. He found in her an incomparable interpreter. Adriana, who had sung his madrigals in the past, excelled herself in his compositions. She performed them at the concerts which Monteverdi arranged every week, by order of the Duke, in the Mirror Hall at the ducal palace. This hall, which was in reality a wide gallery, was the most sumptuous apartment in the palace. Its vaulted roof was adorned with frescoes and its walls were decorated with mirrors and precious stucco reliefs. It was here that the court assembled every Friday to hear the *virtuosi*. The throng was so great at these meetings that Monteverdi was forced to insist that the Cardinal Gonzaga should have strict guard placed at the doors to avoid too great a crowd.

The popular *virtuosi*, Madame Europa, Caterinuccia Martinelli, Settimia Caccini, and now Adriana Basile had in turn shone at these concerts. Madrigals for five voices were sung as arias in the new recitative style. The instruments united with the voices. Chitarroni, lutes, and other stringed instruments combined with the small positive organ (*di legno*) for the thorough-bass. Adriana was especially brilliant in recitative and often accompanied herself on the lute. It seems that she sang all the new music, arias by

Jacopo Peri, Caccini, Sigismondo d'India, and Monteverdi, who sometimes asked her to render compositions by the Cardinal Gonzaga, who was considered a good musician.

Concerts of wind instruments were also given in the Mirror Hall, for the Duke kept an excellent band of cornetti, flutes, oboes, bassoons and trumpets,* which also performed with marvellous effect in the chapel of Santa Barbara on solemn occasions, and it is for them that Monteverdi wrote the magnificent *Sonata sopra Sancta Maria*, which is contained in the Collection of sacred music published in 1610, and in which wind instruments are felicitously combined with violins and viols.†

We know little of the operatic performances which were given during these years. Chiabrera seems to have written various libretti for Mantua, but we have no reason to believe that they were performed. On February 16th, 1612, the old Duke Vincenzo died, and Francesco succeeded him. This prince was still more debauched than his father, and his brief reign of a few months' duration was marked by a series of follies. We do not know the exact circumstances of his quarrel with Monteverdi, whose surest ally he had been for years. It was perhaps on the occasion of a strange spectacle in the Florentine fashion entitled the Rape of the Sabine Women, in which the various phases of a tournament and equestrian display were commented upon by music and recitations. The fête given in honour of the election of a new Emperor took place on July 19th and 20th, 1612. Ten days later, Monteverdi left the court of Mantua with an agreement of release in good form, and bearing in his pocket the total sum of his savings for twenty-three years of service— *twenty-five crowns !*

While Monteverdi had little cause to regret the Gonzagas, the Gonzagas soon regretted him. Francesco died on

* See Note 85.　　　　　† See Note 86.

December 22nd, 1612, leaving the throne to his brother Ferdinando, who cheerfully renounced his Cardinalate to become Duke. Ferdinando had a profound and sincere admiration for Monteverdi; he made many attempts to get him into his service, and kept up with him, as we shall see, the most cordial relations. For that matter, Francesco himself had not been slow to realize his loss. It was perhaps in the hope of enticing Monteverdi back to Mantua that he ordered a performance of the *Arianna* in the ducal theatre in September 1612, two months after his departure. Monteverdi was then in Milan. Envious people were circulating a rumour that he had gone there to request the post of *Maestro di Cappella* of the Duomo, but that he had met with a humiliating set-back. It was said that he could not maintain discipline among the musicians. This was pure calumny, as the singer Campagnola informed the Duke, but it proves that the great musician had made powerful enemies at the court.

After some months of retirement at Cremona with his family, during which he was probably in negotiations with various cities to obtain a situation worthy of a man of his genius and reputation, Monteverdi (on August 19th, 1613) was to his great joy, appointed Master of the Music of the Most Serene Republic of Venice.

PART III
MONTEVERDI AT VENICE, 1613–1643

I

THE CHAPEL OF SAN MARCO

WHEN Monteverdi was nominated *Maestro di Cappella* of St. Mark's at Venice, this church was renowned throughout Italy for its music. The Venetians were justifiably proud of it, and made the greatest sacrifices to maintain it in the state of splendour which it had attained under the direction of masters such as Adrian Willaert, Ciprian de Rore, and Zarlino. The regulations demanded that the *Maestro di Cappella* should be a man of mature age, of worthy life, and of sober character. His musical attainments had to be such that he could inspire the respect of the artists who formed the *Cappella*, amongst whom there were not only singers of note, but talented composers. Before appointing a successor to the late Martinengo, the Procurators had written to the ambassadors and residents of the Republic at Rome, Milan and Mantua, to consult them as to the musician most capable of filling this exalted position. All three had named Monteverdi. On August 19th, 1613, Monteverdi was invited to Venice to give a trial concert, which was entirely successful.* The Procurators were so satisfied with the trial that, of their own free will, they raised the salary of the post to 300 ducats, Martinengo having received only 200. There were many benefits accruing from the position, and the *Maestro di Cappella* was lodged in the Canons' residence. A sum of 50 ducats was, moreover, immediately granted to Monteverdi to cover the expenses of the journey which he had just undertaken to comply with the Procurators' invitation.

* See Note 87.

Monteverdi returned to Cremona, and then went on to Mantua to settle up all the business he had in that town, and to assure himself that the pension granted him by the late Duke would continue to be paid. He even had a quarter paid in advance to cover his travelling expenses. Yet another misfortune lay ahead. The roads were unsafe, and Monteverdi set out for Venice in the company of the courier. He had with him his son Francesco, now fifteen years old, and a servant. Near Sanguanato, brigands surprised the little company, forced them with armed threats to surrender, and robbed them of all they possessed. The fact that the brigands left the courier unmolested made Monteverdi suspect him of connivance. Monteverdi lost more than 100 ducats in this affair. The end of the journey was clouded by the incident, but he soon forgot it in the warmth of his welcome at Venice and in the material and moral satisfaction which he found in his new post.

Monteverdi's correspondence testifies to the change in his life. His letters from Mantua had been a long series of complaints and recriminations; he rebelled against his poverty, he was indignant that he was not properly paid. Proud and conscious of his genius as he was, he was continually hurt by the Prince's ungenerous dealings with him. At the court, they knew that they could rely on him, that he might grumble, but that he would not abandon his post, and therefore they considered it unnecessary to treat him with consideration. Money difficulties, family expenses, his wife's illness, the undermining of his own health by the fever-laden air of Mantua, all this contributed to embitter his character and to make him profoundly unhappy.

The letters written from Venice bear witness to the serenity of which his restless and unhappy nature was capable. He was housed with his sons in the *Canonica* like the canons. His residence was certainly diminutive; his own room was little larger than a monk's cell, but profound calm reigned in this vast monastic building with its double cloisters.* He was only a few steps away from the church. Wandering along the canals or through the narrow streets, their gaiety and animation offered a delightful contrast with the gloomy stagnation of Mantua, where the entire activity of the city seemed concentrated in the court. The whole of Venice was in cheerful movement, with merchants busy at their stalls, displaying to foreign buyers the most sumptuous fabrics of the East, or holding up for their admiration glittering glass-ware or rich ornaments. The people seemed to work with joy. They felt and knew that they were free, for it was the nobles themselves who had voluntarily accepted the state of servitude in which they lived. To the stranger, surprised at the entire liberty which all enjoyed, the Venetian artizan proudly replied, " This is Venice." Save that he must take no hand in politics, and speak no ill of the Doge and the Ten, there was no restraint upon his liberty. Endowed with a truly Cremonese independence of spirit, Monteverdi delighted in this atmosphere of freedom which contrasted so strikingly with the servility of the Mantuans. And in Venice he breathed air which, though it could not equal that of Cremona, was none the less famous in Italy for its purity. He suffered no longer from the headaches caused by the marsh vapours. He felt better, morally and physically.

He had suffered at Mantua, not because his talent was not recognized, for he was celebrated among the musicians, but because he was not treated with the respect to which his genius entitled him. At Venice, he was admired and beloved by all. Of their own free will, the Procurators raised his salary from time to time. Three years later, his salary amounted to 400 ducats, double what his predecessors had received.† He received, moreover, various sums from private

* See Note 88.   † See Note 89.

persons, and from the superiors of convents where he directed
the music. It was not wealth, for he had heavy expenses,
but at least it was not poverty. He was able, though not
without occasional difficulty, to meet the expenses of his sons'
education. Fearing for them the "perilous liberty" of
Venetian life, he had them and their tutor to live with him
at the *Canonica* and supervised their studies. His obligations
were not too severe. He was not even required to appear
in chapel if he did not wish to. No one would reprimand
him on that score. He reigned supreme over the personnel
of the choir. No musician, no organist, no *maestro* could
be appointed without his consent. Appeal was always made
to him to settle differences between singers. He was
free to suspend from their functions the musicians placed
under his orders, and could grant or refuse leave which they
asked.*

The cathedral of St. Mark's was placed under the perpetual
superintendence of the Procurators. The dignity of *Procuratore di San Marco* was, by reason of the prerogatives and
privileges which it carried with it, "the highest object of
the ambition of the Venetian nobility." There were nine
Procurators for life charged with the administration of the
church and of the considerable domains belonging to it.
Three of them, called *Procuratori di sopra*, took charge of
everything which concerned the church. Housed in the
magnificent new *Procuratorie* on the Piazzetta, they wore
the ducal robe with its long sleeves sweeping to the ground.
All the difficulties which arose in the administration of the
church music were submitted to them, and there was no
appeal against their decision. Monteverdi was also under
the authority of the *Primiciero* as to the arrangement of the
religious ceremonies. The *Primiciero* was a Venetian noble
appointed to his high functions by the Doge. He was at

* See Note 90.

the head of the twenty-six canons of the church, and officiated with mitre and crosier like a bishop.

The religious ceremonies were remarkable for their splendour. During Holy Week, the ritual of the Alexandrian Church was followed. On Good Friday, the Holy Sacrament, enclosed in a black velvet casket, was carried in solemn procession round the Piazza, which was " lit by a million torches." All the town guilds followed with their banners, and penitents " with pointed caps two feet high upon their heads, walking backwards before the Crucifix," scourged themselves till the blood flowed.*

At Christmas, mass was sung at six o'clock, not at midnight. The ceremony attracted an enormous crowd which overflowed on to the Piazza to hear the music sung by four choirs, according to the fashion adopted at the end of the sixteenth century. On solemn occasions, numerous instruments, cornetti, trombones, viols, accompanied the voices.†

At the end of the basilica rose the musicians' gallery, octagonal in shape and supported on nine columns.‡ It was there that mass and vespers were sung on ordinary days, but on great festivals the singers were divided into several choirs. Andrea and Giovanni Gabrieli had definitely introduced the use of numerous choirs which sang antiphonally, or in dialogue, or united in superb *ensembles*, while instruments played *ritornelli* or symphonies at intervals, or reinforced the voices.§ It was only upon solemn occasions, however, that masses or motets were sung by several choirs with the assistance of the orchestra. For the ordinary services, mass was sung *a cappella* in strictly traditional fashion. Two organs renowned for the beauty of their tone were situated opposite each other in the transepts. The first, manufactured by Brother Urbano of Venice, dated from 1490; the other, more modern, was smaller, but the

* See Note 91. † See Note 92. ‡ See Note 93. § See Note 94.

suavity of its tone was admirable.* It had been decorated with shutters painted by Giovanni Bellini. It was on this organ that the famous and universally regretted Giovanni Gabrieli had performed. Up to the present, the list of names of the musicians of St. Mark's has not been found, and the only information available is that given in the proceedings of the Procurators' meetings. Monteverdi, on taking up his post, found the post of *Vice-Maestro* occupied by a composer of talent, Marc Antonio Negri, composer of Psalms and of delightful secular two-part compositions in the Roman style entitled *Affetti Amorosi.*† In 1620, Monteverdi appointed to succeed him Alessandro Grandi, the singing-master of the ducal seminary, pupil of the famous Giovanni Gabrieli, himself a composer of genius whose name belongs more particularly to the history of religious music and of the cantata. In 1627, Grandi left St. Mark's to take up the position of *Maestro di Cappella* at the Duomo of Bergamo, where he died of plague three years later. He was succeeded by G. Rovetta, who had been a singer in the chapel since 1683. Monteverdi was therefore ably seconded. He could, if need be, go to Bologna, Parma, Mantua, Cremona without any anxiety. The personnel of the chapel comprised, besides the Master, the Vice-Master and the two organists,‡ some thirty singers and about twenty-five instrumental performers.§

When Monteverdi was appointed *Maestro di Cappella* it seems that traditional church-singing was entirely neglected. The fashion for solo-singing, and the rapid decline of music *a cappella*, had led to the complete abandonment of polyphonic singing. Caberlotti tells us that the musical direction of the chapel was in a state of complete disorder. Indeed, a glance through the record of the Procuratorial proceedings for this period shows that the return to the traditional practice was

---

* See Note 95.   † See Note 96.   ‡ See Note 97.   § See Note 98.

periodically recommended. Monteverdi probably received
the same recommendation when he took up office, and we
know through Caberlotti that he succeeded in restoring singing *a cappella* to all its ancient glory, having recourse rather
to persuasion and example than to the authority to which his
office entitled him.*

Yet the singers who formed the choir were by no means
easy to keep in order. They had, with the consent of the
Procurator, formed an association, and stubbornly defended
their privileges.† The *Vice-Maestro*, Marc Antonio Negri,
had unpleasant proof of this in 1613. He claimed the right
of conducting the choir even when they performed in churches
other than St. Mark's. After prolonged discussion, the
Procurators and the Doge decided for the singers. They
were obliged to recognize the authority of Marc Antonio
Negri in the church of St. Mark, but once outside the church
he was their equal. On May 30th, 1612, they had elected
as their Chief Canon Gaspare Locatello, author of villanellas
and madrigals, who obstinately maintained the prerogatives
of the association. From time to time, doubtless with the
object of keeping them better in hand, they were forbidden
to sing in other churches,‡ but these orders were never
enforced.

The majority of the singers played various instruments ;
viols (soprano, alto, tenor, bass and double bass), violins and
bass violins, cornetti, trombones, flutes. They alternately
sang and played in the orchestra, though naturally at great
festivals instrumental performers approved by the Procurators
were called upon to complete the orchestra.

The Guild of Minstrels and Players, whose patron saint
was San Silvestro, claimed that they had the right to force
such musicians of St. Mark's as practised instrumental music
to inscribe themselves upon their register and to pay their

* See Note 99.   † See Note 100.   † See Note 101.

dues. The result was countless lawsuits. Finally, acting upon the Procurators' report, the Doge intervened and expressly forbade the Minstrels to exercise any claim upon the singers of St. Mark, who came under his authority only. The singers were authorized to play various instruments in churches and other places, and to give lessons in their schools or at private residences. They were forbidden only to accept engagements for balls at public or private celebrations.* Twenty years later the Minstrels returned to the charge, and attempted, though unsuccessfully, to enrol in their association the organists of St. Mark's.†

Certain of the singers were exceedingly difficult to get on with, and continually made trouble. There are, in particular, in the records of the secretariat, references to accusations and complaints by one Domenico Aldegati.‡ This singer, conceiving that he had been injured by Claudio Monteverdi, had the insolence to stop him in the Piazza and pull his beard. Monteverdi, who must have already been ordained at the time, is careful to specify that he claims punishment for the insult, not as priest, but as *Maestro di Cappella*. Aldegati was properly chastised by the Procurators.§

This scandalous incident was an event in Monteverdi's life, for, as a general rule, the singers showed him the profoundest respect. He never had disputes with them, such as his predecessor Martinengo had constantly had, and we shall see how sincerely he was regretted and mourned by the singers placed under his orders.

Monteverdi devoted himself entirely to his duties, and never ceased to exercise them with energy. He applied himself to replacing the old singers by younger men. He discovered such men as Francesco Cavalli or Giovanni Rovetta; he recognized the talent of Alessandro Grandi

* See Note 102.   † See Note 103.   ‡ See Note 104.   § See Note 105.

whom he made his second in command. He maintained strict discipline in the church, requiring the attendance of the musicians at all rehearsals and performances. He considerably extended the musical library, procuring the works which seemed to him worthy to figure in the repertory of the *Maîtrise*.*

Theoretically, he was by the terms of his appointment obliged to teach figured song, counterpoint and choral singing not only to the choir-boys, but also to the pupils of the seminary.† Actually, it was the *Vice-Maestro* and the singing-master of the seminary who performed this thankless task ‡; but Monteverdi took his pedagogic duties seriously and interested himself personally in any talented pupil. He was truly a *maestro* in the complete sense of the word.

In addition to the duties of his office, he accepted a series of well-paid engagements. He gave regular concerts three times a week at the house of the Dean of the Chapter, the *Primiciero*, on Wednesdays, Fridays and Sundays, which were attended by " half the aristocracy of Venice " §; he directed the private chapels of several Venetian nobles. We shall have to consider later his secular occupations, and we shall see how absorbing they were, particularly towards the end of his life. In fact, it is a wonder that he had any time for composition, yet his creative activity was at no period of his life at a higher pitch than in Venice. For St. Mark's, he continually composed music *a cappella* in contrapuntal style, and formal music with orchestra for the great festivals. He was, moreover, regularly asked by Venetian noblemen, by the governors of religious institutions, and by superiors of monasteries to compose masses for their chapels. We know by one of his letters that he earned more than 200 ducats a year in this way, and that he constantly received marks of gratitude and admiration.

* See Note 106.   † See Note 107.   ‡ See Note 108.   § See Note 109.

It is only by reading his correspondence that it is possible
to realize how busy he was. He was ceaselessly occupied in
composing sacred or secular music for Venice and for foreign
courts. One day, for example, having performed chamber-
music at the English Ambassador's house all the afternoon, he
had to go on to the *Carmine* for the festival of the Madonna
del Abito, and conduct Vespers there till late at night.* In
March 1625 he states that he is much occupied with both
sacred and secular music for the King of Poland.

With remarkable ease, he managed to do it all, and found
time to write secular compositions for public and private
festivals, operas for foreign courts, or Venetian theatres,
cantatas, madrigals, arias, songs, which were sung throughout Italy. During the thirty years spent in Venice he produced a prodigious quantity of music which has mostly
disappeared. What is left bears witness to the inexhaustible
fecundity and variety of his genius.

* See Note 110.

II

MONTEVERDI'S SACRED MUSIC

WITH the exception of M. Charles van den Borren's brief but pregnant preface to the edition of the *Missa a 4 da Cappella*, no general study of Monteverdi's sacred music has yet been made. The task is difficult, for three-quarters of such compositions as have survived are still unpublished and scattered throughout the libraries of Europe. Sometimes one part is to be found in Bologna, another in Breslau, another in London or Paris. These parts would have to be copied or photographed if the whole score were to be restored I shall restrict myself to defining the characteristics of Monteverdi's sacred music as exemplified by the works which I have been able to consult at first hand.

Monteverdi's religious compositions can be divided into two groups, those written in the traditional polyphonic style, and those composed in concerted style. He seems to have practised both styles with perfect freedom, in spite of the fact that they are different and even antagonistic. Nothing authorizes one to believe that a mass such as the *Missa da Cappella* is anterior to the highly dramatic motets with instruments which subsequently formed part of the *Selva Morale* in 1641. Not only does Monteverdi in the more important of his religious works refrain from those audacities of harmony which characterize his madrigals and lyric dramas, but he surpasses all the purists of the epoch. He uses a style of archaic austerity.

His attitude is all the more surprising in view of the fact that the innovators were then concentrating upon introducing into church music the methods of monody and the use of concerted instruments.   Andrea and Giovanni Gabrieli had, moreover, opened the way by substituting for the intimate expression of a profound religious sentiment the pursuit of decorative effect, the continual interpretation of the text. The madrigal had first invaded church music, and rendered every licence possible.   Composers were seeking to strike the imagination and the senses by the powerful tone-effects produced by choral masses in dialogue.   The Roman school, though profoundly conservative, was influenced by this new musical ideal, and the school descended from Palestrina finally produced gigantic constructions such as the mass of Orazio Benevoli, with its fifty-three vocal and instrumental parts.   Monteverdi was surrounded by composers writing in the new concerted style, amongst others, his colleague at Mantua, G. Gastoldi, *Maestro di Cappella* of Santa Barbara. In his masses and motets, Gastoldi distributes the voices into two choirs which carry on a dialogue in broad vertical chords.   There is nothing less polyphonic than this style. For that matter, the style of Monteverdi's master, Ingegneri, is harmonic rather than contrapuntal, and Monteverdi notes with approval that he always had regard to the intelligibility of the text, which is destroyed when the voices are engaged in inextricable contrapuntal patterns.

Finally, it must not be forgotten that Monteverdi had been for several years in Mantua in touch with the celebrated Grossi da Viadana, who was one of the musicians who contributed most to introduce the recitative and concerted style into church music.   As early as 1602, in his *Concerti Ecclesiastici* Viadana had given very successful examples of motets in recitative style for one, two, three or four voices, accompanied by the *basso continuo* on the organ.   Viadana's principal object was to simplify the task of the organist, who frequently had only two or three singers to perform a motet for four or

five voices and was obliged to reduce the other parts at sight
for the organ, but the introduction of the Florentine system
of the *basso continuo* brought about the ruin of the polyphonic
style. Vertical harmonies replace the interwoven designs
of counterpoint, and a clearly defined melody is heard above
the discreet chords of the organ.

We shall see that Monteverdi did not disdain these innovations, and gave brilliant examples of the concerted style in
his church music but it is astonishing that he should at the
same time have written masses and motets in a disconcertingly
archaic and contrapuntal style.

Why, then, did Monteverdi show himself so conservative
in his church music ? Why did he, who had propagated with
such zeal the *nuova prattica*, feel obliged to conform to obsolete
methods of composition which contemporary musicians were
abandoning ? We have seen that, from the moment of his
arrival in Venice, he had endeavoured to restore church
music to the polyphonic tradition which had already fallen
into disuse. Doubtless he was complying with the desire
of the Procurators, who stubbornly held to traditional methods,
but it is possible that he was glad of the opportunity of giving
public proof that, in spite of Canon Artusi, he was capable
of writing a mass or a motet in the strictest style, and that
the liberties he allowed himself in his secular compositions
were due not to his ignorance of the technique of counterpoint,
but to a new sense of the expressive power of harmony.

It must be noticed that Monteverdi had given evidence of
his talent for religious music both in contrapuntal and in
concerted style before leaving Mantua. His first religious
works are written indifferently in the one or the other, but
the severe style predominates. In this, Monteverdi doubtless conformed to Lombard custom and taste. It is remarkable that the beautiful religious compositions of his compatriot
Costanzo Porta show the same regard for the archaic style.

The pupils of Palestrina, Anerio, Nanini, Giovannelli, also remained faithful to the polyphonic tradition. But the austerity of Monteverdi surpasses theirs. He took infinite pains over the composition of the mass included in his first collection. Bernardo Casola testifies to this : " Monteverdi," he writes on July 16th, 1610, " is at present engaged upon the composition of a mass for six voices which gives him great difficulty and much labour, for he has set himself to introduce all possible contrapuntal combinations, weaving together in ever-increasing *stretto* the eight fugal themes contained in Gombert's motet *In illo tempore*." *

The mass *In illo tempore*, to which Bernardo Casola here alludes, written by Monteverdi in 1610, is contained in the collection dedicated to Pope Paul V under the title : *Sanctissimae Virgini Missa senis vocibus ac Vesperae pluribus de cantandae con nonnullis sacris concentibus*. It is composed according to the old practice on the melody of a motet by Gombert divided into ten motives which are used singly or in combination.

EXAMPLE 33

These musical motives are treated in the various parts in strict imitation. In the *Crucifixus* for four voices, for example, the tenor, alternating with the alto, twice gives out the theme of Gombert's motet, while the *superius* and the *sextus* sing in imitation a melody consisting of a variation of another motive

* See Note 111.

from the same motet. This style is a pure anachronism, and it is difficult to conceive that this passage, which is of great beauty, was composed in 1610, and not a century earlier.

EXAMPLE 34

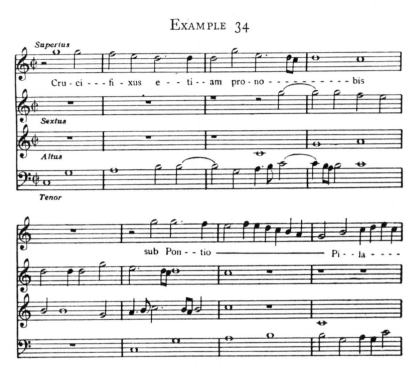

The archaic effect is still further augmented by the fact that several passages of this mass are written in the ancient ecclesiastical modes, and are only very slightly influenced by modern tonalities. The entire opening of this *Crucifixus*, for example, is composed in the authentic mixolydian mode, sufficiently rare even in Palestrina's time, the majority of musicians, as Glareanus remarks, sharpening the F.

The *Christe eleison*, composed on the fourth theme of Gombert's motet, is, in its austerity, a passage of genuine grandeur, moving yet unpretentious. Master of dramatic music as Monteverdi is, he here intentionally abstains from any theatrical effect, and interprets the liturgic text as Josquin Deprés himself might have done.

EXAMPLE 35

If the author of this mass were unknown, one would be tempted to attribute it to some composer of the Roman school, contemporary with Palestrina. The *basso seguente* is the only sign that the work is posterior to 1607, for it was in that year that Adriano Banchieri used it, apparently for the first time, in his *Ecclesiastiche Sinfonie dette canzoni in Aria francese per sonare et cantare et sopra un Basso seguente concertare con l'organo.* We know that the *basso seguente,* which must not be confused with the *basso continuo,** was not necessarily intended as an organ accompaniment to the voices, but served the *Maestro di Cappella* as a kind of guide to direct the voices and regulate their entries.

Taken as a whole, the mass *In illo tempore* is a work composed in view of *a cappella* performance, without the intervention of any instrument. With the exception of the *Crucifixus,* which is for nine voices, the mass is written for six voices. It bears no trace of the Venetian influences one would have expected to find in it, but is obviously related to the Romano-Lombardian school. Its archaic style, its scholastic processes of development and imitation, recall the early masses of Palestrina, and it is quite possible that Monte-

* See Note 112.

verdi may have taken these masses as his model in attacking a genre which was, after all, new to him.

The *Missa a 4 da Cappella*, published in 1641 in the *Selva Morale e Spirituale*, and republished by Tirabossi and Van den Borren, is rather different from the *In illo tempore*. While Monteverdi persists in his ascetic archaism, while he avoids dramatic and immediate expression, while he is careful not to employ the harmonic style which is habitual in his secular compositions, he betrays himself in certain methods of composition somewhat unusual in sacred music, more particularly in the systematic use of sequences. As Van den Borren very rightly remarks, he also manifests " that sense of development by gradation of expression which is one of the essential characteristics of his genius." On the other hand, there is no trace in this work of the ancient ecclesiastical modes. The tonal plan is perfectly clear. The work is written in F major, with modulations to the dominant and the relative minor.

The frequent cadences on the dominant still further accentuate the tonal character of the work. Van den Borren quotes a few examples of dissonances which have escaped Monteverdi, but they are exceptional, and the counterpoint is quite traditional. The only dissonances which Monteverdi allows himself are those resulting from retardation, or from appoggiaturas, as was the practice of the masters of the sixteenth century.

The construction of the work reveals that logical, systematic spirit which inspires everything Monteverdi wrote. He no longer uses the various musical motives of an anterior motet upon which to construct this work, as in the mass of 1610, but a very short and simple theme of six notes :

EXAMPLE 36

which he varies and develops by every scholastic process imaginable. He inverts it, decorates it, varies it by mutation, augmentation and diminution, changes its rhythm. "In fact," remarks Van den Borren, "there is little save the cadences, and two or three passages of a few bars which eludes the tyranny of the thematic unity."

From beginning to end the work is treated in very vigorous imitation. There is little homophony, but when it appears, especially in the *Incarnatus est*, the *Gratias*, the *Resurrexit*, it produces the most magnificent effect. These passages recall the fine successions of chords which are to be found in the work of Monteverdi's master, Ingegneri. As a whole, the work is inspired with sincere and profound feeling. It breathes tenderness and mystic love.

The *Missa a* 4, published at Venice in 1650, seven years after Monteverdi's death, differs little from the preceding Masses. It is archaic in character, and is written throughout in very strict imitation. It was printed, like the others, with a *basso seguente*.

The opening of the *Kyrie* will suffice to show the severity of its counterpoint.

EXAMPLE 37

Yet it must not be thought that all Monteverdi's religious
works are written in this archaic style. We know from contemporary evidence that he had composed masses of quite a
different nature, one in particular, dated 1631, to celebrate
the end of the plague, in which " *trombe squarciate* " accompanied the voices in the *Gloria* and the *Credo*, producing
" exquisite and marvellous harmony." *

What is still stranger is that the mass of the *Selva Morale*
bears a note authorizing the substitution for the *Crucifixus*,
the *Et resurrexit* and the *Et iterum* of three pieces printed in
the same book, and composed in a totally different style.
Not only have the melodic themes no relation to that running
through the whole mass, but the style is *concertato*. It is
the style of the cantata, and is no longer Palestrinian. The
ease with which Monteverdi passes from one style to the
other is astounding. It is simple to attribute this to a concession to contemporary taste, but the question is, Was this
concession made when Monteverdi was writing in the popular
style, or in scholastic polyphony ? In point of fact, Monteverdi's technical skill was marvellous ; he was versed in all
the subtleties of his art. When he had to write a mass or
a motet for the great public religious ceremonies which were

* See Note 113.

frequent in Venice, he wrote in the *concertato* style, but when he had to write a mass for some strictly liturgical service, he contrived to write in the style of the old masters, and used the occasion to display his marvellous dexterity. A glance through the Motets, Psalms, Magnificats, or fragments of his masses which are still extant leaves no room for doubt that he practised the two styles with equal facility. It is difficult to understand how a man could write works so different in character. Nor can it be said that Monteverdi betrays any preference in the matter, for during his lifetime he had works of both styles printed in the same collections.

The collection of 1610, dedicated to the Pope, contained, in addition to the mass *In illo tempore,* motets of very varied style. There are no traces of Venetian influences in the mass, which is conceived in the spirit of the old Flemish masters. But such traces are to be seen in several of the *sacri concentus* which follow. The *concertato* style popularized by Gabrieli may be recognized here, but it has been strangely perfected by Monteverdi. In these works there is to be found, in M. André Pirro's happy phrase, " the gravity of ancient polyphony combined with the inventions of the opera." *

Here, for example, are the vespers : *Vespero da concerto composto sopra canti fermi* for six voices and six instruments. They are typical of the music performed at St. Mark's during magnificent ceremonies. The music is sumptuous and brilliant. While the voices are occupied merely with a rhythmic plain-song, harmonized for six voices, the instruments, cornetti, *viole da braccio,* trombones and *viole da gamba* disport themselves with the most secular gaiety. In point of fact, Monteverdi here uses the triumphal theme of the symphony which preceded the rise of the curtain at the performances of the *Orfeo.*

* See Note 114.

Example 38

The psalm, *Dixit Dominus*, for six voices and six instruments, is in the same style. There is the same contrast between the Gregorian psalmody and the quite secular style of the instrumental score. Monteverdi, moreover, takes liberties with the plainsong, and sometimes terminates a plainsong verse with *fiorituri*.

EXAMPLE 39

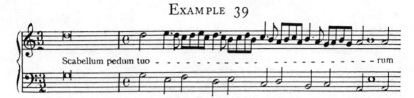

Plainsong verses alternate with verses treated in figured style.   After each verse the instruments play a brief *ritornello*.

The influence of the monodic style can be recognized throughout, particularly in the motets for one, two or three voices with thorough-bass.   It is clear from the embellishments of the voice-parts that they were written for performance by *virtuosi*.

EXAMPLE 40

An *Ave maris stella* for eight voices divided into two groups recalls Gabrieli's style.   *Ensembles* for eight or four voices alternate with solos, and the instruments play *ritornelli* in the intervals.

The *Magnificat* scored for six voices and six instruments is a superb composition of extraordinary variety. It presents one curious peculiarity which has just been pointed out to me by Prof. Francesco Vatielli, who, at my request, has been kind enough to study this work from the manuscript at the library of the *Liceo Musicale* of Bologna. The thorough-bass part, destined for the organ, contains indications of organ-stops, for example, "*Magnificat, Principale solo, principale, e ottava-principale, ottava e quintadecima,*" "*Qui fecit ! Principale e registro delle zifare o voci umane,*" etc. There are also precise indications for execution. The *Et exultavit* is to be accompanied by the "principal" alone, played slowly, because the tenors here perform rapid runs.

The work is written in *concertato* style. Some verses, certainly, are sung *a cappella* with the organ, but the majority are treated in cantata style, the *Fecit potentiam*, for example, for one voice and three instruments, the *Quia fecit* for three voices and two instruments, the *Sicut locutus* for a solo voice and six instruments in dialogue. Interludes separate the verses of the *Magnificat*, and the cornetti and violins echo each other.

To obtain an idea of the splendour of Monteverdi's instrumental style in his church music one must read, in the Torchi edition, the *Sonata sopra Sancta Maria*, taken from the collection of 1610, written for a solo voice and eight instruments. viols, cornetti and trombones. The constantly recurring figures, the powerful sequences, give the impression of a triumphal ascension.

Yet there is something meagre in the melodic figures executed by the instruments above the liturgic theme chanted by the voices in unison : *Sancta Maria ora pro nobis*. Monteverdi realized that the methods of instrumental polyphony could not be the methods of vocal polyphony, and, intent upon discovering them, he sometimes neglected matter for form. Whilst his madrigals and monodies are always richly expressive, there is at times something hollow, something mechanical, in his instrumental style. As with Veronese, the subject disappears in the preoccupation with dazzling colouring.

He has a predilection for the brass, for the profound sonorities of the trombones, for the cornetto whose tones, softer than the trumpet, more colourful than the flute, seem, as Padre Mersenne has said, like " a ray of sunlight shining in the gloom when they are heard among the voices in the Cathedral churches." *

To these compositions must be added the psalm, *Laetatus sum*, for six voices with the accompaniment of two violins, two trombones and a bassoon, and a thorough-bass for the organ. It was published after Monteverdi's death in 1650, with the *Missa a 4* of which we have already spoken. It presents a most perfect contrast with the archaic style of that work. It has been published by La Fage in his excellent *Essais de Diphtérographie musicale*. The psalm is divided into four sections. The first is sung by two soprani with a concerted accompaniment of two violins and thorough-bass, the second by two tenors supported by two trombones and the organ, the third by two basses in dialogue with a bassoon. Finally the six voices and five instruments echo each other, before uniting in a powerful homophonic *ensemble* to the words *Gloria Patri et Filio*. Monteverdi seems to have defied the laws of musical possibility in thus constructing the entire work on a *basso ostinato* consisting of four notes (G-G-C-D) indefatigably repeated for nearly two hundred bars. He only quits it for twenty bars at the words of the *Gloria* in order to modulate from G to A major.

Yet let no mistake be made. It was works of this type, and not the masses and motets in counterpoint, which made

* See Note 115.

Monteverdi's reputation as composer of sacred music. It is obvious from contemporary records that his great popular successes were the big works in which voices and instruments are combined.

Caffi has quoted one of Strozzi's letters describing the solemn mass celebrated in the church of SS. John and Paul, in honour of the Grand Duke of Tuscany, on May 25th, 1621. It had been composed by Monteverdi for the occasion. It is clear that instrumental music played an important part in it. Strozzi emphasizes the moving character of the symphonic passages written in the mixolydian mode, which seemed " like to draw tears of grief " from all that heard it.

By the very words he uses, one can see that the work was sumptuous, with an external brilliance well calculated to delight a people who loved all kinds of splendour. He gives special praise to the suave *De Profundis*, sung at the elevation in the form of a dialogue, as it were, between " souls in Purgatory and angels come to visit them." *

Monteverdi cannot get away from his epoch. It would be a misconception to regard him as a " Gothic " who has· strayed into the splendour of the dying Renaissance. He is of his age, which is the age of Bernini. Like the great Neapolitan artist, he has a passion for real life, a powerful sensuality, a restless soul tortured by one desire : to give powerful expression to human emotions. Sincere mystic as he was, he knew contemplation and even asceticism, but they were with him transitory crises. Monteverdi feels his soul rising to God upon the sound of voices and instruments, the perfume of incense, beneath the gilded vault of St. Mark's, within its glittering walls. The fervour which overflows in his soul expresses itself in religious effusions. His motets and spiritual cantatas are, for the most part, identical with his arias and secular cantatas. To express his love of God and

* See Note 116.

the Blessed Virgin, he uses melodic phrases which could well
be addressed to some passionately adored mistress. One can
imagine nothing more sensuous and passionate than the
motet *O quam pulchra es*, extracted by M. Vatielli * from
Simonetti's collection (1625), with the languorous tones of its
melismata and its chromatic descents.

EXAMPLE 41

Ve - - ni   Ve - - ni   quia a - mo - re   lan - - gue - - - o

The *Salve Regina*, extracted by Tirabossi from the *Selva
Morale*, resembles at moments a love-duet.

EXAMPLE 42

A *Salve Regina* for solo-voice, published by M. Pineau,†
is an operatic aria, and a very beautiful one, but it might well
belong to the *Orfeo*. There is the same dramatic feeling, the
same declamation, in short, the same " representation " of
passion. The motet *Currite populi*, which appeared for the
first time in 1625, is strangely in advance of the epoch at
which it was composed. It contains something like a fore-
taste of the *Incoronazione di Poppea*. It is written in cantata
style, and is insistently reminiscent of the compositions of

* See Note 117.   † See Note 118.

Luigi Rossi and Cesti of twenty years later. The return of
the phrase *currite, currite populi*, with its characteristic sequences,
divides the motet into three sections in a way frequent in
Lulli's work.   The theme of rejoicing, *Alleluia*, is quite in the
style of the canzonette of Luigi Rossi and Marazzoli.

EXAMPLE 43

Al-le - - - lu - jia Al-le   lu - jia   Al-le - - - lu - jia &c - - - - -

Monteverdi does not fear to introduce the methods of
opera into sacred music if the occasion demands it.   In the
Selva Morale there is a *Salve Regina con dentro un Ecco voce
sola, risposta a' Ecco e due Violini.*   The tenor sings *Audi
Coelum, Verba mia audi*, the heavenly voice replies in distant
echo *audio*, and the dialogue is continued at length, interspersed with *ritornelli* by three violins.

EXAMPLE 44

Tenor (Forte)   Eco

gau ———————————— dio ——   Au ———————————— dio

There are, in the collection of the *Selva Morale* (1641),
many motets constructed in the same way as secular cantatas.
For that matter, Monteverdi was only conforming to general
custom.   His disciple, Alessandro Grandi, whose religious
compositions met with even more public favour than his
own, was writing about the same time regular spiritual
cantatas.   In his first book of motets (1647) he divided the
O vos omnes, written in recitative style, into three parts separated by the repetition of a *sinfonia*.   At other times, he
combined the voices with two violins and a bassoon or a

trombone.   He also used the ornaments, the *fiorituri* which
Monteverdi loved to use, and delighted in expressive chromatic
figures for the violins.

EXAMPLE 45

It was an epoch in which everyone was striving towards
originality, in which genres were ceasing to have clearly
defined limits.   In his church music, Monteverdi uses all
the modern inventions, Italian and foreign.   He writes a
Confitebor " *alla francese* " for five voices.   The upper part
can be sung by a solo-voice, the other four being played by
violins.   This composition is modelled on the plan of the
French *airs de cour*.   A single voice chants *Confitebor tibi,
Domine*, etc.   The chorus then repeats the phrase, which is
developed with alternating *solo* and *tutti*.*

It has sometimes given cause for astonishment that, towards
the end of his life, Monteverdi should have adapted some of
his arias or madrigals to religious words.   Certainly it might
appear strange to find in the *Selva Spirituale* under the title
Pianto della Madonna the admirable *Lamento d'Arianna*,
but we have no reason for assuming that if Monteverdi had
had to set to music the Virgin's Lament for the death of
Christ, he would not have invented something very similar
to the complaint of the forsaken Ariadne.   The only real
cause for regret is that these adaptations necessarily lead to
faults of prosody.   Indeed, there is no fundamental difference
between his secular and his religious compositions, save in
the few masses and motets which, by a personal peculiarity,
he contrived to compose in an archaic style which was then

only cultivated by a few composers who had remained faithful to an obsolete form of composition.

This conception of religious art conflicts with our modern ideas, but we must not forget that Monteverdi lived in Venice, in the country of Titian and Veronese, where, every year, when carnival ran wild through the town, priests went masked through the streets, nuns crowded to the parlour to hear the jests of extravagantly costumed cavaliers, and to laugh at their buffooneries, while at the gates of certain monasteries nuns were to be seen dressed in the height of fashion, or even " disguised as men, with a plume in their hats, making their bows with grace." Strange convents, those of Venice, where " the nuns go to choir when they want to, get up and go to bed when they think fit." * A considerable part of their time was passed in making music, eating sweets, or chattering between themselves or with friends in the parlour.

The churches themselves were mere concert-halls, where people met to discuss the most secular matters, or to pass the time listening to splendid music. " These assemblies," remarks Saint Didier, " seem anything but religious gatherings," and he describes the fine ladies seated in their arm-chairs, talking to their friends during the services, or conversing in signs with the gentlemen on the other side of the church, who paid far more attention to what the ladies were doing than to the religious ceremony.

It was for these monasteries and these churches that Monteverdi wrote his sacred music, so that we cannot be surprised at the secular spirit of compositions written for such frivolous congregations. What is astonishing is that, in so worldly an atmosphere, he should have given any time to the composition of so large a number of masses and motets in the severe style.

But there are strange contrasts in Monteverdi. Grave,

* See Note 120.

religious, austere as he was, he can write, if the occasion demands, madrigals or arias of lively grace, of burning passion. His genius was capable of any form of expression, and his imagination allowed him to express with equal mastery, with equal sincerity, the most contradictory emotions in incredibly diverse forms.

III

OPERAS AND COURT SPECTACLES (1615–1630)

ALTHOUGH much absorbed in his duties as *Maestro di Cappella*, Monteverdi nevertheless continued to compose operas, ballets and interludes for the princes or nobles who counted it an honour to produce the works of the most famous composer of Italy. From about 1615 onwards, his fame spread throughout the Peninsula. However great his reputation as composer of sacred music, it was eclipsed by the popularity of his dramas and madrigals.

With the exception of the ballet *Tirsi e Clori*, we possess nothing of the dramatic music composed by Monteverdi between the *Arianna* (1609) and the *Ritorno d'Ulisse* (1641). Yet we can gather some notion of his dramatic style from his madrigals and from his correspondence, which gives the most enlightening information upon his conception of the opera.

Although he was several times invited to work for the court of Florence, Monteverdi only wrote operas for the Dukes of Mantua and Parma, and for the patricians of Venice. Ferdinando Gonzaga, from the moment of his accession, made every effort to persuade Monteverdi to return to Mantua, but the musician had always eluded the invitation, comparing no doubt the brilliant situation he occupied in Venice with the hard servitude in which he had passed twenty years of his life at Mantua. Yet the Duke of Mantua remained his sovereign lord. Monteverdi did not forget that he was a citizen of Mantua, and that his sons had been born there. The commands of the Duke were sacred to him. He only rebelled when Ferdinando seemed to forget that he was no longer in the service of Mantua, and that he was now under the control of the Most Serene Republic.   In February 1615 the Duke, who had asked him for a ballet for the Carnival, sent him orders to leave at once for Mantua.   But Monteverdi was no man to suffer such cavalier treatment.   His reply to Councillor Striggio is extremely witty.   To comply with the Duke's command, he says, he would have had to be booted and spurred and ready to step into the courier's boat when the letter arrived.   He has no desire to pass a bad night, and perhaps catch some illness, particularly as the weather is so rainy that it is almost impossible to go out.   So he prefers to wait, and would be glad if the libretto could be sent to him at Venice so that he may write the music for it at his leisure.

The lesson was not fruitless, and when, in the autumn of the same year, the Duke of Mantua called upon Monteverdi to write the music for the ballet *Tirsi e Clori*, he ordered his ambassador to make a personal visit to his former *Maestro di Cappella* so as to persuade him to undertake the work.* This ballet has been preserved.   It is to be found in Book VII of the Madrigals.   The charming text was very probably written by Alessandro Striggio.†

In a very gay tune to 6/4 time, Thyrsis invites Cloris to dance, but the amorous Cloris begs to stay apart with him. Her languorous supplication contrasts with the cheerful song of the shepherd.

EXAMPLE 46.

Dol - - - cis - - - - - si - mo   Tir - - - - - - - - cl

However, the shepherd insists and prevails.

* See Note 121.   † See Note 122.

EXAMPLE 47

Su Clo-ri mio   co - re An-di-a-mo a   quel lo - co ch'in-vi - ta -
- no in - vi - ta - no al gio-co   le Gra-tie coi A - mo - - - ri

The lovers sing a duet on the same theme, then the ballet
begins. It is a madrigal for five voices. The voices are
supported *se piace* by a certain number of instruments, violins,
spinet (*spinetta-arpata*), small lutes. Like all the *Balletti*
sung at the time in Italy or England, it comprises a certain
number of movements (eight in all) with reprises. After a
brief introduction in common time, the dance begins in 6/4.

EXAMPLE 48

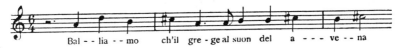

Bal - - lia - - mo   ch'il gre - ge al suon del   a - - - ve - - na

The melody and rhythm vary in the two succeeding stanzas,
but the 6/4 time is maintained until the fourth " change,"
then the rhythm is that of the dactylic metre (◡◡—◡◡—).
The 6/4 time is resumed, and the ballet concludes in rapid
common time, with a final *cauda lente*.

EXAMPLE 49

Bal - - -li - am'e giriam Corri - - am'e   sal - ti - a - mo Bal - - -li - - a - mo

As to the way in which the ballet was performed, we have
only the suggestions given by Monteverdi in a letter of
November 21st, 1611, addressed, it appears, to Striggio.
He wishes the musicians to be arranged in the form of a

crescent, at one point of which there is to be a harpsichord, at
the other a theorbo, the first to accompany Cloris, the latter
Thyrsis. The singers are to accompany themselves on the
theorbo. Cloris's theorbo might well be replaced by a
harp.

After the dialogue, when the dance is about to begin, the
other voices will join with Cloris and Thyrsis in the *ballet à huit*,
accompanied by eight violins, one *contrabasso di viola*, one
spinet (*spinetta-arpata*). Two small lutes would make a
happy addition to the orchestra.

It is not at all certain that this ballet, which Ferdinando had
ordered for his wedding with Camilla Faa, was ever performed,
and Monteverdi does not appear to have been invited to contribute to the coronation celebrations which took place in
Mantua at the end of April 1616. Some months later, the
Duke suggested that he should set to music the *Favola di
Peleo e di Teti* of Conte Scipioni Agnelli. Monteverdi, in a
frequently published letter, dated December 16th, 1616,
began by refusing on the ground of his distaste for the mythological libretto. This letter is of capital importance for the
comprehension of Monteverdi's art. It shows that while the
musical drama was manifesting an increasing tendency to
transform itself into a purely spectacular genre in which the
musician played second fiddle to the scene-shifter, and had to
concentrate far more on delighting the ear with picturesque
and pleasing music than upon emotional expression, Monteverdi, whose aim was always to give powerful expression to
human emotion, remained faithful to the realism of which he
had given such marvellous examples in the *Orfeo* and the
Arianna.

"How can I," he writes, "imitate the language of the
winds, which cannot speak, and move hearts through their
mouths? Ariadne was moving because she was a woman,
and Orpheus because he was a man, not a wind. These

mythological personifications, these Tritons, these Sirens, are not capable of interesting and moving the spectator." This does not mean to say that Monteverdi despises the lovely style of the *canzonette* and *cantate* which were delighting the court of Rome, but he feels that it has no place in lyrical drama. Some weeks later, Striggio having defined his position, and made it clear that the *Nozze di Tetide* was not, properly speaking, a lyrical drama to be set to music, but a series of musical scenes to be inserted as interludes between the acts of a comedy, all Monteverdi's objections disappeared. As soon as he realized that the business in hand was music, not drama, to " sing, speaking," not to " speak, singing," the subject seemed made for him. He only desired that there should be added a final *canzonetta* in praise of the noble couple, which could be arranged to serve for a general ballet.*
It is clear from the alterations he requires that he is no longer concerned with dramatic expression but with pure music. In the place of three stanzas sung by a solo-voice, he suggests that the first stanza should be sung as a solo, the second as a duet, the third as a trio. He thinks that Venus's narration after the complaint of Peleus should be entrusted to Signora Adriana, whose powerful voice could carry on a dialogue with the united voices of her two sisters. He also goes into questions of costume, and desires that Signora Adriana should change her dress in the course of the performance. He is about to set to work on the spoken narrations; he will subsequently compose the passages for singing (*quelli che si cantano di garbo*), and elsewhere he alludes to the fact that these passages are to be ornamented with runs and *fioritori*.
The scenes of the *Nozze di Tetide* were to serve as interludes sung between the acts of another piece, perhaps the *Galatea* of Chiabrera. The Duke had hurried on the work for the

* See Note 123.

fêtes due to take place at Mantua at his marriage with Caterina de' Medici, sister of the Duke of Tuscany.

The first idea was that these celebrations should be particularly splendid. The *Galatea* of Chiabrera, slightly retouched by the author, was to be sung on this occasion, set to music by Sante Orlandi. An opera, *Endimione*, was also to be performed, and the Duke Ferdinando was said to have himself collaborated both in the text and in the score ; finally there was to be an opera *Ati e Cibele* by the famous singer Francesco Rasi. Quite suddenly the Duke gave up the idea of the *Nozze di Tetide* when Monteverdi had almost finished the score. He wanted a genuine opera. Scipione Agnelli proposed a subject the pathetic character of which was well suited to Monteverdi, *La Congiunta d' Alceste e d' Admeto*, but the Duke countermanded the order when the work was well advanced, and the only piece given was the *Galatea* of Chiabrera, which was performed without particular splendour. The Duke told Monteverdi, who was awaiting from day to day the order to come to Mantua, that he would not be required.

Monteverdi felt very bitter about this, and does not attempt to hide the fact in his letter to Striggio of February 18th, 1617. He had not only lost time and work in setting to music interludes which would never be performed, but to fulfil this order he had refused his friend Ottavio Rinuccini's invitation to Florence. The Grand Duke and all the court desired to make his acquaintance, and Rinuccini had hinted that he would be expected to contribute to the marriage celebrations. He had been badly rewarded for his zeal in Ferdinando's service.

The same year, 1617, Monteverdi, in collaboration with Salomone Rossi, Muzio Efrem, and Alessandro Giunizzoni, composed interludes for the *Maddalena* of G. B. Andreini. This curious composition marks a stage between the Florentine pastoral and the great spectacular performances which were to be popular in Rome. From the confusion of different genres, tragedy, comedy, tragi-comedy, religious drama, there gradually emerges a new form called *melodramma*, that is, modern opera. *La Maddalena* already marks the final stage of this transformation, since there is no doubt that the major part of this piece was not recited, but sung.* Monteverdi does not seem to have attached any importance to this piece. He was an old acquaintance of Andreini, whose wife Virginia had created the rôle of Ariadne, and sung the lament of the *Ballo delle Ingrate*. He probably wrote some passages for the *Maddalena* simply to oblige Andreini.

Monteverdi reveals in his correspondence the difficulty he had in keeping up with the work which was heaped upon him. In 1618 the hereditary prince, Vincenzo Gonzaga, commissioned him to write an opera, *Andromeda*, to a libretto by his secretary, Ercole Marigliano. Monteverdi set to work, but was constantly interrupted. Easter was coming on ; he was occupied from morning to evening by services at St. Mark's ; then for Ascension Day he had to complete a great mass, some motets, and a cantata to be sung on the Bucentaur when the Doge cast his ring into the sea in renewal of the eternal pact with the Adriatic. He hoped to have more time during summer, but he suffered from violent headaches during the hot weather, and his work seemed heavier than ever. " I never see Saturday come," he writes, " without a sigh that it comes so soon." †

While we can form no idea of the music of the *Andromeda* from Monteverdi's letters, we can at least realize to what an extent he had bound himself by the conditions of its execution. He asks the Prince how many voices will be at his disposal for the choruses, whether he may write a *ritornello*, and upon what instruments he may count. Can the chorus, *Il fulgore onde resplendono*, be sung and danced at the same time, and what instruments are to accompany it ? ‡

* See Note 124.   † See Note 125.   ‡ See Note 126.

The orchestration was similar to that of the *Orfeo*, the author making use of all the instruments at his disposal to produce tone-colour. This explains how Monteverdi was able later to adapt himself with ease to the exceedingly restricted resources of the Venetian theatres.

The *Andromeda* was to have been produced at Mantua by Monteverdi himself at the carnival of 1620, but the musician was dismayed at the brief time allotted to him for the production of a work of such dimensions. He explained to Striggio that if he were forced to complete it in a few weeks, the result would be deplorable. On January 16th he still had four hundred lines to set to music. He foresees " verses badly recited, instruments badly combined, harmonies badly conceived." This sort of thing cannot be done in a hurry, and he reminds Striggio of the five months of rehearsals which had been found necessary for the *Arianna*. Prince Vincenzo having insisted, Monteverdi writes to Striggio on February 1st that he will not come to Mantua, as he wishes to have no responsibility for a performance which cannot, in the circumstances, be anything but execrable, in view of the conditions imposed upon him.

Simultaneously with the *Andromeda*, Monteverdi had been setting to music an eclogue by his friend Striggio on the subject of the Loves of Apollo and Daphne. The most important passage of this composition was a lament of Apollo for the death of Daphne, which Monteverdi frequently produced with success in the Venetian salons. He seems to have wished that this *divertissement*, which comprised only a small number of performers, should be produced at the carnival of 1620 instead of the *Andromeda*, but his wish does not appear to have been fulfilled.

Ferdinando Gonzaga always regretted that he had not succeeded in getting Monteverdi into his service. On the death of his *Maestro di Cappella*, Sante Orlandi, in 1619, he renewed his efforts to induce Monteverdi to accept the vacant post, but Monteverdi was not at all attracted to the idea of leaving Venice.   He was even much troubled by the fact that the advances made to him by the Duke of Mantua were known to the Procurators of St. Mark's, who feared that he would leave them, and only very unwillingly gave him leave of absence when business called him to Mantua.   To put an end to all these difficulties, he wrote to Striggio the long and frequently quoted letter, in which he contrasted the honour and material advantage of his post at Venice with the constant difficulties which he had met with in Mantua, and which still continued, since the pension granted him by the late Duke was only paid to him with evident unwillingness.   Yet, desirous to spare the feelings of the rulers of Mantua, in December, 1619, he dedicated his seventh book of madrigals to the Duchess Caterina, who rewarded him with a gold necklace.   For that matter, the Duchess was favourably disposed towards him.   It was by her influence that he was able to enter his son at the college of the Cardinal di Montalto at Bologna.

The Duke continued to show the same want of decision. In March, 1620, he suddenly decided to give a great fête to celebrate the birthday of the Duchess, which fell on May 2nd. He wished to revive the *Arianna* of Monteverdi, and produce Peri's *Adone*.   Monteverdi hastened to send him a copy of the score, but excused himself from going to Mantua to superintend the performance.   It was well for him that he did so, for at the last moment the Duke decided upon a simple *ballet*.   Monteverdi had profited by the occasion to petition for the conversion of his pension into a capital grant, but without success.   During the summer, he went to Mantua, and begged Ferdinando to grant him at least a few months' advance on his pension.   His request was granted without difficulty, and this enabled him to establish his son Massimiliano, who had just finished his medical course, at Mantua.

Monteverdi, for that matter, always regarded himself as one of the Duke's subjects, and rendered him a host of minor services.   He kept him informed of the compositions which might be profitably performed by his musicians, and sometimes, even at the risk of offending the Procurators, he arranged that certain singers or instrumentalists should offer their services to the court of Mantua instead of entering St. Mark's.

It is noticeable, however, that the relations between Monteverdi and Ferdinando Gonzaga became less close after the failure of certain of the former's artistic enterprises.   There is, in fact, no proof of Ademollo's supposition that some of Monteverdi's compositions were performed at the carnival of 1620 on the occasion of the marriage of the Princess Eleanora with the Emperor of Austria.   In May, 1623, Ferdinando went to Venice, accompanied by the Duchess and the entire court. Monteverdi must have contributed to the celebrations which marked the occasion, and doubtless heard his own madrigals sung on the Grand Canal by the admirable musicians of Mantua.   The famous Leonora Baroni was in the Duke's suite, and resided in the palace of the patrician Mocenigo, Monteverdi's chief patron, where, three years later, was performed the *Combattimento di Tancredi e di Clorinda*.

The few letters which we possess written by Monteverdi between 1619 and 1626 show that he was busy supplying the court of Mantua with singers and instrumental performers, but contain no allusion to any commission for operas.   He is principally in communication with Conte Ercole Marigliani, the favourite of the hereditary prince Vincenzo.

Vincenzo Gonzaga, who had always shown Monteverdi much admiration and affection, invited him to collaborate in the court fêtes at his accession in 1626.   Monteverdi offered to compose either interludes to be performed between the acts of the comedy which was given annually, or an opera.   He suggested, in the first case, scenes from the

Jerusalemma Liberata, which he was then composing; in the second, a piece by Giulio Strozzi, *La Finta Pazza Licori*, of which the subject appeared to him both interesting and original. The Duke accepted the latter suggestion.

The character of Licori, who feigns madness, and appears sometimes dressed as a man, sometimes as a woman, appealed particularly to Monteverdi, for it rendered possible the expression of varied emotions. Now at this time, as we shall see when considering the madrigals, he was intent upon finding direct and exact expression for ideas and images. " When Licori speaks of war," he writes, " then the sounds of war must be heard; when of peace, then the music must express peace; when of death, then the impression of death must be conveyed, and so on." * We can easily form an idea from the *Combattimento* of the way in which Monteverdi expressed these various impressions in music.

The loss of the *Finta Pazza Licori* is irreparable, for Monteverdi devoted his entire energy to its composition. It provided him with a whole field of dramatic experiment. To his friend Striggio he speaks of the work with enthusiasm. We can gather from his letters that he collaborated in the libretto, for he required Giulio Strozzi to recast certain scenes, and we can feel his pleasure in creating new musical effects.

It seems astonishing that Monteverdi should have admired the extravagant inventions of Strozzi. They are much inferior to the rather stilted majesty of Rinuccini's or Chiabrera's Greek creations. Strozzi, like G. B. Andreini, aims principally at astonishing his audience. The highest praise he can conceive, is that his compositions should be considered *bizarre*. The explanation is that Monteverdi, concentrated upon realistic expression, finds, in these preposterous situations, excellent occasion for displaying his talent. The incoherent ravings of the pretended madwoman give him the

* See Note 127.

opportunity for a rapid alternation of brilliant and soft
harmonies.

This desire for realistic and varied expression gradually
took precedence over all other considerations. Monteverdi
refused Rinuccini's *Narcisso* because, although its literary
beauty was great, it offered no situation of dramatic intensity,
and because there was danger of monotony in its continual
dialogues between shepherds and nymphs.* On the other
hand, in 1627 he enthusiastically accepted a commission from
the court of Parma to compose a prologue, some interludes,
and the music for a tournament.

The text of these *divertissements* having been published by
Angelo Solerti, we can only with difficulty understand the
obvious interest with which Monteverdi set them to music.
The verses of the interludes particularly delighted him.
Written by Ascanio Pio di Savoia, they are, he says, animated
by varied emotions (*tutti variati d'affetto*). The text of the
prologue and the tournament, by Claudio Achillini, pleased
him much less. " Where I have been able to find no variety
in the emotions," he writes, " I have at least sought to bring
variety into my music." † It is this passionate search for
dramatic effect which subsequently led Monteverdi to that
Shakespearean conception of opera of which the *Incoronazione
di Poppea* is the masterpiece.

It was in September 1627 that Monteverdi received from
the Marchese Bentivoglio the invitation to collaborate in the
magnificent fêtes which were to accompany the celebration of
the marriage of the Duke of Parma with the Princess Margherita of Tuscany. Charmed with the interludes of Ascanio
Pio, he accepted the invitation with enthusiasm. A glance
through one of them, on the subject of Diana and Endymion,
sufficed to give him an idea of its general arrangement. He
established his plan, deciding in advance the colour he was to

* See Note 128.   † See Note 129.

give to each scene. He realized that the *Endymion* would require four types of music, or, more exactly, four styles. The first style was to form the introduction and lead up to the scene of the quarrel between Venus and Diana, the second would express the quarrel, the third would begin with the arrival of Pluto, who came to restore calm, and the fourth would express Diana's love for Endymion.*

It is very regrettable that the music of this interlude should have disappeared. We should no doubt find in the quarrel scene an example of that *concitato* style which Monteverdi had used for the first time in the *Arianna*, and of which he made systematic use in the *Combattimento*.

These fêtes gave Monteverdi a great deal of trouble. He was obliged to go to Parma several times, more particularly to view the Farnese theatre,† and the amphitheatre which was being specially constructed on the Piazza San Pier in view of these performances, in order to adapt his music to their vast dimensions. The newly-married couple were due to return to Parma in November, but the ceremonial entry could only take place at the end of December, and Monteverdi was obliged to ask for an extension of leave to direct the performance of these works, in which the most celebrated *virtuosi* from every town in Italy were to take part.

The prologue, *Teti e Flora*, which represented, with much stage-craft, the liberation of Roger from the palace of Atalanta, the Loves of Dido and Eneas, Diana and Endymion, the Argonauts, and the other interludes, were an immense success, and rather distracted the attention of the audience from the pastoral *Aminta*, between the acts of which they were played.

The tournament, *Mercurio e Marte*, was given in the huge hall of the Farnese theatre, which had been specially designed for spectacles of this type. A mythological story, sung on the high stage, served as pretext for the jousts of the cavaliers

* See Note 130.   † See Note 131.

which took place in the semicircle reserved between the stage and the spectators.

The best singers of Italy distinguished themselves upon this occasion, among others the famous Loreto Vittori, who later became the favourite of Pope Urban VIII and the idol of the Romans, who thronged the churches to hear him. This was also the beginning of the career of the famous soprano Marc Antonio Pasqualini, surnamed Malagigi, who, little more than a child at this time, had been brought from Rome by his tutor. All the parts were taken by *virtuosi* of repute who had been rehearsed by Monteverdi. He hated anything like hasty performance, and must have been delighted to see his work performed with such perfection of detail.

For that matter, the performances at Parma were a triumph for him, too, and Luigi Inghirami, who has left us a detailed description of the fêtes, voices general opinion when he calls him " the first Italian composer of the day."

Of these interludes and the *torneo*, only the poetic text remains.* The music composed two years later by Monteverdi to celebrate the marriage of Giustiniana Mocenigo with Lorenzo Giustinian has also disappeared. Monteverdi must have written it with great care. Mocenigo had always been his patron, and we know by his correspondence how affectionately disposed he was to the young Lorenzo Giustinian. To please him, he went to great pains to get the famous actors of the ducal company to come from Mantua, and always showed himself ready to serve him.†

The poetic text was by Giulio Strozzi, who had already provided him with the libretto of *La Finta Pazza Licori*, the ballets had been arranged by the choreographer Girolamo Scolari, the scenery and stage effects had been designed by Giuseppe Schioppi. The performances took place in the

Mocenigo palace.*   It is possible that the music was destroyed by accident, for Strozzi's play was performed in 1644 in the Teatro San Mosé with new music by Francesco Sacrati.   The *Arianna* had just been successfully revived, and it is highly probable that if Monteverdi's score had been available, no other would have been performed in its place.

After 1630, the sack of Mantua and the plague diverted Monteverdi's attention for many years from operas and court spectacles.   But he returned to them at the end of his life.   In 1641, at the request of the Duke of Parma, he agreed to write the ballet *La Vittoria d'Amore*, which was to celebrate the birth at Piacenza of an heir to Odoardo Farnese.

Only Bernardo Morandi's libretto has been discovered and published by Angelo Solerti.†   The subject is the rivalry of Cupid and Diana.   Love, naturally, conquers the chaste goddess.   It is interesting to speculate to what degree Monteverdi, who had doubtless already begun work on the *Incoronazione di Poppea*, had been inspired by this trite subject. In any case, the ballet remains a proof of Monteverdi's adaptability.   At sixty-three years of age, he was able to comply with all the whims of his noble patrons, finding in the most futile intrigue an idea for a picturesque scene.   To judge from the libretto, Monteverdi must have treated the entire score in the manner of a vast cantata, with a multitude of songs, ariettas, duets, trios, choruses, not to speak of dances played and sung.

* See Note 134.   † See Note 135.

IV

FROM THE MADRIGAL TO THE CANTATA,
1615–1638

THE inventions of the recitative style, which the Camerata
Bardi had destined exclusively for the theatre, had brought
about, in less than twenty years, a complete revolution in taste
and habits. On every hand, musicians had attempted to
write for the concert-room or for the church arias for solo-
voice with thorough-bass. Caccini, Sigismondo D'India,
Luzzasco Luzzaschi, Ortensio Naldi, Ottavio Durante, Saraceni, Kapsberger, S. Pietro de Negri, Belli, and, a little later,
Alessandro Grandi, Giuseppe Rovetta, Sances, Manelli, Benedetto Ferrari, Milanuzi, and still others whose names are forgotten to-day, produced the first examples of these compositions, which were more melodious and more ornate than the
first recitative *melopeia* and moved more freely and more
definitely in the modern major and minor keys. Soon,
throughout Italy, madrigals were neglected for *canzoni, canzonette, arie* for solo-voice; instrumental polyphonic music
was replaced by music for a solo-instrument accompanied by a
thorough-bass. Monteverdi did not give up the madrigal
all at once. Preoccupied with the profound expression of
feelings and ideas, he despised neither the acquisitions of the
past nor the inventions of the present. We have seen how
he enriched tragedy in recitative with all the resources of
vocal and instrumental polyphony; he now endows the madrigal with all the inventions of the homophonic school. The
madrigal, which has already served him as a field of experi-

ment for the attainment of a powerfully expressive harmonic style, in which the feeling for major and minor keys, then quite new, makes itself felt, is now to be transformed by him into a new genre, the Cantata. Monteverdi was certainly not the sole creator of this form. Others, between 1620 and 1630, had given the first examples of it, taking the monody as their point of departure, but it is curious to see how Monteverdi, starting from the old madrigal, arrives at the same result as they, and at the same time.

This transition from the madrigal to the cantata was made in three stages, marked by the publication of Book VI of the Madrigals in 1614, of Book VII in 1619, and of Book VIII in 1638.

The very title of Book VI testifies to the decay of the polyphonic ideal : " *Il sesto libro di madrigali a cinque voci con un dialogo e sette, con suo basso continuo, per poterli concertare nel clavicembalo e altri stromenti.*" * The thorough-bass, indeed, permits of the various parts being reduced for the harpsichord, a single voice remaining. It is not surprising that Ariadne's lament, here arranged for five voices, should find a place in this collection. With very slight modifications of the rhythm, with the prolongation of certain passages to permit of the play of imitations, the original melody is to be found throughout, predominating in one or other of the voices. The accompaniment, which is formed by the other voices, cannot be very different from that played by the viols at the performance of 1608.

The major part of the collection is taken up with the set of six madrigals, *Lagrime d'amante al sepolcro del amata*, composed by Monteverdi in 1610 to words by Scipione Agnelli, in memory of Caterinuccia Martinelli. The first part is one of Monteverdi's most moving pages. A single voice evokes the fragile spirit, " *Incenerite spoglie, Avara Tomba,*"

* See Note 136.

while the other voices act as orchestra. The harmonic style,
the insistent rhythm, give the impression of a funeral
symphony :—

EXAMPLE 50

The grief-stricken lover calls on the dryads, the nymphs,
the whole. of nature to share in his grief. " A moment of
serenity shows heaven, where doubtless the dead Corinna
lives ; but the earth is desolate and the woods are deserted since
she left them." The lover gives full voice to his despair.
He invokes the Muses, and pours forth his lamentations.
Then he grows calmer. It is of no use to mourn. An
ocean of tears will not give life to the dead. The opening
rhythm (—◡◡—) reappears, practically in its original
form ; and while a single voice is heard in sad resignation,
the other parts form an accompaniment of instrumental
character.

EXAMPLE 51

"This is truly Latin art," writes M. Tessier, "the art of Virgil, very moving by reason of the sincerity of the emotion expressed, but both true and beautiful in form." Like the great classics, Monteverdi maintains his right to interpret nature, but, transposing the real on to the plane of the ideal, he ennobles without deforming it.

In Book VI, Monteverdi has collected pieces of very different style. *Misero Alfeo* is a madrigal of the type of those which are contained in Book V. While the melody is always clearly defined in one of the parts, the feeling is polyphonic, and the master delights in the subtle play of imitations.

Zefiro torna, which has been popularized in a very mutilated form in A. Mendelssohn's edition (Peters), seems to be one of Monteverdi's very early compositions. It is written in imitations on a charming pastoral theme of somewhat popular atmosphere, and is delightfully fresh and spring-like. The principal part, written in recitative and dramatic style, is accompanied by the other parts in ingenious and expressive counterpoint.

The new arietta and cantata style appears quite clearly in the madrigal *Qui rise o Tirsi*. Above the *basso continuo* first the two high voices, then the two low voices sing in duet. At rare intervals, the five voices sing a few chords together, but the style of this madrigal is essentially the same as that which later was adopted by composers of operas when they wished to show off two or three voices in a duet or trio. The voices pursue each other lightly, borrowing from each other brilliant and rapid runs, and at the end unite and interweave in long concatenations of thirds and sixths. A duet of the same type appears in the middle of the madrigal *Batto qui pianse Ergasto*, which is, however, taken as a whole, more polyphonic than the other.

Addio Florida bella cannot be regarded as a madrigal. It is a dramatic sketch which might be detached from an opera, like the *lamento* of Ariadne, which it closely resembles. It is a classic farewell scene. A lover (tenor) bids farewell to his lady ; she (soprano) replies to him in despair. The monodies are accompanied by a thorough-bass. The chorus only enters to discuss the departure of the lover, and even then the soprano voice continues to predominate, the other parts being restricted to supporting it discreetly with strong single chords. The conclusion only, at the word *Addio*, is treated in contrapuntal style. The dialogue is in recitative, and certain passages embellished with vocalises show the first appearance of the ornate style which was to become characteristic of the cantata and the opera.

EXAMPLE 52

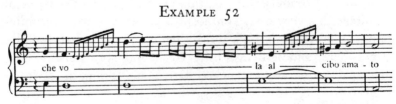

This madrigal comprises, in addition to the *basso continuo*, a *basso seguente* which doubles the principal part throughout. It is probable that it served as score to the *maestro* who conducted the performance. The seven-part dialogue, *Presso un fiume tranquillo*, is a kind of prototype of the dramatic madrigal and of the cantata for several voices, of which the *Combattimento* is the most perfect type. The *ensembles* play the same part as the antique chorus, *i.e.* of the narrator who recounts what is about to happen. They are silent where, in the text, one of the characters speaks. A solo-voice accompanied by the *basso continuo* then sings the words which the poet has allotted to his hero. Towards the end, there is a love duet between the soprano and the tenor, decorated with passionate vocalises, and the *finale*, for seven voices in contrapuntal style, celebrates the happiness of the lovers in tones of voluptuous joy.

The form of the cantata, which is essentially a concert-opera, can already be recognized in this piece. The composer gives full scope to the virtuosity of the performers. It is a grave error to imagine that Monteverdi, in virtue of some kind of asceticism, despised anything which could contribute to the beautification of musical forms. He was as passionately fond as any Luigi Rossi of fine contours, beautiful lines, ornate vocal passages. It is clear that he gladly adopted the plastic inventions of the Romano-Neapolitan school. There is a tendency to exaggerate somewhat the novelty of the methods he employed ; what is really new is the way in which he adapted processes already known to express feelings and ideas. The peculiar stamp which is borne by everything Monteverdi ever wrote is not attributable to the use of any particular harmonic formula, nor to any particular turn of the melodic phrase, but to its dramatic feeling, to its own peculiar atmosphere.

Far from showing any hostility to the new fashion for ariettas for one or two voices, Monteverdi adopted it with enthusiasm. Perhaps he realized that he had got out of the madrigal everything of which the genre was capable and even more. Perhaps, pure musician as he was, he delighted in seeing music revenge itself on poetry, to which the Florentines had wished to subject it. In point of fact, from about 1615 onwards, he neglected the madrigal, and even the recitative, and composed a large quantity of songs for one, two, or three voices with thorough-bass in cantata style. The seventh book of the madrigals, dedicated to the Duchess of Savoy in 1619, is full of them, and contains practically no madrigals properly speaking.

The ballet *Tirsi e Clori*, composed, as we have seen, in 1615, for the court of Mantua, comprises some arias and a duet with accompaniment by the harpsichord and chitarrone, followed by a madrigal for five voices. The " love-letter," *Se i languide miei sguardi*, for solo-voice and thorough-bass, is exceedingly interesting, and G. B. Doni was justified in quoting it as a perfect model of Monteverdi's representative style, for it reflects the slightest shades of meaning and even the *sous-entendus* of the text. The rest of the collection contains only *Canzonette* for two voices in the new melodic style, brilliant, ornate and rapid, which was beginning to find public favour. Most frequently, each song comprises three or four verses, which, unlike the *villanelle* or *airs de cour*, are sung each to a different melody. The bass alone remains unchanged in each different verse. It is extremely interesting to see the ingenuity with which Monteverdi, quite unembarrassed by this constraint, has ceaselessly varied his melodies. There is a subtle interplay of imitations between the two voices, and the hand of the master-contrapuntist of the *Missa a 4 da cappella* is to be seen in a perfectly secular passage such as the two-part *romanesca : Ohime dov'è il mio ben.*

In these songs, as in the *Scherzi Musicali*, Monteverdi reveals all his capacity for pure grace. The tendency is to

regard him as master only of the sombre and powerful style
of the *Orfeo.* In that terrible and charming city of Venice,
ruled in turn by political intrigue and outbursts of gaiety,
Monteverdi sings of love and its delights with voluptuous
ardour. The sensuality which informed the love madrigals
of his youth here appears in lighter form in the ariettas for
two voices, composed to verses in artificial style. He delights
in expressing the dying flames of the unhappy lover, or in
comparing his fate with that of the bird who sings to his captor.
In *O come sei gentile, caro augellino,* he amuses himself by
imitating, in fantastic *roulades,* the song of the captive night-
ingale. It is a far cry from this to the sublime lament of
Ariadne, or the complaint of Orpheus. Monteverdi changes
his tone, and, without abandoning anything which he has
acquired, takes pleasure in outdoing the musicians of Rome and
Naples, whose songs were being sung throughout Italy. He is
capable of incorporating into his style the inventions of the
younger school, and of using them at the opportune moment.
L'Incoronazione di Poppea is a marvellous example of this style.

The collection entitled *Quarto Scherzo delle Ariose Vaghezze,*
by Carlo Milanuzzi, organist of Santo Stefano at Venice, published in 1624, contains several songs and cantatas by Monteverdi quite akin in spirit to the graceful compositions of
Milanuzzi himself.* The collection also contains two airs by
Monteverdi's son Francesco. These compositions are less
interesting in themselves than on account of the tendencies
they reveal in Monteverdi's work. He would seem tempo-
rarily to have neglected the ideal of dramatic expressiveness
which he had always pursued, and to have concentrated upon
composing *chansonnettes* of sprightly grace.

The melodies are essentially diatonic and tonal ; chromatics
appear only very incidentally to give expressive force to
certain words, for example in the canzonetta, *La mia turca.*

* See Note 137.

EXAMPLE 53

This air comprises several stanzas, then, as a conclusion, *Prendi l'arco invitto* is sung to the same melody, which is slightly modified and developed towards the end.

Ohime ch'io cado is a cantata in the sense in which the word was understood about 1624. The six verses are written over the same bass, and separated by the repetition of the same *ritornello*, but the melody shows ingenious variations, of which the opening bars of three of the stanzas give an idea.

EXAMPLE 54

The song, *Si dolce è'l tormento*, is extremely interesting in its simplicity. It is somewhat akin to the melancholy *villanelle* of Kapsberger. Monteverdi creates an original effect by repetitions; the melodic line scarcely deviates, yet remains very expressive. One feels that Monteverdi is intent upon the creation of a new monodic style, which shall be more melodious than the recitative, and more general and less particularized in its expressive effect.

EXAMPLE 55

Si dolce e'l tormento ch'in seno mi stà ch'io vivo con - tento Per cruda bel-tà

Nel ciel di bel - lez-za S'ac - - creschi fie - - rez-za Et man-chi pie -

- tà che sempre qual scoglio All' on-da d'Or - goglio mia fe-de sa - rà

In 1632 a collection of *Scherzi Musicali* for one and two voices was published at Venice by Magni.*   The title is the only thing they have in common with the songs in *mesuré* style which we have already considered. They consisted for the most part of simple songs, the various stanzas of which differed, though they were sung to the same bass. They are sprightly, rhythmic, and resemble those which Luigi Rossi was then beginning to compose in Rome.

EXAMPLE 56

E - ri già tut - ta mi - a quel al - ma e quel co - re

Some of them are frankly popular in spirit, and contain a suggestion of the future " buffo " style in opera.

EXAMPLE 57

Ma - - le - det - to Sia — l'as - pet - to che m'ar-de tris - to me

The hand of Monteverdi can be recognized here and there in characteristic harmonic effects, in powerful rhythms, in poignant silences. The *canzone* for two voices, *Armato il cor*, which Heinrich Schütz later took as subject of one of his

* See Note 138.

compositions, already anticipates Cavalli's famous Conspiracy
of Medea (*Giasone*, 1646) * and recalls at the same time the
warlike effects of the *Combattimento*.

EXAMPLE 58

Armato il cor   Armato il cor   Armato il cor d'adamantina   fede nell'amoroso

The highly developed *canzone*, *Et è pur dunque vero* comprises six different stanzas sung to the same bass, and separated
by charming instrumental *ritornelli*. This work is exceedingly finished in form, and astonishing in its range of expression. While it is not a cantata, the style is already that of the
cantata. This is not surprising. While the word *cantata*
only appeared after 1620 in titles of works by Grandi, Rovetta,
Milanuzzi, etc., the genre existed long before that date.
There are madrigals in Book VI which, as we have seen, have
already the form of cantatas for several voices, and Domenico
Mazzochi was, about this time, writing dramatic scenes for
concert performance, in which the combination of solos, duets,
and *tutti* shows the characteristics of the cantata for several
voices. Between 1620 and 1638, Alessandro Grandi,
Giuseppe Rovetta, and Benedetto Ferrari, to quote only three
musicians with whom Monteverdi was in touch, published
small cantatas for solo-voice, as yet slightly developed, and
consisting for the most part of several stanzas each sung to a
different melody, though on the same bass, and separated by a
ritornello ; a little later, the genre consisted of a *canzone* or
an aria preceded by an important recitative.

The cantata is, in point of fact, a literary rather than a
musical invention. It consists of a new grouping of well-
known forms, and it is not surprising that one of the first to
have used it, Benedetto Ferrari, was as much a poet as a

* See Note 139.

musician.   In the cantata for several voices, a narrator, who is sometimes replaced by a chorus (in the work of both Monteverdi and Domenico Mazzochi), exposes the subject, and the characters intervene in turn.   Thus there are linked up recitatives, arias, *chansons*, duets and *ensembles*.   The cantata for one or two voices consists of *canzonette* and arias connected with each other by scraps of recitative.   The whole forms a little lyrical or dramatic scena, though *senza gesto*, without dramatic action.   In its origin, in the work of Ferrari and Manelli, the recitative occupied a large part of these compositions, but was later cut down to give place to passages in fixed forms.   The cantata style was an exercise in elegance, in plastic beauty.   Matter was certainly of less importance than form, but musicians such as Luigi Rossi or Carissimi were able to create marvels of music in this genre.   Above all, it must not be imagined that the art of these masters was without expressive power.   On the contrary, it was exceedingly expressive, but frequently inopportunely so.   The disproportion between the feelings expressed by the text and their transposition into music is disconcerting.   The gallant badinage of a lover, who implores the eyes of his mistress to refrain from wounding him with their conquering darts, becomes a cry of anguish, an ardent, desperate supplication. It is partly the temperament of the Southerner at work ; still more it is the result of that baroque taste, tumultuous and excessive in all things, which has given us the upturned eyes of penitent Magdalenes, the tortured bodies of St. Sebastians gleaming in the moonlight, in a strange mixture of sensuality and sentimentalism.

About 1630, though the cantata hardly existed, the cantata style existed, not in the form it was to take in the hands of such men as Luigi Rossi, Marazzoli, Abbatini, Cesti or Stradella, but, though a little heavy, already showing the tendency to rounded contours, to symmetrical construction, to delicate ornamentation which characterizes the baroque style in music as in architecture, and anticipating the development of voluptuous melody of the Romano-Neapolitan school.

Monteverdi wrote a host of *arie*, of *canzone*, of *ariette*, of *cantate* for one, two and three voices, which were sung in every home in Venice and Italy. The majority have not been republished; they can be consulted in the collections published during the master's lifetime, or shortly after his death, in Books VIII and IX of the Madrigals (1638 and 1657), in the *Selva Morale* (1641), and in the contemporary collections of airs by various authors, printed or in manuscript.

By the side of the dramatic cantatas of which he gives the model in the madrigals of Book VIII, there are sprightly *canzonette*, full of wit and fire,

EXAMPLE 59

quando dentro'l tuo se - no   vi - - - bra amo - ro - so sguar - -
- do il primo dol ce dardo,   o che gioir! che gioir! gioir!   o che gioir!

and little drawing-room cantatas of various forms. One of them, *Alcun non mi consigli*, for three voices, is ingeniously arranged.* The tenor first sings his lover's complaint, to the accompaniment of the thorough-bass, then the three voices unite to sing in chorus, *Non me n'adiro, non me ne doglio* (I rage not; I grieve not). The second tenor then enters proclaiming that love can never die, then the trio is resumed;

* See Note 140.

finally, the bass intervenes, and the conclusion is sung by the trio. Thus the three *virtuosi* who perform this composition each has the opportunity of displaying his vocal technique. These compositions show a new and gayer Monteverdi. He delights in inventing lovely melodies for gallant verses as a relaxation from the composition of masses and motets in the severe style. With his passionate love of life, he was, till the end of his days, curious of all that was new. At more than seventy years of age, he was in touch with all that was going on, and readily adopted new forms. He did not, however, attach exaggerated importance to them, and never forgot that the essential point is music, and not the varying forms it adopts. It is exceedingly difficult to distinguish precisely between his inventions and his borrowings. At this time musical technique was continually being enriched by the discoveries of a whole group of artists. Monteverdi was certainly the predominating figure among them, but he did not disdain occasionally to borrow new processes from them. His influence on Francesco Cavalli was enormous, but it would seem that he himself was influenced in his turn by his disciple in his Venetian operas. The same might be said of G. Rovetta, whose little airs, characterized by extreme simplicity of form and by a very marked sense of tonality, may have served as models to Monteverdi in his own *canzonette*.

Monteverdi attached considerable importance to certain of his technical inventions, and he takes care to indicate these in the prefaces to the *Scherzi Musicali* (1607) and the *Madrigali Guerrieri e Amorosi* (1638). It is prudent to abide by what he says and not blindly to attribute to him innovations which belong not to any one man, but to a whole generation of passionate seekers, who followed the same road, and worked in contact with each other.*

Book VIII of the Madrigals, published at Venice in 1638,

* See Note 141.

contains work of quite a different character. There is no need here to go back upon the *Ballo delle Ingrate* of 1608, nor is it necessary to consider the madrigals, which tell us nothing we do not know already. The madrigal is dead. The compositions for six voices with two violins and thorough-bass, which, in this collection, take the place of the madrigals for five voices, are conceived from a standpoint which is only very slightly polyphonic. They are choruses in vertical harmonies, in syllabic counterpoint, with passages for one, two, or three voices. The two and three part compositions are written in *canzone* style. Monteverdi was himself so completely persuaded of the decrepitude of a genre from which he had extracted everything it could give that he again turned to France for ideas through which to rejuvenate it.

The Duke of Mantua was interested in the compositions of Guédron, Superintendent of Music to the King of France, whom he had perhaps seen during his journey to Paris in 1608, and ordered the compositions of this musician to be sent to him as they were published by Ballard.* There was nothing exceptional in this, and airs by Guédron are to be found in the principal court libraries of Italy.

Monteverdi was certainly in touch with foreign music, either through the Duke of Mantua, whose musical director he was, or through his friend, the poet Rinuccini, who was constantly in Paris, and had already introduced the *Ballet de cour* from France into Italy. In the collection of 1638 there already figure two madrigals *alla francese*, composed on the model of the *airs de cour*. A solo-voice sings the first line, or the first group of lines, and all the voices echo the same phrase, after which the development is carried out with contrasts between *soli* and *tutti*. The soprano sings:

> *Chi vuol haver felice et lieto il core*
> *Non segua il crudo Amore,*

* See Note 142.

and the phrase is repeated textually in syllabic counterpoint by the soprano, *quinto*, alto, tenor and baritone.   Then the soprano resumes with *Quel lusinghier ch'ancide*, and the *quinto*, alto, tenor and baritone sing the same motive in turn.   Then comes a short homophonic passage, showing the alternation of 3/4 and common time so prevalent in French music, and again the soprano and the chorus borrow and reborrow phrases from each other until the conclusion, in which all the voices unite.

A comparison of technique shows how puny Guédron appears by the side of Monteverdi.   When he wishes to, Monteverdi develops his ideas *alla francese* far better than contemporary French composers could do, but the interest of these compositions resides in the indefatigable curiosity of mind which ceaselessly incited Monteverdi to adopt new or foreign methods.

These madrigals in the style of the *airs de cour* are among Monteverdi's most delicious and sweet compositions.   A delightfully pastoral impression is given by the *Dolcissimo usignuolo*.   A shepherd speaks to a bird, envying its lot: " Why have I not wings that I might fly to my love ? "   The melodic phrases are ample, and of set purpose simple.

EXAMPLE 60

In his madrigals, Monteverdi never makes use of the vague, ill-defined rhythms beloved by the French composers of the *airs de cour*, but he specifies that they are to be sung very

freely, especially in expressive passages. Thus the voices
which murmur the accompaniment of the Nymph's complaint
in the madrigal *Non avea Febo ancora* must conform exactly
to her song, which is to be directed by " her emotion, and not
by the beat of the conductor's hand." *

EXAMPLE 61

The collection of *Madrigali Guerrieri e Amorosi* (Book VIII)
opens with a kind of prologue in honour of Emperor Ferdinand, to whom it is dedicated. It is scored for six voices,
four viols, two violins and a spinet. Monteverdi again sings
of love in this book, but also of the cruelty of war. The words
Di Marte furibondo e fiero i duri incontri are sung to repetitions
of semiquavers. Later, a solo-voice supported by a viol and
a spinet sings to the glory of the Emperor crowned with
immortal laurels. Monteverdi gave minute attention to the
details of the execution ; for example, at one point he requires
that the " bowing " shall be carried out in prolonged and soft

* See Note 143.

strokes (*Viole sole toccate con arcate lunghe et soave*).   Precise
directions of this kind are quite exceptional at the time.

A ballet *Movete al mio bel suon* sung by five voices with two
violins recalls *Tirsi e Clori* and the *Ballo delle Ingrate*.   A
scene in recitative between the Poet and a Nymph precedes
the dance-music proper which, according to current usage,
comprises a certain number of time-changes, corresponding
to the various figures of the ballet.   Monteverdi even provides
for the insertion towards the end of some instrumental dances
to be composed by the ballet-master.

This collection includes a work of capital importance, the
Combattimento di Tancredi e di Clorinda.*   It had been composed twelve years earlier, and performed in 1626 at the house
of the patrician Girolamo Mocenigo, one of the accepted
patrons of the musician.   In his frequently quoted preface,†
Monteverdi considers at length the conditions which led him
to invent the agitated (*concitato*) style.   He had been struck
by the fact that musicians ordinarily expressed gentle, sweet,
sad, or joyous feelings, never anger or martial rage.   Now
Plato expressly says that music must be capable of expressing
the feelings of those who march valiantly to war.   Monteverdi therefore sought the solution of the problem in the use
of an appropriate rhythm.   It is very possible that on this
occasion his interest in antique metres, which had been aroused
by the French *musique mesurée*, may have stood him in good
stead.   Indeed, his point of departure is the pyrrhic foot ᴗᴗ,
which seemed to him the exact contrary of the spondee − −.
Now, as the spondee expresses calm, the pyrrhic foot should, he
considers, be a marvellous method of expressing agitation.   For
that matter, it had been used by the Greeks in warlike dances.
His next idea would certainly have caused considerable
astonishment to the ancient Greeks; he juxtaposed pyrrhic
feet in such a way that he obtained sixteen quavers in a single

* See Note 144.   † See Note 145.

bar. The effect of these repeated notes, known to-day as
" *tremolo*," did, in fact, render impressions of agitation, anger
and terror in the most picturesque and expressive way. His
love of contrast led him to seek a text which would give him the
opportunity of expressing in turn the fury of war, religious
emotion, and death. He found it in the episode of the Combat
of Tancred and Clorinda in Tasso. He set it to music,
modifying the poetic text slightly in places.

For the first time, it seems that the orchestra is quite
independent of the voices. It creates an atmosphere round
the drama which is being played ; it expresses what the voices
suggest. It is, moreover, exclusively composed of stringed
instruments (*viole da brazzo, basso e contrabasso da gamba*)
with the harpsichord, which played the thorough-bass.

The characters are Tancred, Clorinda, and the Narrator
(Testo). The last-named opens in recitative style, singing
Tasso's beautiful verses to a melody in which the melodic
line is singularly even, the voice moving nearly all the time on
the same degree of the scale. Tancred, believing Clorinda
to be a warrior, wishes to provoke her to combat. The
orchestra, as his challenging words are pronounced, reinforces
their effect with appropriate music. There is something
miraculous in Monteverdi's art. A common chord, repeated
for a long time in a certain rhythm, suffices to give the impression of the galloping of horses, of the charge of the impetuous
horsemen :

EXAMPLE 62

or, a little further on, the wary approach of the adversaries, *a passi tardi e lenti*, or the warlike frenzy which
animates them.

EXAMPLE 63

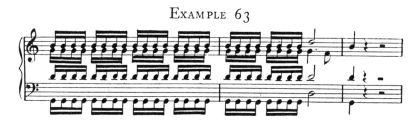

Monteverdi disdains any harmonic artifice ; rhythm suffices
him, and by means of rhythm alone he obtains marvellous
effects.   Now the narrator declaims the Invocation to Night,
which is preceded by a moving instrumental prelude, and the
combat begins, the swords clash and resound.

EXAMPLE 64

The rhythm becomes abrupt and breathless.   One feels the
enervation, the fatigue of the antagonists.   They are weaken-
ing, but pride revives them and urges them to vengeance.
Again the repeated semiquavers appear, both in the voice
parts and in the orchestra.   For a moment the struggle is
interrupted.   Tancred calls on Clorinda to reveal her name,
but her only answer is in scornful words.   The adversaries
throw themselves upon each other, and the powerful and
poignant description of the struggle is carried out by means
of the same rhythmic effects until the moment of Clorinda's
defeat.   Then, abandoning the *concitato* style, Monte-

verdi depicts the death of the warrior maiden in tones worthy
of Tasso. The dying Clorinda can scarcely speak, her breath
comes fast. Her heroic ardour has died down; her soul is
filled with a vast desire for peace. " Love, thou hast con-
quered. I pardon thee. Pardon me, and give me the baptism
that effaces all sin."

EXAMPLE 65

A·mi - co   hai vin-to   Io ti perdon   Perdona tu anco-ra

Tancred, withdrawing his enemy's helmet, sees the golden
hair fall round the lovely face, and his heart is broken with
grief. This is a page of admirable beauty. There is no pomp.
The recitative faithfully reflects all the meaning of the text.
The dying Clorinda sees heaven opening to receive her, and
murmurs in ecstasy:

EXAMPLE 66

S'a - - pre il ciel   io   va - - do   in   pa - - - - - - ce

Violino: Viola soprano

Viola alto: B.C.

We can well say, with M. Tessier, that " Tasso has not
been betrayed by the admirable and cultured musician who
set to music the episode of Tancred's combat. The two artists
are worthy of each other."

The *Combattimento* is destined neither for dramatic nor for concert performance. Monteverdi has given precise data for its execution. There is to be no special stage. Clorinda and Tancred, in costume, are to enter unexpectedly into the *salon* in which the performance is to be given. Whilst the narrator is relating the action, they are to mime it in exact time to the music, and their voices will be heard only in the few phrases the composer has allotted to them. Above all, there are to be no trills, no *roulades*. The Narrator will only permit himself these ornaments in the Invocation to Night. The orchestra is to adapt itself to the dramatic expression of the text.*

As one can see, the work is a kind of drawing-room opera, or cantata, in which pantomime was employed ; it is a hybrid genre, which is, however, sufficiently interesting to make it seem somewhat surprising that no subsequent musician was inspired by it.

Nothing has survived of the great secular cantatas composed by Monteverdi for public or private ceremonies. It is exceedingly regrettable that we do not possess the one written for the Ascension and sung upon the Bucentaur when the vast ship was rowed across the lagoon to bear to the Adriatic the age-old homage of the golden ring of her spouse, the Doge of the Most Serene Republic.

In 1628 Monteverdi composed madrigals to verses by Giulio Strozzi for the reception and banquet given to the Grand Duke of Tuscany at the Arsenal of Venice. Caffi also mentions a cantata of his composition, *Il Rosaio fiorito*, which he says was sung in 1629 at the *Accademia dei Concordi* of Rovigo to celebrate the birth of a son to the Governor, Morosini.

These great cantatas, which were performed in the open air, must have been particularly suited to the decorative side of Monteverdi's genius, and certain motets in concerted style,

* See Note 146.

with *sinfonie* of cornetti and drums, permit us to form at least an approximate idea of them.

In the absence of these cantatas, as of the operas composed during the twenty-three years which separate the *Arianna* from the *Ritorno d'Ulisse*, the sacred works, the dramatic madrigals, the *canzoni*, the airs *alla francese* enlighten us upon the evolution of Monteverdi's genius. All these compositions bear witness to his indefatigable intellectual curiosity, his unquenchable desire to invent or adopt new methods of expression. At more than seventy years of age, he remains young among the young, and vies with them in the use of the most audacious formulæ. He was to give, before his death, a supreme proof of the vigour of his genius in writing a lyrical drama in which is reflected the whole evolution of his talent and its inexhaustible richness : *L'Incoronazione di Poppea*, his masterpiece, and incontestably the masterpiece of lyrical drama in the seventeenth century.

V

THE VENETIAN OPERAS

It was at Venice that the first public opera-house was opened in 1637.* Till then, opera had been " a spectacle for princes," whether in Rome, Florence, or Mantua. Henceforward, the success of the performance was no longer to depend on a few great nobles, but entirely on the audience who had bought, with the price of their seats, the right to criticize the work presented to them.

The San Cassiano theatre, which was the first to be used exclusively for opera, was the property of the patrician family Tron, who had built it. In accordance with the custom which was adopted by all the other theatres, the boxes were rented by the year, and frequented exclusively by the nobility and foreigners of rank. The parterre was open, for four Venetian lire, to anyone possessing that modest sum. The theatre was sometimes managed by the Venetian family who owned it, and who engaged a company of singers to whom were conceded all receipts, except the rent for the boxes, which belonged to the family. Sometimes it was handed over completely to an *impresario*, as in the case of the first company to perform at San Cassiano, which was directed by two Romans, Benedetto Ferrari and Francesco Manelli.

There were two opera seasons each year ; the first took place in the autumn, the second lasted throughout carnival-time. The latter was the more brilliant. It was a season at which Venice seemed to run wild, when everyone was in costume, even the priests on their way to mass, even the austere

* See Note 147.

councillors; a time when the ladies of the Venetian nobility could at least go in search of the adventures of which they dreamed for the rest of the year, shut up in their palaces.   And what an atmosphere of liberty and joy filled the theatres. Only the fear of the armed and masked *bravi* of the noble proprietor at the entrances prevented the animation from degenerating into tumult.   Though the theatres were privileged places in which the least act of violence was a state offence, grave acts of violence were in fact perpetrated.   A Mocenigo once shot a Foscarini in his box.   However, as a general rule, these little disputes were settled outside, and it was prudent to be on one's guard in any altercation with a noble.   The quays were so dark when the performances were over, that it was a simple matter to slip into the lagoon with a dagger in one's body just as one was stepping into a gondola. Yet the opera was better behaved than the theatre.   The presence of ladies of quality in the boxes restrained somewhat the impetuosity of the youth of Venice.   The singers were held in greater respect than the actors.   They were received with the utmost enthusiasm.   The theatre was filled with the cry " *Mi butto, cara* " of the young Venetians, who, leaning out of their boxes, protested their readiness to throw themselves into space for love of the singer who was delighting them. The gondoliers, who were given the seats which were empty when the performance began, expressed their enthusiasm in delighted cries.   When they recognized an actor, they called to him.   Saint Didier relates that in his time there was a priest who frequently sang at the opera.   When he appeared in the guise of an old woman, the cry arose " *Ecco Pre Pierro che fà la vecchia.*" *

Monteverdi's last masterpieces were written for these tumultuous audiences, who seemed entirely given over to a furious desire for enjoyment.   The conditions of the per-

* See Note 148.

formance differed as widely as the audience from anything he had known before. At Mantua, Parma, Florence or Rome, the performances were given in a sumptuous setting. The halls shone in the light of thousands of wax torches. Nothing was too splendid for these magnificent princes, and the most extraordinary inventions of the scene-painters were carried out with incredible refinement. At Venice, the *impresario* had to attract the public, but he also had to balance his expenditure and receipts. Throughout the performance, the auditorium was in semi-darkness. The lantern by the light of which people took their seats was extinguished when the curtain rose. To read the libretto, people were obliged to light little wax candles (*cerini*) which were sold at the door with the scenario. The scenery was much simplified. Whilst Giacopo Torelli performed incredible feats with the scenery in the Teatro Novissimo after 1644, it must be admitted that the decorations, during the first period, at any rate, were somewhat poor, compared with the admirable settings of the princely stages in the rest of Italy. The orchestra was reduced to a small number of stringed instruments grouped round a harpsichord and a few theorboes. On the other hand, no expense was spared as regards the singers, and the most illustrious *virtuosi* in Italy were invited for the season.

Monteverdi was able to accommodate himself marvellously to these new conditions. His librettists, moreover, who were perhaps retained by him, did not multiply extravagant scenic inventions in their libretti, and his operas show no trace of that *capriccio bizzarro de' Veneziani* which, some years later, the poet Aurelio Aureli delighted in indulging.

It must, moreover, be recognized that the first operas played in Venice differed little as regards either the music or the libretto from those played in Rome. It could scarcely have been otherwise. The authors were two eminent Roman musicians, Benedetto Ferrari and Francesco Manelli. The former was as well known for his poetry as for his music. The first works performed by his company in Venice, *Andromeda* and *La Maga Fulminata*, have disappeared, but it is certain that they were typical productions of the Roman æsthetic. Whilst in Florence and Mantua the recitative tradition had maintained itself until this date, the Roman type of opera had been influenced from its very origin by the cantata style. It is extremely interesting to compare a Florentine opera such as the *Galatea* of Vittori (1639) with essentially Roman operas, such as those composed by Domenicho Mazzochi or Stefano Landi. In Vittori's work, the recitative is the very backbone of the drama. Through that medium, feelings and passions are expressed ; the airs, choruses and ballets serve only as a diversion. On the contrary, in the *Catene d'Adone*, Mazzochi clearly writes the recitative without interest. He loses no opportunity of inserting airs in fixed form, and songs, and the principal interest of the work is, for him, contained in these passages. The scores are flooded with little notes, and the recitative soon came to occupy less space than the *canzonette*. These brisk, lively, and sometimes touching songs generally show a delightful melodic freshness and grace, but they all seem to be copied from each other. The same stereotyped formulæ of runs, sequences and cadences are to be found in all of them. They invade opera, as earlier they had invaded the cantata. Any subject, whether sacred or secular, serves as pretext for exquisite songs. One may say that in Rome the dramatic sense rapidly declines, while pure music triumphs. It is the victory of formal beauty over profound feeling and thought.

About 1640, however, things had not reached this stage, and the musicians of the Romano-Neapolitan school were creating melodies which were at the same time emotionally appealing and of marvellous formal beauty. They no longer attempted to find an equivalent in music for the isolated word, but sought to render the general feeling of the poem. It is very regrettable that Ferrari's operas, which preceded Monteverdi's in Venice, should have disappeared, for there are in his cantatas dramatic arias which, for power and plastic beauty, would not be unworthy of the greatest masters. The opening of this air from the *Scherzo libro delle musiche* is characteristic.

EXAMPLE 67

O Monumen-ti   a-pri-te - vi a – pri-te-vi   non ve-de-te ch'io

moro ch'io mo - - ro in lasciando colei che tanto che   tanto a-do - - - - - - ro

Moving passages of this kind are to be found here and there in the Roman operas of the epoch, but the sense of dramatic unity is lacking. It was certainly the splendid stage-settings of the Barberini which brought about the ruin of lyrical drama as it had been created in Florence and Mantua.

About 1635, a Roman opera consisted of libretto which was generally absurd, the intrigue being almost impossible to follow. The fantastic subject gave occasion for constant changes of scene, and for *divertissements* in song and dance. It was a splendid display for the delight of the senses, but appealing little to the mind or the heart. Contemporary records show that the spectators were principally interested in the extraordinary stage machinery and the marvellous voices of the great singers.

This was the conception of opera which Ferrari and Manelli introduced into Venice. They soon found a rival in Francesco Sacrati of Parma. The Venetian audiences were essentially popular. These highly spectacular operas, the solos, the tuneful duets and trios were better calculated to please them, it would seem, than the lyrical tragedies of the Florentines.

The intervention of Monteverdi was destined to bring about a durable change.   Up to a certain point Monteverdi accommodated himself to these libretti, the variety of which had much charm for him.   He too felt the delight of the pure musician in writing, under the influence of the cantata style, airs and *ensembles* of fixed form.   But he always maintained the rights of the recitative.   In his hands it never degenerated into the poor and languishing declamation which made the Florentine operas insufferable.   His recitative is expressive, powerful, full of music.   It is an organized whole, with a beginning, a middle and an end.   He can extract from words the melody they contain within them.   The last operas of Monteverdi are a kind of fusion between the style of his earliest operas and the Roman conception of the cantata-opera.

In order to understand properly Monteverdi's last works, they should not be compared, as is generally done, with his first operas, written thirty-five years earlier, but with the operas which were being performed in Italy at the time of their production.   There is nothing more typical from this point of view than the *Palazzo d'Atlante* of Luigi Rossi, produced *con amore* by the Cardinal Antonio Barberini, at the Quattro Fontane theatre during the carnival of 1642.   It is the triumph of the cantata style in the drama.   It contains airs of admirable form, very melodious recitatives, *ariosi* and a host of touching or sprightly *canzonette* of various forms.   The orchestra accompanies the airs, it represents the murmuring waves evoked by the air of the Prologue, and executes charming ballets which are danced by the captives of the sorceress.   The poem, from the fertile pen of a future Pope, Giulio Rospigliosi, has none of the incoherences of the ordinary libretti of the Roman school, but it has little dramatic power.   The action stagnates, and obviously interests nobody.   The audience listens to the airs and the *canzoni* without inquiring into the place they occupy in the drama. This is the form of opera ridiculed by Benedetto Marcello, in which the airs by the composer can be replaced by popular items from the repertory of the various singers taking part in the performance. The opera tends to become a kind of concert performed amid magnificent scenery, in the course of which the audience applauds airs, duets, trios without any heed to their appositeness.

But this much must be said of Luigi Rossi and his rivals, that they created melodic forms of ideal beauty and expressive power. From the point of view of variety and perfection of form, Rossi may be confidently regarded as Monteverdi's superior. What he lacked was dramatic instinct. One might establish an analogous comparison a century later between Hasse, whose melodies, with their harmonious periods, are among the most beautiful that musical genius has ever created, and Gluck, a composer far less subtle, and even, in some respects, somewhat clumsy, yet gifted with that natural greatness which Hasse entirely lacks. But the analogy must not be accepted literally, for Monteverdi is totally different from Gluck.

This *Palazzo d'Atlante*, voluptuous, elegiac, of subtle melodic beauty, but devoid of force and life, may be contrasted with the first operas of Monteverdi's disciple Francesco Cavalli, which preceded Monteverdi's own in the Venetian opera-house.

Pietro Francesco Caletti Bruni, called after his patron Francesco Cavalli, was born in Crema in 1602. On January 18th, 1617, he entered the Chapel of St. Mark's as singer, was in 1640 appointed second organist, and subsequently director. He developed entirely under the influence of Monteverdi. His talent, powerful, rich and unequal, offers a complete contrast with that of Luigi Rossi. Rossi and

Cavalli were, after the death of Monteverdi and Mazzochi, considered throughout Italy as the greatest musicians of their generation. The former is an aristocrat by nature; his delicate music is written for an *élite* ; the second is a genuinely popular genius, seeing things in broad outlines, with no mind for detail. His music is animated by a dramatic power which even to-day has lost nothing of its effectiveness. His broadly designed melodies, his wilfully simple harmonies, which vigorously emphasize tonality, contrast with the subtle experiments of Luigi Rossi, with their curious development of new chromatic effects, of luscious dissonances, of rich frictions.*

It is particularly in his first operas that Cavalli is seen as Monteverdi's disciple. These are to be found in his work the rhythmic effects, the impressive silences which give so peculiar a stamp to the orchestral work of his master, but his style is looser. He can, without effort, paint vast instrumental tone-pictures, and has not his equal for composing, in a style, easy, flowing, and consistently expressive, a narration in which ample periods develop naturally. No musician of the epoch possesses to the same degree as Cavalli the sense of the decorative quality of music. While Monteverdi may be compared with Titian, his pupil corresponds, to a certain extent, with Veronese.

Monteverdi certainly followed with interest the productions of the new generation. Cavalli had to submit to him his *Nozze di Teti e Peleo* in 1638, and his admirable *Didone* in 1641. The master possessed in the highest degree qualities which both Luigi Rossi and Cavalli lacked, a superior intelligence, and a genius for conceiving his characters as living beings with distinctive characteristics, their own foibles, their own manias. A more powerful dramatist than Luigi Rossi, a more subtle musician than Cavalli, Monteverdi in his last operas employed with equal skill the operatic and the cantata

* See Note 149.

style, profiting by all the inventions of the art of his epoch.

Venetian opera was not left for long in the hands of foreigners. Benedetto Ferrari, who had inaugurated the theatre of San Cassiano in 1637 with his *Andromeda* set to music by Francesco Manelli, and produced his *Maga* in the following year, had, in 1639, to make way for Francesco Cavalli, who, from 1639 to 1645, composed all the operas played in this theatre with the one exception of Monteverdi's *Ritorno d'Ulisse in Patria*. The sumptuous theatre of SS. Giovanni e Paolo having been opened in 1639, Benedetto Ferrari and Manelli transferred their activities there, and produced *Delia* (poem by Strozzi, music by Manelli) and *Armida* (poem and music by Ferrari); but, in the autumn season, they were ousted from the theatre by Monteverdi, who there produced his *Adone*, which was so great a success that it ran throughout the following season, and the *Nozze d'Enea con Lavinia* (1641). Meanwhile, the theatre of San Mose was inaugurated in 1639 with the *Arianna*. Thus Monteverdi's operas were being played simultaneously in all the theatres of Venice.

The first operas written by Monteverdi for the Venetian theatres are lost. Of the *Adone*, we have only the libretto of Paolo Vendramin, printed in 1639, and dedicated to the founder of the theatre of SS. Giovanni e Paolo, the patrician Antonio Grimani, whose sons were destined to be still more celebrated for their crimes than for their passion for opera.* The only idea we can get of the *Nozze d'Enea con Lavinia* comes from a detailed scenario. The poem was written by a Venetian noble, Giacomo Badoaro, who, in the same year, gave Monteverdi the libretto of the *Ritorno d'Ulisse in Patria,* the score of which has been preserved.†

At the Carnival of 1641 the master produced two operas simultaneously, *Il Ritorno d'Ulisse* at San Cassiano, and

* See Note 150.　　　　† See Note 151.

Le Nozze d'Enea at SS. Giovanni e Paolo. It is not astonishing that in these circumstances their style should show some slight negligences. Monteverdi seems to have written *Il Ritorno d'Ulisse* under the influence of the first operas of Cavalli and to have regarded with some envy his disciple's prodigious power of melodic invention, the large and powerful construction, the spontaneous outpouring of music which characterize both the *Nozze di Teti* and the *Didone*. He was at the same time under the spell of the style of the *canzonette*, and, with advancing age, gave evidence of an increasing taste for the folk-song from which he drew his inspiration in his work. The *Ritorno d'Ulisse* must be considered not as a work finished at leisure, but as a kind of improvisation of genius, a vast sketch, certain parts of which have been elaborated, while others are of set purpose only roughly indicated.

Monteverdi seems to have been on friendly terms with Badoaro, and to have collaborated in the libretto. Badoaro was a mediocre poet, but his ideas on dramatic art were not without interest. His libretti, with those of Busenello, were the first to give historic tableaux highly animated, to combine comedy with tragedy and tears with laughter. Men such as Aureli and Minato later did little more than to readopt and develop this conception of musical drama. One wonders, however, whether it was really Badoaro's invention, or whether Monteverdi had not suggested it to him.[*]

The characters are drawn with the vigour of outline peculiar to the art of Monteverdi. By the side of Ulysses and Penelope, whose characters are depicted in the most lively fashion, inspired rather by Homer than by Badoaro, there are divine characters which are very important, but sometimes tedious. They express themselves pompously in a solemn and bombastic style. Some secondary characters are sketched with spirit; Melanto, Penelope's lovely servant, in love with

[*] See Note 152.

the servant Eurimaco, Eumeus the shepherd, whose songs are in popular style, and finally Iro the beggar, a court buffoon, gluttonous and cynical.* Indeed, Badoaro has introduced *buffo* scenes in imitation of the fashion which had obtained in Rome for several years past. It must be admitted that Monteverdi has treated them somewhat clumsily, and that the scenes lack the verve of a Cavalli, the wit of a Marazzoli or a Giacopo Melani. In the *Incoronazione di Poppea*, on the other hand, he gets positively Shakespearean effects from the combination of comic and tragic scenes.

The opera opens with a prologue of the greatest beauty. Human Frailty laments her weakness. Time vaunts his terrible power. He attacks everything, and nothing escapes him. He limps, but he has wings. The curious descriptive effects at the words *zoppo* (*lame*) and *ali* (*wings*) are worthy of notice.

EXAMPLE 68

se   ben   zop - - - po   ho   l'a - - - - - - - - - - - - - - - - - li

L'Umana Fragilità resumes her complaint. She is the sport of *Destiny*, who at once intervenes, singing an exceedingly curious air built up on a single phrase repeated in different keys, the repetitions giving the impression of the relentless turning of a wheel.

EXAMPLE 69

Mia   vi-ta   son voglie le   gioje, le doglie le   gioje le doglie le   do - glie

Human Frailty sings a third stanza, still to the same bass. The recitative, the dolorous and grave accents of which recall the songs of Orpheus, relates the misery of the man who is

† See Note 153.

the prey of love. Cupid then begins a hymn of triumph
in his own honour, and after a last stanza by Human Frailty,
Love, Destiny and Time, in a superb trio, threaten Ulysses
with the cruelties which they inflict upon mankind.

Throughout this prologue, Monteverdi is at his best.
Its construction is marvellously solid. The three airs of
Time, of Fortune and of Love, composed respectively in
C major, G major, and A minor, are united in the reprise of
the complaint of *L'Umana Fragilita*, and the trio in D minor
forms a marvellous conclusion to the tableau. This artistic
choice of keys, and the manner in which they are linked, this
skill in the construction of a scene had become familiar to
musicians by their use of the cantata style, but Monteverdi is
here again in the vanguard.

The play opens with a monologue by Penelope interrupted
by the comforting words of the nurse. It is a superb dramatic
narration, finely developed in three parts, and reminiscent of
the songs of Orpheus and Ariadne. Monteverdi accumulates
expressive dissonances and brusque modulations in order to
express the feelings which overwhelm the unhappy queen.

To create a diversion, and in accordance with the principle
of the alternation of sad and gay scenes which was to be the
rule in Venetian opera, Melanto and Eurimaco appear,
singing of their love.

The scene changes, and one sees the vessel of the Phæacians
which bears Ulysses to Ithaca to the sound of a very suggestive
orchestral passage. Jupiter persuades the angry Neptune
to renounce his vengeance. The Phæacians bring the sleeping
Ulysses to land.

From this moment onwards the music maintains a pastoral
character until the end of the act. Ulysses awakens; he
relates his pretended shipwreck to Minerva, who, appearing
in the form of a young shepherd, conducts him to the house
of the shepherd Eumeus. Songs of popular character, grace-

ful *canzonette* adroitly introduced into the action, contribute
to the creation of a rustic atmosphere, and form a contrast
with the dramatic narration in which Ulysses describes the
tempest which has destroyed his ship. Here appears the
dramatic air, the result of the representative style inaugurated
by Monteverdi in the songs of Orpheus, the form of which
had gradually been rendered more flexible by the development
of the cantata. Using the sequence as a method of pathetic
development, Ulysses depicts the violence of the raging seas
which have thrown his ship on the coast.

EXAMPLE 70

fummo   a   forza a forza cac - cia-ti cacciati cac - cia-ti cacciati in questo   li - - do

In Act II, Minerva brings Telemachus back to Ithaca
on a cloud, and conducts him to Eumeus. The stupefied
delight of the shepherd on seeing the son of his master is
rendered in most striking fashion ; the shepherd first utters
only a stifled cry, which he repeats on a higher note, and
finally cries with all his strength, " Oh ! Oh ! Oh ! great son
of Ulysses," while the bass hammers out a descending run in
a powerful rhythm in triple time, the instruments crashing
out solemn chords. Ulysses reveals his identity to Eumeus,
and this is the occasion for a delightful duet to a ground-bass.
The scene of the meeting between Ulysses and Telemachus
is moving. The father clasps his son to his breast. The
voices alternate and interweave in passionate effusions. The
general arrangement of this duet for male voices is the same
as that of the admirable duet between Nero and Poppea.
Then the action drags a little. The suitors exhort Penelope
to marry one of them, but she refuses with dignity. They
plot the death of Telemachus, but the sight of Jupiter's eagle

flying above them terrifies them.   The semiquavers of the *stile concitato* express their terror at the menace of the god.*

In the fields, Eumeus finds Ulysses, and tells him of the terror of the suitors.   Ulysses derides them, and in a very odd piece of dramatic realism, actually bursts into laughter at the end of the air : *Godo anch' io ne so perchè rido.*

Finally, Monteverdi depicts in masterly style the scene of the massacre.   The suitors try to draw their bows.   Ulysses, disguised as a beggar, fights with Iro to the sound of a *ritornello* in which is already announced the *Sinfonia di guerra* which bursts out a moment later when Ulysses, drawing his bow, utters his war-cry.   The terror of the suitors is strikingly rendered.   They cry aloud, and Monteverdi merely indicates the note of the cry, without fixing its duration.   The voice of the hero exhorting his comrades to fight soars above the warlike sounds of the orchestra.

Act III is the least interesting.   The long dialogues in which Eumeus, Telemachus and the Nurse convince Penelope that the victor is really Ulysses, the discourses of the Gods—all this is somewhat tedious.   On the other hand, when Penelope at last recognizes Ulysses, and calls upon the whole of Nature to share in her happiness, the genius of Monteverdi finds its full expression.   The opera terminates with a superb love-duet.

The score gives us no details of the composition of the orchestra of the San Cassiano theatre in 1640, but it is almost certain that Monteverdi was obliged to accommodate his music to the small number of instruments which were all that the exigencies of a commercial undertaking could permit.   For that matter the simplification of the orchestra due to economic reasons coincided with the efforts of composers to give the orchestra a centre of gravity.   The cantata style, and the rise of the solo, quite naturally led musicians to relinquish the mass

* See Note 154.

effects of the rich instrumental polyphony of the sixteenth century. The harpsichord, to which was confided the thorough-bass, becomes the centre of the orchestra. With one or two theorboes and basses (*violoni*) it suffices for the accompaniment of narrations and airs. Sometimes the violins combine with the voices and attack brilliant runs. Composition in five parts tends to disappear; the orchestral passages are written mostly in four or even three parts. Sometimes, though in picturesque passages only, such as scenes of war or scenes in the infernal regions, the brass—trumpets, cornetti, and trombones—appears. This impoverishment of the orchestra was indispensable to the establishment of a new balance of sound. The harpsichord and the string quartet were to become the pivot on which the whole orchestra rested; in the course of the succeeding centuries, all the instruments ruthlessly ejected at the beginning of the seventeenth century gradually re-enter the orchestra around the quartet, and a new order is established.

For the same economic reasons, choruses were to be eliminated from Venetian opera. They still appear in 1641 in the *Didone* of Cavalli and the *Ritorno d'Ulisse* of Monteverdi, but there is none in the *Incoronazione* (1642) nor in Cavalli's *Egisto*. The composer was obliged for these choruses to substitute *ensembles* rendered by the combined voices of the actors on the stage. The cantata had been for musicians an admirable preparation for this sudden change of habit. With all the accustomed flexibility of his genius, Monteverdi accepted these changed conditions. " Symphonic passages and choruses were no longer desired," writes M. Romain Rolland, " so he wrote no more of them. He was typical of that great race of Latin artists who can always accommodate their genius to practical conditions." *

* See Note 155.

In the autumn of 1642, *Il Nerone ossia l'Incoronazione di Poppea* was played in the theatre of SS. Giovanni e Paolo. Monteverdi and the poet Francesco Busenello collaborated in the work. The latter was a librettist after Monteverdi's own heart. Great power of imagination, a fine faculty for realistic observation combined with great vigour of expression, these were qualities which served the composer well. From the strictly dramatic point of view, the *Incoronazione di Poppea* may be regarded as the unrivalled masterpiece of the new genre, the historical opera.

The action is divided into a large number of scenes distributed into three acts.

In Act I, Otho, the lover of Poppea, returns from a journey, and goes by night to his mistress's house, trembling with joy at the thought of seeing her again.

EXAMPLE 71

E pur io torno   e pur io torno   qui   qual   li - nea al   cen - tro

The music reflects intimately the meaning of the text, and is moulded upon the words. This is not the Florentine recitative, nor is it melody in symmetrical periods : it is the arioso, finely elaborated, of finished workmanship, such as may be found in the cantatas of the epoch, but with an additional element, which is the stamp of genius. As Otho is about to cross the threshold he stumbles over a sleeping man, and recognizes him to be one of Nero's guards. He understands, and, in his grief, utters angry complaints. The soldiers are awakened by the disturbance and call, " Who speaks ? Who goes there ? " Otho disappears into the night, and the two sentinels, with mutual excuses for having slept, begin a dialogue of astonishing realism, in which they bewail their own fate and the state of Rome. The day dawns, and Nero appears on the threshold, accompanied by Poppea, who embraces him and tenderly holds him back. From their first words, the characters are defined with remarkable vigour, that of Poppea especially, a woman more ambitious than passionate and above all frivolous and wanton. One feels in her caressing *vocalises* her affectation and her desire for admiration. Nero is a toy in her hands. It is Monteverdi who, in this scene, has given life to the dialogue by interrupting Nero's narration with eager questions. The whole scene is treated in cantata style. Arias and songs alternate, linked by *ariosi* and recitatives with such skill that instead of an impression of a mosaic of fragments, we have the feeling that here is a mighty whole powerfully welded together. This is characteristic of the entire opera.

The scene changes. Beneath the porch of a palace, Octavia laments her fate in a recitative full of nobility and energy. Offended in her wifely dignity, she conceives the idea of revenging herself upon Poppea and Nero. The character of Octavia, a great Roman lady, proud and torn by jealousy, is admirably rendered. Seneca appears and offers her moral consolation. He is a strange figure, certainly attractive in his nobility and uprightness, but unable to resist the sound of his own voice, and fixed in an attitude of stoic virtue which he will maintain unto death. All this is expressed rather by Monteverdi's music than by Busenello's text. Seneca speaks grandiloquently, and the pompous way in which he preaches resignation to the unfortunate Octavia is a little ridiculous. Octavia's young page, who is at once ingenuous, cunning and ardent, can make nothing of all this. He grows angry, and replies sharply to the philosopher, calling his fine speeches nonsense, and threatening childish revenge. The fury of the irreverent page is expressed with dazzling verve.

Octavia leaves the stage, and Seneca is meditating the lot of the great ones of the earth when the Goddess Pallas appears to him and announces his approaching death. However, Nero appears, and a moving dialogue begins. In a few brief words, Nero acquaints his tutor with his decision to repudiate Octavia and to wed Poppea. Seneca tries to dissuade him, but Nero, whose nervousness is evident from the opening of the scene by the hesitating way in which he speaks, and by the way in which he constantly repeats himself, enters into a fury, an opportunity which allows Monteverdi to write a page in the *concitato* style which is his invention. Nero, exasperated by Seneca's worthy replies and wise counsels, dismisses him. Poppea immediately enters, as though she had been spying for the philosopher's departure. Cajoling, seductive, playfully rebellious, she approaches the Emperor, who is pale with rage, and tenderly recalls the memory of their last night of love. Nero is moved. Profiting by her lover's distress, Poppea cleverly gets him to order Seneca's death. Shakespeare himself could not better have depicted the contrast between these characters than Monteverdi has done with the aid of Busenello : Nero, impetuous, brutal, sacrificing everything to sensual satisfaction ; Poppea, the incarnation of feminine coquetry, cunning and ambitious.

Otho has arrived towards the end of the conversation and, from a hiding-place, has heard everything, He bitterly reproaches Poppea, who receives his complaints coldly. She leaves him to his despair. Then enters Drusilla, one of Octavia's maids of honour, who has long loved Otho secretly. In his desire to forget Poppea, Otho lavishes promises of love upon Drusilla. Left alone, he reflects sadly, " I speak but of Drusilla, I think but of Poppea."

Act II opens somewhat frigidly with the apparition of Mercury to Seneca. The god announces his death but promises him immortality. Then the captain of the Prætorian guard appears, and, with precaution, tells the philosopher of Nero's decision. Then follows the celebrated scene in which

Seneca cheerfully informs his friends of his departure for Olympus. The servants mourn in a chromatic chorus which is powerfully effective, but Seneca bids them be silent, and orders them to prepare the bath in which he is to open his veins.

To relieve the tension, we are transported, in the next scene, to a gallery in Nero's palace, in which Octavia's page teases a pretty serving-maid and asks her, with feigned naïveté, why he is so troubled in her presence.

EXAMPLE 72

Sento un cer-to   non so che   che mi piz-zi - - - ca e di-let-ta

Dimmi tu che   co-sa è   Da mi-gel-la a - - - mo - - ro - - set-ta

The *Damigella* promises to cure him. This duet is incontestably the masterpiece of the *canzonetta* style in drama. There are to be found a little later, in the work of Marco Marazzoli and Giacopo Melani, dialogues written in this witty, light, graceful and playful style, but none reaches so high a degree of perfection. The Page of the *Incoronazione* has often been compared with Cherubino, but that is a grave misconception. Doubtless, he is as susceptible as Cherubino, but there is nothing sentimental in his ardour; he is purely sensual, and one must not be taken in by his protestations of ignorance.

The following scene shows us Nero among his familiars, Lucian, Petronius, Tigellinus. They lie on couches round the banqueting table. "Now that Seneca is dead," begins Nero, "let us sing to Love;" and he utters passionate *vocalises* in which the voice of Lucian first mingles, then predominates. The poet celebrates in ornate style the graces of Poppea;

Nero, enchanted, with tears in his eyes, intersperses his favourite's song with delirious exclamations.

EXAMPLE 73

The next scene takes place in Octavia's apartments.   Otho,
his heart torn by jealousy, meditates the death of Poppea.
Octavia appears, and asks him to rid her of her rival.   Otho
is troubled, and at first hesitates, but in the end promises to
obey.

In the garden of her villa, Poppea falls asleep to dream of
the throne.   Arnolta the nurse lulls her with an exquisite
song.*   Otho, disguised as Drusilla, creeps towards Poppea ;
his courage fails him, but he has just resolved to strike the
fatal blow, when Love awakens Poppea, who utters a cry.
The nurse rushes in and urges on the slaves to hunt down the
criminal.

Act III, which is shorter than the preceding acts, shows the
arrest of Drusilla for the attempted murder, and her interroga-
tion by Nero, who threatens her with the most dire punish-

* See Note 156.

ments. Drusilla, to save her lover, accepts the accusation, and is ready to be led to death, when Otho throws himself at the Emperor's feet and reveals the truth. Busenello gave no words to Drusilla in this scene, but Monteverdi, to intensify the dramatic interest, makes her constantly interrupt with denials the narration of her lover. Otho, to palliate his crime, weakly reveals that he has only carried out the Empress's commands. Nero, delighted to have found at last a reason for repudiating Octavia, punishes Otho with exile only. Drusilla will accompany him, and this punishment will mean happiness for them. A voluptuous love-duet between Nero and Poppea terminates this scene. In Scene VI, Octavia sings her farewell to Rome. This is one of the most famous passages in the opera, and is the most frequently heard in concert programmes. Octavia's complaint is akin to the Lament of Ariadne, but the style has not that archaic stiffness which is not the least attractive element of the Lament. It has become softer. The periods of the discourse obey a kind of symmetry; it is rather a dramatic air than a recitative, yet there is profound realism in its details. The unfortunate woman, choked with tears, is at first unable to speak; she falters :

EXAMPLE 74

A - A - - - A - - - Adio Roma   A - A - - - - Adio patria   A - - A - mi-ci

Bold dissonances enhance the poignant quality of her complaint. This is pure feeling expressed in the most immediate yet the most harmonious fashion. Grief has become music.

Scene VIII is a vast historical tableau. Nero invites Poppea to mount the steps of the throne. She wavers now, overcome with the weight of all this honour, and seems to fear

a reverse of fortune.   Having nothing more to desire, she is
to know fear.   This feeling is admirably rendered by the air
Il mio genio confuso, which she sings to humble herself before
her lover, and to express her gratitude.   Nero sings his radiant
love to a very free passacaglia rhythm (without ground-bass).
A symphony bursts out, a true triumphal march to which
advance the Consuls and the Tribunes, who solemnly crown
Poppea.   Busenello followed up this scene with an apotheosis
of Love on Olympus, but Monteverdi has preferred to close
the drama with a love-duet between Nero and Poppea.   This
duet offers curious analogies with that of Ulysses and Telemachus in the *Ritorno d'Ulisse*, but is quite different in spirit.
It is a page of voluptuous ardour ; the voices, murmuring
words of love, interweave, seek each other, embrace, in passionate effusions.   The powerful sensuality of the aged
Monteverdi is expressed in this passage in the same way as
Titian's in his last pictures.

EXAMPLE 75

We have already had occasion to emphasize the psychological
truth of the characters.   They all live intensely.   As in real
life, comedy and tragedy are seen side by side.   The idle talk
of the nurse Arnolta, the heedless chatter of the page contrast
with the stilted gestures and pompous language of Seneca ; the
coquetry of Poppea with the pride of Octavia.   We can
realize the truth of G. D. Doni's remark that Monteverdi was
even greater in comedy than in tragedy.   By comedy, he

understood familiar drama drawn from life. A drama such as Shakespeare's *Julius Cæsar* can alone sustain comparison with the *Incoronazione* for the impression of reality given by the action. Monteverdi has seen Imperial Rome with the eyes of genius, and has been able to recreate it for us. No book, no chronicle, could bring Nero and Poppea so vigorously home to us as this opera.

The work contains a synthesis of all Monteverdi's finest qualities.* His technique was never richer, more satisfying. Every element is here combined, inexhaustible invention in the melody, expressive force and audacity in the harmonic structure. There is no praise too great for the balance established between the new melodic forms (airs of various forms, *canzoni* and *canzonette*) and the recitative, without which fine pieces of music can exist, but not a musical drama.

L'Incoronazione is the masterpiece of Italian drama in the seventeenth century, and a masterpiece which established a tradition. It marks the triumph in Venice of the historical opera which had been inaugurated by Cavalli. Mythological and pastoral subjects were thrown aside. Francesco Cavalli developed the principle of the *Incoronazione* to its farthest results. In particular, he developed the comic element which Monteverdi had used with as much felicity as sobriety.

The *Incoronazione* was played in the principal towns of Italy, and was chosen for the inauguration of the first public opera-house opened at Naples in 1651. In 1646, three years after the master's death, the work was revived with great success in Venice. Even to-day it gives an impression of vigour and radiant youth. The caprice of fashion is powerless against it, and it remains one of the most precious ornaments of musical drama.

* See Note 157.

VI

LAST YEARS AND DEATH

THE only portrait of Monteverdi we possess, which figures as the frontispiece of the *Fiori Poetici* published in his honour in 1644, shows him as he must have been at about sixty years of age. An energetic countenance, a high forehead crowned with short thick hair, a thin face barred by a moustache, a chin elongated by a short greyish beard, a long nose, and, beneath thick eyebrows, great black eyes whose dreamy, melancholy expression contrasts with the resolute impression given by the whole face. In the vast forehead there is the sign of powerful will, but the whole portrait gives the impression of profound sadness. This may be the author of the *Arianna* and the *Orfeo*; it is difficult to believe that it is the author of the amorous madrigals, of the voluptuous songs. One cannot believe that that mouth has ever smiled. We are in the presence of a man whose soul is worn with grief, who can never know joy again. That this man, who was for the greater part of his life profoundly unhappy, who seems to have led a chaste, orderly life, could, by the force of his genius, have composed so many lively songs, so many playful and witty madrigals, so much music overflowing with sensual pleasure, this is hard to conceive, and, indeed, it is one of the mysteries of genius. Handel and Mozart too, in their dire distress, could create a world of joy and light.

From Monteverdi's correspondence, we get the impression of a lively intelligence, of a penetrating mind, prompt to seize the weak point of an argument. He seems to have received a good education in his youth, but most of his culture was self-acquired. He writes with a certain difficulty. His sentences are long and ill-formed, yet there are sudden images and expressions which strike the imagination. As he says in one of his letters, he is ignorant of the art of translating his thoughts into a precise, concise style ; to say what he has to say, he must cover much paper, but he forgets nothing, and his arguments are irresistible. His sound common sense can be perceived in all his remarks. Moreover, his correspondence confirms the impression given by the portrait—of a man grave, almost austere, without gaiety. If he meets with a difficulty, if he feels that a slight injustice has been done him, he is resentful, and speaks with concentrated bitterness. One feels that he is proud, very sure of his genius, conscious of the rights which it confers upon him. His letters to the sovereigns, once stripped of the consecrated formulæ of politeness, are full of dignity and nobility. Occasionally he will request a favour which he considers he has deserved, but he always refuses to beg it with servility, as was then the custom. Desiring to obtain the canonicate of Cremona, where he wished to end his days in peace, he refuses to use the letters of recommendation given to him for the Empress Eleanora di Gonzaga by her brother the Duke of Mantua. These letters describe his situation too gloomily, and he is humiliated by them. " I am not rich," he writes to Striggio, " but I am not poor either," * and he describes the advantages of his office in Venice, where his salary is paid with absolute regularity every two months, not to speak of accessory payments he receives for music composed for private citizens. He is no man to speak of his poverty without reason, and the court of Mantua must, in 1609, have shown him base ingratitude to make him quit his haughty reserve.

One feels that it is extremely painful to him to be obliged

* See Note 158.

continually to make complaints in order to receive payment of
the pension bequeathed him by the Duke Vincenzo. He begs
no favour, but claims a strict right, and feels very bitter at
being obliged to have recourse to the intervention of his
friend Striggio.

Though a self-educated man, yet his culture was profound.
He knew the classics, read and meditated Plato, and drew
from him new ideas on art. His literary taste was sure, his
dramatic instinct infallible. Monteverdi lived to create and
to act. His power of work was formidable. At Venice, the
headaches caused by the fever-laden air of Mantua ceased,
but his health remained precarious. During the winter of
1623 an attack of rheumatism completely crippled him ; he
could not move a limb. On several occasions he contracted
chills which went to his eyes. In 1627 and in 1638 he could
neither write nor read, a privation which was intolerable to
him, for he brooked no restriction of his activity.

Ceaselessly occupied with his compositions, his only diversion was to conduct at St. Mark's the rehearsals of a motet,
or to take part in the celebration of a service. During the
last years of his life he was obliged, in addition, to supervise
the performances of his operas. In four years there were
performed in Venice *L'Adone*, *Le Nozze d'Enea*, *L'Arianna*,
Il Ritorno d'Ulisse, and *L'Incoronazione di Poppea ;* but he
nevertheless had time to publish in 1641 the voluminous
collection of the *Selva Morale*, and to write a ballet for the court
of Parma. He also managed to direct the chapels of several
private citizens. In 1620 he conducted music three times a
week in the Oratory of the *Primiciero* of St. Mark's, and gave
real concerts at the house of his patron, the noble Mocenigo.
But this is not all. He carried on an active correspondence
with several princely courts, for whom he procured singers and
instrumentalists ; for, owing to his reputation as judge of such
matters, many had recourse to him in case of need.* He was

* See Note 159.

always willing to help. He put himself to much trouble to procure actors for Giustinian ; he supervised the printing of a book by the Duke of Bracciano, Paolo Orsini, a passionate lover of music who was also something of a poet, and had formerly given Monteverdi a kindly welcome in Rome.* He also had disciples to whom he gave advice, if not regular lessons. Rovetta, Cavalli, G. C. Bianchi, seem to have worked under his direction.

To get a fair idea of his astonishing activity, one must peruse the considerable number of letters which we possess for the year 1627. In April he is occupied in setting to music both the scene of Armida and Rinaldo from Tasso, and the opera *La Finta Pazza Licori* which he is writing for Mantua. A short time after come the interludes for the fêtes at Parma, and the tournament *Mercurio e Marte*. In October he has to arrange the solemn festivals at Chioggia, ordered by the Senate to commemorate the victory of Lepanto. He naturally continues to direct the Chapel of St. Mark's, and is even obliged to return to Venice from a stay at Parma in order to conduct the Christmas Mass. As if that were not enough, he agrees to correct the proofs of a new edition of the madrigals of Arcadelt,† the great Flemish master, in whose work he loves the simplicity of style, the transparent harmonies, the broad, well-defined melody.

His letters show him in a state of positively feverish activity. He has a hundred ideas, and, whilst continually creating music, supervises all the details of its performance, recommends a singer for a part, or goes himself to Parma in order to get a first-hand idea of the dimensions of the hall in which the tournament is to take place. One wonders how he could bear up under such mental strain, such physical effort, and yet in this very year he complains that he is suffering from a film over his eye.

* See Note 160.   † See Note 161.

Monteverdi seemed not to know what rest or amusement was. His only recreation was alchemy. As soon as he had a moment's leisure, he occupied it with seeking the great secret. He was very proud of having fused gold with mercury, but seems otherwise to have had few illusions as to the success of his experiments.*

Whilst it was difficult for him to be absent from Venice for any length of time, he obtained leave for short journeys to neighbouring districts. Thus on several occasions he went to Mantua on business ; perhaps his pension was not paid, and, his letters remaining without effect, he was obliged to make the journeys to obtain payment of arrears ; on other occasions he had family business to settle. In 1624 his father-in-law, Giacomo Cataneo, the violist, died in Mantua, bequeathing to Monteverdi's children his house on the Via del Mastrino and his furniture, which, among other objects, comprised some thirty musical instruments. A second heir disputed the will, and Monteverdi was obliged to solicit the Duke in person before he could enter into possession. The litigation lasted over a year.†

It was particularly to Bologna that Monteverdi made frequent visits. He was publicly welcomed there on June 13th, 1620, the day of St. Anthony, patron-saint of Lombardy, by the Members of the *Floridi de San Michele in Bosco*. His friend and rival, Adriano Banchieri, arranged an enthusiastic reception for him.

His two sons studied in turn at Bologna, and this was the reason for several short visits which Monteverdi made to that university.

His elder son, Francesco, born in 1600, had at first been intended for the Church. Monteverdi had tried in 1610 to enter him at the seminary in Rome, with a scholarship, but he had not been able to obtain this favour from the Pope,

* See Note 162.   † See Note 163.

and Francesco had remained with him in Venice, along with his brother Massimiliano, who was five years younger. Monteverdi supervised attentively the education of his children.* He had a tutor for them, and made great sacrifices for their studies. Although he taught them music, he had no idea of seeing them take it up as a career. He wished to make Francesco a lawyer and Massimiliano a doctor. Francesco had a fine tenor voice, and gradually became so passionately attached to music that his father had to resign himself to seeing him abandon law. In 1619, Francesco, who was studying at Bologna in the monastery of the Servite Fathers, suddenly decided to take Orders, and became a Carmelite monk. This decision did nothing to impede his musical career—quite the contrary.

It must not be forgotten that at this time it was not rare to see a monk sing in the theatre. Padre Filippo Melani, a *castrato* of the order of the Servites, even went to Paris in 1660 to sing the rôle of Queen Amestris, lover of King Xerxes.

Monteverdi had his son admitted as tenor to the Chapel of St. Mark's on July 1st 1623. Francesco had already sung there on occasions; in particular, he had sung with considerable success in April 1615. Francesco Monteverdi was destined to be one of the most brilliant of the *virtuosi* of the Chapel. He also acquired some reputation as a composer, and, as early as 1624, Milanuzzi's collection contained some agreeable *canzoni* of his composition.

Massimiliano had been educated at Bologna, first at the seminary, then at the college of the Cardinal di Montalto, to which he had been admitted on the recommendation of the Duchess of Mantua.† Having obtained his university degrees, he established himself in Mantua in 1623, and thenceforth practised his profession there. He was curious of astrology and secret sciences. In December 1627 he was

* See Note 164.   † See Note 165.

denounced to the Inquisition for possessing forbidden books, and thrown into prison. Count Striggio, who had intervened on his behalf immediately Monteverdi appealed to him, had hard work to get him released from the Inquisitorial prison. This affair caused Monteverdi grave concern. He had spent too many happy years in Venice, and, as he said himself, fate never failed to mingle bitterness with the few favours she granted him. He received two pieces of bad news at the same time, the arrest of his son and the death of the Duke of Mantua after a reign of fourteen months. With Vincenzo, the dynasty of the Gonzagas of Mantua died out. A younger branch of the family was to succeed. What could Monteverdi hope for from the new Duke, Charles de Nevers, who had spent most of his life in France ? It is quite comprehensible that he should have felt some anxiety about the pension of a hundred crowns which formed the basis of his personal income. But Charles loved music as much as did his predecessors. He confirmed Monteverdi in his pension, which he converted into a permanent annuity.* But events stultified his good intentions. Charles had scarcely spent three years in Mantua when he was obliged to take flight before the Imperial armies. In spite of its ramparts, its natural defences, its marshes, the town was taken and sacked on July 18th, 1630, by the Imperial troops. For several days the conquerors gave themselves, up to murder, pillage, burning and rapine. A large part of the population was annihilated, the churches profaned, the monuments and houses devastated by fire.

The news produced a feeling of profound horror, not only throughout Italy, but throughout Europe. Rubens wrote to Peiresc, " My grief is extreme, for I have long served the house of Gonzaga, and, in my youth, have enjoyed the delights of living in their country." Whilst Monteverdi had had less cause for gratitude to the Gonzagas than Rubens, he must have

* See Note 166.

been profoundly moved by the calamity which had overtaken the country in which a decisive phase of his existence had been passed. It was in Mantua that he had first known fame, that he had been married, that he had produced the *Arianna* and the *Orfeo*, which still lived in the public memory. It was in Mantua that he had most passionately loved, suffered, struggled. He could not remain indifferent to the misfortunes of a city which he regarded as his second and beloved home : " *Questa patria da me amata.*" * From the financial point of view, the ruin of Mantua involved the cessation of the pension which he had had so much difficulty in obtaining, and compromised certain interests which he still held in the town.

But the grief which he felt at the terrible news soon gave place to other preoccupations ; plague was enveloping Venice. For nearly a year, from the end of 1630 to the autumn of the following year, the malady ravaged the town. Nearly one-third of the population perished. Monteverdi made a vow to the Madonna di Loretta to make her a pilgrimage of grace if he escaped.

On November 28th, 1631, there was sung at St. Mark's a solemn Requiem composed by Monteverdi to render thanks for the end of the plague. We know that this mass was written in the modern style, and that trombones accompanied the *Gloria* and the *Credo*. During this terrible trial, Monteverdi had re-entered into himself. His religious faith had grown stronger. He decided to take Orders, after the example of many of the *Maestri di Cappella* who had preceded him. But his ordination brought no change in the conditions of his creative activity. It was at this time that Monsignor Rospigliosi, who later became Pope Clement XI, wrote for his patrons, the Cardinals Barberini, operatic libretti, occasionally on religious, but more frequently on amorous subjects.

* See Note 167.

Monteverdi therefore continued to compose madrigals and operas, and there is no reason to believe that he devoted himself more particularly to religious music after his ordination.

He continued to meditate profoundly upon his art. The preface to the *Madrigali guerrieri et amorosi* is sufficient proof of this. Four years earlier, he had been engaged upon a book, some details of which are contained in two letters, addressed, probably, to G. B. Doni in 1633 and 1634.* He wished at last to publish the work announced in the preface of Book V of the Madrigals, which his brother had commented in advance in the manifesto which prefaced the *Scherzi Musicali*. The title was to be *Melodia, overo seconda pratica musicale*. This work was to be divided into three parts, the first treating of discourse, the second of harmony, the third of rhythm, and the whole book was to illustrate the principle of the imitation of nature.

When one knows Monteverdi's work, and has some acquaintance with his correspondence, it is easy to form an idea of what this book would have been. Yet it would have been interesting to see the systematic exposition of the under-lying ideas which an analysis of the work of the great musician reveals. The title alone is sufficient to prove that Monteverdi wished to demonstrate that the reign of counterpoint considered as an end in itself was over, and that melody must succeed polyphony. This involved a whole theory of dramatic expression and of the manner of rendering ideas and images by means of melody, harmony, and rhythm. We have, moreover, had occasion to recognize these foundations of Monteverdi's doctrine in considering the dramatic madrigals and the operas.

*   *   *   *   *   *

During the last twenty years of his life, Monteverdi had at least the satisfaction of seeing his genius universally recog-

* See Note 168.

nized and admired. " Age, which is decadence for ordinary beings, is, for men of genius, an apotheosis." * His fame spread throughout Italy, and his name was celebrated abroad. Heinrich Schutz, marvelling at the originality of the work of the " ingenious " master, came to visit him in Venice in 1628, and composed in his honour one of his spiritual songs on the themes of the two ariettas for two voices published in the collection of the *Scherzi Musicali* in 1632 † : *Zefiro torna* and *Armato il cor*. Prætorius in Germany, Huyghens and Albert Ban in Holland, Thomas Gobert and Mersenne in France, studied his work with curiosity and admiration.‡ The French violinist Maugars, who was travelling in Italy in 1639, acclaimed in him the inventor " of a new and most admirable manner of composition both for instruments and for voices," and considered him " one of the first composers in the world." His influence extended throughout Europe. In England he had disciples, Tomkins and Walter Porter, both of whom reveal his influence.§

His madrigals were published by P. Phalèse in Antwerp, and even in Denmark, and his sacred or secular compositions are to be found scattered in numerous collections published in Germany. His popularity in the Teutonic countries was so great that he was frequently invited there, but he does not seem to have left Italy during the last years of his life.

In his native country he was practically without a rival. Only Domenico Mazzocchi, Gagliano or Giacopo Peri were sometimes quoted along with him. The last-named expressed the most sincere admiration for Monteverdi's work, and did not escape from his influence. It is evident in many airs of his last period, and particularly in a great dramatic narration, *Uccidimi dolore*, which is constructed practically on the same plan as the *Lamento d'Arianna*.¶ For that matter, traces of

* See Note 169.   † See Note 170.   ‡ See Note 171.
            § See Note 172.   ¶ See Note 173.

Monteverdi's influence may be seen in the work of a host of musicians of the epoch, particularly in that of the strange Claudio Saraceni, who, in 1620, dedicated to Monteverdi a pathetic air from his *Seconde Musiche* ; * in that of Kapsberger, and of Rovetta, who openly proclaimed himself his disciple.   Even those who remained faithful to the madrigalesque style, such as Adriano Banchieri, admired him.   The imitation of the master's methods is chiefly to be seen in the search for the passionate expression of emotion, and in the use of bold modulations and chromatics.   His exceptional power of emotional expression strikes all his contemporaries.   Caberlotti expressly says that Claudio is the only musician with all emotions at his command, who can at will awaken them in the heart of his audience : " Who can withhold his tears when listening to the complaint of the unhappy Ariadne?   Who can refuse to respond to the joy of his madrigals and his exquisite *Scherzi* ? Who can fail to feel true religious devotion in hearing his sacred compositions?   Can he whose ears are charmed by his spiritual and moral songs not meditate a more orderly life ? And in the variety of the works performed on the occasion of princely weddings or in the theatres of Venice, do not the emotions expressed change at every moment ?   At the very moment of laughter, tears arise, and when the mind is inspired by revenge, by some new variation, a suave harmony disposes the heart to mercy."

By the side of these tempered praises, panegyrics abound. Badoaro having produced in 1644 a second opera on the subject of Ulysses, *Ulisse errante*, testifies in these pompous terms to the sorrow he felt at the death of his first collaborator. " *Il Ritorno d'Ulisse* was adorned with music by Claudio Monteverdi, an artist of supreme glory, and one whose name will live for ever.   From this present work that splendour is absent, for the great master has departed to chant with the

* See Note 174.

angels the praises of God. But as compensation, we have the glorious productions of Francesco Sacrati, and indeed it was necessary that the sun should set before the glories of the moon could be perceived." *

To tell the truth, the innumerable poems, sonnets or songs composed in his praise by the poets and musicians of the epoch attest his personal popularity rather than anything else, for very mediocre composers were at that time extolled in dithyrambic language. The verses of Bellerofante Castaldi, and the *Fiori Poetici* offer, however, a certain interest in that they give us some information about the last years of Monteverdi. The *Laconismo delle alte qualità di Claudio Monteverdi* by Caberlotti in particular gives us some details of the circumstances of his death.

In the spring of 1643, Monteverdi, then seventy-five years old, felt his strength failing. Tortured with the desire to revisit Cremona and some other cities which he had not seen for many years, he asked for leave, and set out with the Procurators' permission. For six months he travelled in Lombardy, receiving everywhere a triumphant welcome. Perhaps he hoped, by personal intervention, to receive the canonicate of Cremona for which he had applied unsuccessfully in 1627, and the revenues of which had now become necessary to him if he wished to retire to his native town. He knew very well that the time of rest was come. But he realized it too late. He fell ill on the way and, " like the swan who, feeling his end near, returns to the water," he desired to reach Venice to die in peace. He did not linger long, and died after twenty days of fever on November 29th, 1643.

The death of the great musician brought sorrow to the whole of Venice. He was mourned by all who had known him.

* See Note 175.

He was given a splendid funeral. The church of the Frari was resplendent with candles. The best singers of the town took part in the mass conducted by G. B. Marinoni, surnamed Giove (Jupiter), his old travelling-companion of the Hungarian voyage, and one of the competitors for his place. The body was interred in the chapel of the Lombards, dedicated to St. Anthony. At St. Mark's, G. Rovetta, who was to succeed him, had another solemn mass sung in his honour in the presence of a vast and reverent crowd. One can say that the death of Monteverdi was a public sorrow.* His funeral oration was pronounced by the senators Di Marco and Boleano, and for two years poets composed sonnets and elegies to the glory of the great departed.

Yet he was soon forgotten. By the end of the seventeenth century his name was scarcely mentioned. People were convinced that music was a new invention and that nothing counted if it were more than twenty years old. Only a few learned contrapuntists preserved his madrigals and motets as curiosities, admiring their prodigious technique. In the eighteenth century, G. B. Martini published some examples in his treatise, with judicious notes. Burney quoted with astonishment the boldness of his harmonies, and rightly drew attention to them.

It was only in the second half of the nineteenth century that Monteverdi ceased to be a mere name bandied about among musical historians, who knew nothing of the man nor of his work. Fétis, La Fage, Padre Caffi, Davari, Ambros, later Vogel, Goldschmidt, Solerti, and above all, Romain Rolland, have restored Monteverdi to his true place, which is the foremost of his century. M. Vincent d'Indy has published important fragments of the *Orfeo* and the *Incoronazione* translated into French, and has had them performed by pupils of the *Schola Cantorum*. The whole of the dramatic

* See Note 176.

work will shortly be published in its entirety, and it is to be hoped that the publication of the madrigals, songs, masses and motets will one day follow.

This immense work is inexhaustible. It astonishes by its richness as by its incredible variety. Yet the personality of Monteverdi gives to this work, written in styles not only different but incongruous, a surprising unity. Everything bears the mark of his genius; the contrapuntal motets, the madrigals with their barbaric dissonances, the graceful *canzonette*, the dramatic narrations. The slightest arietta by Monteverdi has so peculiar a quality that the composer can be recognized in the very first bars. For, if the methods change, the essential quality of the music does not change. As M. Andre Suarès has so justly said, " No artist has ever been more conscious of his art than Monteverdi." From his youth onwards he pursued an ideal which never changed: the translation of human passions and ideas into the language of sound. The music of Monteverdi, like that of Bach, is never empty of thought and feeling; it does not find its end in itself, but in the emotions it expresses. His vehement soul is revealed entire, with its passionate sadness, its powerful sensuality, its love of life; for this great Latin artist, who suffered so greatly, preserved to the end that love and feeling for life. This is doubtless the reason why even to-day his music has for us the irresistible attraction of life itself.

APPENDICES

NOTES.

(1) The birth certificate has been published by Vogel.

(2) Cf. G. Sommi Picenardi, *Claudio Monteverdi a Cremona* (Ricordi). This pamphlet of 36 pages contains all the documents so far discovered concerning the family of Monteverdi and the youth of the musician.

(3) Davari, *Claudio Monteverdi*, p. 4.

(4) Scotti, *Itinerario d'Italia*, Roma, 1650, p. 166.

(5) Baldassare Monteverdi had five children : Claudio (1567), Maria Domitia (1571), Giulio Cesare (1573), Clara Massimilia (1579), and Luca (1581). Sommi Picenardi has published their birth certificates.

(6) The authorship has been definitely established by Haberl, who has drawn attention to the Venetian edition of 1588, published under the name of Ingegneri during the lifetime of the author. See Michel Brenet's *Palestrina,* pp. 136—140.

(7) " *Et io non devo aspettare . . . di compositioni cosi giovenili come son queste mie altre lode che quelle che si suole dare ai fiori di primavera.*" Dedication of the First Book of *Madrigali a cinque voci di Claudio Monteverde Cremonese Discopolo dal Sig. Marc Antonio Ingegneri . . .* in Venetia.

Appresso Angelo Gardano M. DLXXXVII (Dantzig Library).

(8) " *Mi fu acenato di venire a farle riverenza mentre fui a Milano. . . . Vidi io affissare Ella il purgato senso al debil moto della mia mano sopra della viola.*" The dedication to Giacomo Ricardi is dated January 1st, 1590.

(9) For Vincenzo, cf. Baschet's article " Rubens à Mantoue," *Gazette des Beaux-Arts*, May 1st, 1866, and Ademollo, *La Bella Adriana*, pp. 26 seq.

(10) Cf. Bertolotti, *La Musica in Mantova*, pp. 39–46, *et passim*.

(11) Gian Giacomo Gastoldi is a very interesting musician, and it is extremely regrettable that no general study of his work has as yet been published. According to Bertolotti, he made his début when a child as singer in Mantua. His first work (*Canzoni a cinque voci*, 1582) is dedicated to the Prince of Mantua. In 1582 he was in Rome, devoting himself to the study of the severe style, and sent sacred music to the Duke. Then he returned to settle in Mantua. About 1591 he was appointed *Maestro di Cappella* of Santa Barbara, and this title figured on the title-page of all his subsequent work, sacred or secular. The fact that he retained the title in 1604 is seen by the dedication of the *Concenti Musicali* to the Duke of Mantua, by which we also know that he had taken Orders. He seems to have left Mantua after the festivities of 1608, to which he had contributed an interlude to the *Idropica*. His last collection is dated 1611.

For the bibliography of his works, see Eitner, Vogel, and the catalogue of the Library of the *Liceo Musicale* by Gasparri.

(12) Cf. Bertolotti, *op. cit.* Rovigo's death certificate states that he was sixty-six years old, and refers to him as organist of the cathedral. Monteverdi, however, in his letter of November 24th, 1601, mentions his name among the successors of Giaches de Wert and seems to regard him as *Maestro di Cappella.*

(13) Professor Torelli has had the kindness to search the Mantuan archives for the death-certificate of Pallavicini, and has communicated it to me : " *Lunedi a di 26 Novembre* 1601, *M. Benedetto Pallavicini, nelle Contrada di Montenegro, è morte di fabre in un mese, de anni No.* 50 " (Registre dei morti, 1601, p. 178, v.)

(14) Quoted by Davari, *Claudio Monteverdi,* p. 5.

(15) " . . . *col nobilissimo essercitio della viola che mi sparse la fortunata porta del suo servizio.*" The dedication to the Duke is dated June 27th, 1892.

(16) Bertolotti gives their names, *op. cit.,* p. 73. That of Monteverdi does not appear among them, but there is the name of his father-in-law, Giacomo Cattaneo.

(17) Solerti, *Musica, Ballo, Drammatica alla corte medica,* p. 49. Corsi writes on March 7th, 1598, " *Quella Musica concertata e di vari strumenti non e in altra luogo.*"

(18) Cf. *La Bella Adriana, passim.*

(19) Francesco was born in 1600 and Massimiliano in 1605.

(20) G. B. Marinone had been in the Duke's service since 1584, and was one of the best bass singers in the chapel. There seems to have been a particularly close friendship between him and Monteverdi. He subsequently entered the choir of St. Mark's in Venice, and remained there under the orders of Monteverdi, to whose memory he wrote a panegyric in 1643. In 1644 he was appointed *Maestro di Cappella* of the cathedral of Padua, and remained there till his death in 1647.

Teodoro Bacchino was a Carmelite monk. In 1594 the Duke had asked the Superior General of his order for permission for him to travel in a long robe, but without a cassock (see Bertolotti, p. 771). Bacchino was a *castrato* singer of wide reputation. He composed several madrigals.

Serafino Terso, surnamed della Vittoria, was an excellent bass singer.

(21) Letter from Monteverdi dated December 2nd, 1608 (Davari, p. 18). See also his father's letter, published by Vogel, dated November 27th, 1608.

(22) For the itinerary and the events of the journey to Spa, see Baschet, " Rubens à Mantoue," *Gazette des Beaux-Arts,* May, 1866 ; and Albin Body, *Le Théâtre et la Musique à Spa,* Brussels, 1895 (2nd edition), p. 151 *seq.*

(23) " . . . *il canto alla francese in questro moderno modo che per le stampe da tre o quattro anni in qua si va mirando, hor de madrigali, hor di canzonette & d'arie chi fu il primo di lui che lo riportasse in Italia di quando venne da li bagni di Spa l'anno* 1599 ? *Et chi incomincio a porlo sotto ad orationi latine a vulgari nelle nostra lingua prima di lui ?* " (1607).

(24) As early as 1585, Plantin published in Antwerp a book entirely consecrated to the Miscellanies of Claude le Jeune. In 1592, Emm. Adriamson, the lutanist, included music by this composer in his *Novum Pratum,* and finally, in 1597 and 1598, Pierre Phalèse published Airs by Du Caurroy and Le Jeune in *Le Rossignol Musical.* There are, indeed, few airs in antique metres among these pieces, but the fact that compositions by the Parisian school

were sung everywhere in Flanders, permits us to assume that the *airs de cour* and the *chansonnettes mesurées* of the same authors found equal favour.

(25) In 1571, Adrien le Roy published an arrangement of *airs de cour* for solo-voice with lute tablature.

(26) Cf. Bertolotti, pp. 93 and 73.

(27) Du Perron seems to have been a musician. De la Borde quotes an air, *Sortez de mon esprit, pensers pleins de délices*, of which he is supposed to be the author. The text is to be found in a printed collection (Res. Bibl. Ye 2055).

(28) For the experiments of Baif and his collaborators see *Le Ballet de Cour en France* (Paris, Laurens 1914).

(29) For the history of the *Riforma Melodrammatica* see the bibliographies by Romain Rolland and Angelo Solerti (*op. cit.*).

(30) The Duke of Mantua had first gone to Venice with a large and magnificent escort. He arrived there on July 14th, 1600. On the 22nd he tore himself from the pleasures of Venice in order to pay a visit to his estates at Montferrat. Thence he went to Milan, and on to Florence, where he made a fairly long stay, and was present at all the marriage festivities. It is very probable that Monteverdi, who, as we have seen, had accompanied his patron to Hungary and Flanders, was also in his escort this time.

After the festivities the Duke went to Genoa with his wife, Eleanora de' Medici, who was going to accompany her sister, the new Queen, to Marseilles; he awaited the return of the galleys and re-entered his dominions just before Christmas. The following summer he went to Hungary again, but this time without Monteverdi.

(31) On the great singer Francesco Rasi and his relations with the courts of Mantua and Florence, see Ademollo, *La Bella Adriana;* and Bertolotti, *op. cit.*

(32) This is the earliest letter of Monteverdi which has been preserved. It has been frequently published.

(33) Davari, *op. cit.*, p. 8.

(34) See particularly his eloquent letter of October 27th, 1604. (Letter I.)

(35) Cf. in the Appendix, Letter II. December 1604. The biographers of Monteverdi state that Massimiliano was born in 1605. The letter shows that the date is correct. It is quite possible that Monteverdi may have taken his wife to Cremona for her confinement in December 1604.

(36) *Tribune de St.-Gervais*, Vol. II, p. 117. It is worthy of note that Ingegneri's reputation was maintained during the new generation. His works continued to be sung simultaneously with those of the innovators. In December 1603, the Duke of Modena charged Alberto Colombo to buy in Venice the Madrigals for four and five voices by the aged Ingegneri along with those of Monteverdi and Sigismondo d'India (Archives of Modena. *Musica Busha* 4. *Bibliografia*).

(37) Madrigal: *A che tormi il ben mio.*

(38) Madrigal, *Ch' ami la vita mia.*

(39) Published by Torchi, Vol. 4 of *L'Arte Musicale in Italia* (Ricordi).

(40) For the madrigalesque comedy, see M. Romain Rolland's illuminating study in *L'Opéra en Europe avant Scarlatti* (chap. 2).

(41) *Revue Musicale,* June 1924, p. 275.

(42) Cf. *Le Mondain se nourrit toujours de Claude le Jeune* in the *Octonnaire de la Vanité du Monde* (published by Henry Expert. Senart).

(43) On the influence of French measured music on Monteverdi, see my article " Monteverdi and French Music " (*The Sackbut,* London, October, 1922). For music measured by syllabic quantity, see the authoritative study by M. P. M. Masson (*Revue Musicale,* S.I.M., 1907) and M. Henry Expert's edition (published by Senart) of the works of Claude le Jeune, Mauduit, and Du Caurroy.

(44) A copy of this very rare work is to be found in the *Liceo Musicale* of Bologna.

(45) Cf. Solerti, *Musica, Ballo, e Drammatica alla Corta Medica, passim,* and *Albori del Melodramma* I, Chap. viii.

(46) This relates, of course, only to the style of the *Euridice.* Caccini, in point of fact, contributed more largely than any other, in his airs for concert performance, to giving melody to the recitative style. The beautiful airs *Amarilli, Fere, Selvaggie,* etc., published in the *Nuove Musiche* of 1601, are well known.

(47) Davari, *Notizie Biografiche del Monteverdi,* p. 9.

(48) Solerti, *Albori del Melodramma,* p. 58 seq.

(49) *Orfeo,* Edition Malipiero, Chester, pp. 50 and 53.

(50) *Ibid.,* pp. 87–89.

(51) *Ibid.,* p. 7.

(52) *Ibid.,* pp. 105–106.

(53) *Ibid.,* pp. 33 and 40.

(54) *Ibid.,* p. 127.

(55) *Ibid.,* p. 92.

(56) *Ibid.,* p. 9.

(57) *Ibid.,* pp. 53–54.

(58) The score gives the composition of the orchestra :

    10 *viole da brazzo.*

    2 *violini piccoli alla francese.*

    3 *bassi da gamba.*

    2 *contrabassi de viola.*

    2 *gravicemballi.*

    1 *arpa doppia.*

    2 *chitarroni.*

    2 *organi di legno.*

    1 *regale.*

    2 *cornetti.*

    1 *flautino alla vigesima seconda.*

    1 *clarino.*

    3 *trombe sorde.*

    4 *tromboni.*

(59) Here is a fragment from this unpublished letter : " *Non voglio mancare d'offerirmi a servir V.A. com'ho Servito l'Altezzo di Savoia et di Mantova et simili, anzi perchè se tutto quelle che si ha da fare in Torino et Mantova, m'offeris co far a V.A. una invenzione poetica da me intitolata Regolamento che non si fara*

cosa simile nelle sudette Corti et spero che non sia disgrata, poichè da i maggiori poeti de tempi nostri et in particolar dal Chiabrera questa mia nova maniera di regalare vien molto comendata et di queste poesie drammatiche et del modo di farle rappresentare in canto, io me m'intendo qualche poco, come attesta Claudio Monteverdo, Mastro di Capella del Duca di Mantova, conferendo meco li suoi componimenti et quando facesse anco bisogna a V.A. di cantori buoni per cantarseli et rappresentar per li affetti dell'animo, come in queste invenzio ni si ricercano, io ne trovero come ho anché trovato per l'Altezza di Savoia."—Milan, March 8th, 1608. Archives of Modena. Canc. Duc. Regolari.

(60) Cf. *L'Opéra Italien en France*, p. xxvi. *et seq.*

(61) For all the details of the fêtes of Mantua see Solerti, *Albori del Melodramma*, and Ademollo, *La Bell' Adriana*.

(62) Letter from Peri, October 26th, 1607.

(63) Letter from Francesco Gonzaga, October 10th (cf. Davari, p. 12).

(64) Solerti has reproduced it in his *Origine del Melodramma*.

(65) For Marco da Gagliano, cf. R. Rolland, *op. cit.*, p. 108, and Vogel, *Vierteljahrschrift*, 1889.

(66) *E in tal guisa Florinda udisti, O Manto,*
    La ne' teatri de' tuoi regi tetti
    D'Arianna spiegar gli aspri martiri
    E trar da mille cor mille sospiri

(67) De Courville, *L'Arianna* (*Revue Musicale*, October 1921).

(68) Published by Gardano at Venice. *Lamento d'Arianna del S. Claudio Monteverde.*

This edition contains some very interesting variants, and the text is preferable to that of the manuscript published by Vogel.

The only known copy is preserved in the University Library of Ghent. I have republished this text in the collection, *Les Maîtres du Chant, Airs Italiens* II, published by Heugel.

(69) Letter of October 22nd, 1633.

(70) "... *gli stormenti collocati dietro la scena, che l'accompagnavano sempre econ la Variazione della musica variavano il suono*" (Follino's description).

(71) *Harmonie Universelle—Des Instruments*. It must be remarked, however, that about 1615 the Italian *Viole da brazzo* are confused with the violins, as Prætorius remarks. Mersenne notes that they have only four strings like the violins.

(72) "Fifteen excellent dancers, dressed as soldiers of Bacchus, executed a dance entirely composed of caprioles." Solerti, p. 100.

(73) Quoted by Romain Rolland, *L'Opéra en Europe*.

(74) Rinuccini. *Poésie*, 1622.

(75) *Le Ballet de Cour en France avant Lully*. Paris: Laurens, 1914.

(76) *Terzo Libro della Musica di Claudio Monteverdi*. Milano, 1609.

(77) Four days earlier, on November 26th, he very probably wrote to the same Chieppio a letter which has not been discovered, in which he declared himself ready to comply with his orders and send him what he asks in spite of his illness, which is the consequence of the excessive fatigue he has suffered.

(78) Galeazzo Sirena had taken part as organist in the fête given on August

10th, 1607, by the Academicians of Cremona in honour of Monteverdi (cf. Picenardi, *op. cit.*, p. 35).

He did not, moreover, leave his native town for Mantua. In 1626 he held the post of *Maestro di Cappella* of the cathedral, and had a collection of Masses published by Gardano at Venice. A motet of his composition had appeared in 1626 in Bonometti's *Parnassus musicus*.

(79) Letter of September 10, 1609. This letter has not been published. Schneider alludes to it, and quotes a passage from it, but, confusing the hereditary prince with the Duke, he gives an erroneous version.

(80) See Letter V (August 24th, 1609), and in Davari (pp. 58 and 59) the letter of March 26th, 1611.

(81) Letter from Casola to the Cardinal Gonzaga, July 26th, 1610 (arch. Gonzaga).

(82) Cf. Solerti, *Albori del Melodramma*, chap. x.

(83) Letter of December 28, 1610, No. VIII.

(84) Ademollo, pp. 155 seq.

(85) Letter from Monteverdi, June 22nd, 1611. Davari, p. 58, and Bertolotti, *passim*.

(86) Published by Torchi. *Arte Musicale in Italia*, I, IV.

(87) Cf. Vogel, pp. 363 seq., and Caffi, 1, pp. 220 seq. Letter of October 12, 1613, No. X.

(88) Cf. *Venetia Citta Nobilissima et singolare descritta gia in XXII libri da M. Francesco Sansovino et hora . . . emendata et ampliata dal M.R.D. Giovanni Stringa canonico della chiesa ducale di S. Marco Venetia* 1604, p. 4. " *Le Stanze sono poco commode e molto anguste.*"

The *Canonica* was reconstructed some years later, from 1618 to 1638.

(89) Decree of August 24th, 1616. Vogel, p. 367.

(90) Letter of March 13th, 1620.

(91) De St. Didier, *La Ville et la République de Venise.* Paris, 1680, p. 158.

(92) De St. Didier, *op. cit.*, pp. 47—48.

(93) " *Il Pergolo dei Musici, il quale è in forma ottangola et in aria da sette colonne di finissima pietra sostuneto e due altre mediocri vi si veggono vicino al muro.*" . . . *Venetia Citta Nobilissima.*

(94) " . . . *alcuni altri Musici che in certi giorni solenni fra l'anno con trombo ni, cornetti et altri varij e diuersi stromenti musical suonano et alla Messa et al Vespro molto eccellentemente, e tutti sono salariati dalla Procuratia onde anco anco l'elettion loro spetta a'i Procuratori.*"—*Venetia Citta Nobilissima*, p. 85.

(95) " *Sotto il predetto volto a punto su'l corritore giace un bellissimo organo. Egli fu opera di Fra Urbano Eccellentissimo Maestro di tali instrumenti et pero trovasi ottimo e perfettissimo : leggendovisi di dentro questre parole in lettere d'oro : Opus hoc rarissimum Urbanus Venetus F. Le canne d'avanti sono in sette ordini et in vaga maniera compartite. Egli è vaghissimamente all' intorno lavora e messo ad oro.*" " *E sonato al presente quest'organo da Paolo Giusto organista salariato dalla chiesa.*" . . . This organ is placed above the altar of St. Peter ; the second organ is situated opposite, but in such a way as not to block the window. " *Il suono di questo organo a soavessimo e tanto piu soave quanto viene dal piu eccellente organista ch' habbia hoggidi la nostra Italia sonato e questo è Giovanni Gabrielli*

*degno d'ognilode per la rara e singolare virtù che regna in lui in simil professione. . . ."
Venetia Citta Nobilissima* (1604).

(96) Marc Antonio Negri had been appointed Vice Maestro on December 22nd, 1612. For the list of his compositions, cf. Eitner, *Quellenlexicon.*

(97) About 1619 the post of first organist was held by G. B. Grillo, who was succeeded in 1623 by Carlo Fillago. G. B. Berti was appointed second organist in 1624; he was succeeded on January 22nd, 1640, by Francesco Cavalli, who had been tenor at the chapel since 1617.

In the sixteenth century there had been as many as three nominal organists. The third organist played " *l'organo piccolo del terzo de' concerti* "—doubtless a regal or a positive which was placed in a corner of the church on festival days. The post was suppressed in 1591, and it was decided that the *Maestro di Cappella* should, in case of need, get outside help. (*Procuratoria di Sopra* 4 f. 68.)

(98) Rovetta, in the Note to the Reader of his *Salmi concertati a 5 e 6,* published in 1626, states that there are, in the service of the Chapel of St. Mark's, " *non tanto trenta a più cantori, ma venti e più Instrumentisti de fiato e da arco.*"

(99) *Laconismo delle alte qualita di Claudio Monteverdi.*

(100) It would be exceedingly interesting to write a history of the musicians of St. Mark's. All the details could be found in the files of the *Procuratoria di Sopra* of the *Cancelleria Inferiore.*

Historians of music seem, up to the present, to have ignored this rich source of information. See, in particular, *Cancelleria Inferiore :* T. 79, f. 108, T. 80, f. 24, 65, 102, 203, 230, 249 and f. 45 ; T. 81, 123 ; T. 82. f. 20.

(101) *Cancelleria Inf.,* T. 80, f. 230, 249.

(102) The decision of the Doge is dated October 29th, 1623. The text is as follows : " *Essendo pervenuto a notizia di S. Ser., certa tal qual pretentione della scola de sonadori eretta nella chiesa di San Silvestro di questa città di voler aggregare in essa loro scola li cantori della cappella della chiesa di santo Marco, il che riuscirebbe a poca reputatione di essi cantori gia eletti et che si eleggeranno dalli Illustrissimi Procuratori, et impossessarsi della suprema autorità della Ser. Percio invigilando alla conservazione della suprema autorità della, Ducale giuridizione et al giusto sollievo et honoravolezza di essi cantori, termina che sià terminato che tutti cantori di essa capella presenti e che saranno de cetero celetti siano e s'intendino assolutamente liberi e esenti di essa scola et non debbono conoscere altro magistrato superiore in tal materia che'l Ser. Principe suo Padrone e Protettore. Terminando in oltre S. Ser. Che essi cantori di detta cappella possino oltre il canto, sonare qualunque instromento musicale in qualunque chiesa e luogo di questa città et parimente insegnare di sonare et cantare si nelle sue scole comme nelle case de particolari, ne possino sonare di ballo nelle feste pubbliche e private mercenariamente.*" *Cancelleria Inf.,* T. 81, p. 123.

(103) Gio. Batta Gualtieri had himself exempted by the Procuratori from the dues claimed from him by the Guild of Minstrels. Proceedings of June 26th, 1684. *Cancelleria Inf.,* Vol. 82.

(104) In 1613 Domenico Aldegati denounced Pietro Savolchi for not being a regular member of the choir of St. Mark's, and denied his right to accompany the members to sing in other churches. Cf. *Cancelleria Inf. Primiceria* 3.

(105) Cf. Caffi, I. 231.
(106) Cf. Caffi, I. 324.
(107) C . Vogel, pp. 361–399, and *Archivio del Stato di Venezia* (March 9th, 1590).
(108) In 1617, Alessandro Grandi had succeeded Gaspare Locatello as singing-master of the Ducal seminary. He was succeeded in 1626 by Andrea Grandi, who was in his turn succeeded in 1637 by Antonio Gualtieri.
(109) Letter of March 17th, 1620. M. Schneider, who quotes this letter, seems to think that " Il Signor Primiciero " is the name of a Venetian noble. The *Primiciero* is the Dean and the first dignitary of the Chapter.
(110) Letter of July 10th, 1627, published by Davari, pp. 84–85.
(111) This is a free translation. The text of this letter, published by Davari (p. 24), is as follows : " *Una messa a sei voci, di studio et fatica grande, essendosi obligato maneggiar sempre in ogni note per tutte vie, sempre più rinforzando le otto fughe che sono nel motetto in illo tempore del Gomberti. Il vespro della Madonna, con varie et diverse maniere d'inventioni et d'armonia, et tutte sopra il canto fermo.*"
(112) The thorough-bass had soon been adopted for church music. Viadana, who was at Mantua at the same time as Monteverdi, and exercised the functions of *Maestro di Cappella* of St. Peter's cathedral from 1594 to 1609, published as early as 1602 his famous *Concerti ecclesiastica a 1, 2, 3 e 4 voci con il basso continuo per sonar nell' organo Nova inventione commoda per ogni sorte de Cantori e per gli organisti.*
(113) Quoted by Vogel, p. 392.
(114) André Pirro, *H. Schutz*, p. 78.
(115) *Harmonie Universelle.* Des Instruments, p. 274.
(116) Caffi, *op. cit.*, I. 227.
(117) Published by Marcelle Capra, Torino.
(118) Published by Senart, Paris.
(119) Selva Morale (1641), p. 14 (soprano) : *Confitebor terzo alla francese a 5 qual si può Concertare se piacerà con quattro viole da brazzo lasciando la parte del soprano alla voce.*
(120) De St. Didier, *La Ville et la République de Venise*, 1680, pp. 386 et passim.
(121) The letter from the Resident, Sordi, containing an account of his interview with Monteverdi, is to be found in the Archivio Gonzaga (Venetia, *Lettere del Sordi*, November 21st, 1615).
(122) The poetic text has been published by Solerti : *Albori del Melodramma*, p. 289.
(123) This letter, which has not been published, is erroneously dated January 6th, 1611, instead of January 6th, 1617. M. Schneider, who quotes it, maintains this date, which is obviously an error, since Monteverdi had not yet arrived at Venice in 1611, and since, moreover, it is a continuation of the letter of December 9th, 1616, quoted above.
(124) Bevilacqua—Andreini : *Giornale storico di letteratura ital.* XII, p. 77 *seq.*
(125) Letter of March 22nd, 1619.
(126) Letter of July 21st, 1618.

NOTES

(127) Letter of July 10th, 1627, published by Davari.

(128) Letter of May 7th, 1627 (No. XLII).

(129) Letter of February 4th, 1628 (No. XLIX).

(130) This letter, which has been published by Florimo, belongs to the year 1627, and not to 1617, as was assumed by Florimo, and on his authority by all those who have reproduced or quoted this letter. Cf. No. XLIV.

(131) Cf. Letter XLV.

(132) Cf. Angelo Solerti, *Musica, Ballo, Drammatica*, p. 193.

(133) Cf. Letters XXXIV–XXXVI.

(134) According to Galvani, this is now the Hotel Danieli.

(135) Cf. *Rivista Musicale Ital.*, 1904, fasc. 1.

(136) For the Madrigals of Book VI, see the very lively and comprehensive commentary by M. André Tessier, *Les deux styles de Monteverdi* (*Revue Musicale*, 1922), where numerous examples taken from these madrigals are to be found.

(137) The only existing copy of this work is to be found in the Library of Hamburg. I am glad to take this opportunity of expressing my profound gratitude to my erudite colleague, Prof. Herman Springer of Berlin, who has been good enough to use his influence to procure for me photographs of this valuable collection, and of various compositions by Monteverdi preserved in German libraries.

(138) The only existing copy is in the Breslau Library. I have published the aira *Maledetto sia l'aspetto* in *Les Maîtres du Chant* (3rd Collection of Italian airs. Published by Heugel).

(139) Cf. *Encyclopédie Lavignac*, II, 716 (musical text quoted by Romain Rolland).

(140) XX *Madrigali e Canzonette a due et tre voci*. Venetia, Vincenti (Libraries of Breslau and Bologna).

(141) I propose to study the history of the cantata in Vol. VI. of the *Encyclopédie Lavignac*, and to reproduce there examples which will complete the limited quotations which have been possible here.

(142) In 1611 he had sent to him " the latest musical airs printed by Sr. Guesdron." Cf. Bertolotti ; *op. cit.*, pp. 73 and 93. Finally, the singer G. M. Lugharo wrote him in 1606 that he had gone to Paris on his account in order to enrich his repertory (*arrichirmi*) with the finest French airs, and to learn how to sing them (*Arch. Gonzaga. Francia, 666–1606. Diversi*).

(143) " *Le tre parti che vanno commiserando in debole voce la Ninfa si sono poste in partitura acciò seguitano il pianto di essa, qual va cantato a tempo del' affetto de l'animo e non a quello della mano* " (*Madrigali Guerrieri ed amorosi*).

(144) Published by Torchi : *L'Arte Musicale in Italia*. Vol. VII. Ricordi. In Book VII, the *partezza amorosa in genere rappresentatio* is to be sung *senza battuda*. See the musical text in Adler's *Handbuch der Musikgeschichte*, p. 376.

(145) It is to be found in Vogel, *op. cit.*

(146) A note is prefixed to the musical text of the *Combattimento* and gives most precise directions for the way in which the work was to be performed. " *Combattimento in musica di Tancredi, descritto dal Tasso ; il qual volandosi esser fatto in genere rappresentative, si fara entrare alla sprovista (dope cantatosi*

madrigali senza gesto) dalla parte della camera in cui si farà la Musica, Clorinda in piedi armata, seguita da Tancredi armato sopra ad un cavallo mariano ed il Testo all'hora comincierà il canto.

Faranno gli passi et gesti nel modo che l'oratione esprime et nulla di più ne meno, osservando questi diligentemente gli tempi, colpi et passi et gli istrumentisti gli suoni incitati et molli, ed il Testo le parole a tempo promuntiate, in maniera che le tre ationi venghine ad incontrarsi in un imitiatione unita. Clorinda parlerà quando gli tocchera, tacendo il Testo ; cosi Tancredi. Gli istromenti, cioie quattre viole da brazzo soprano, alto, tenore et basse et contrebasso da gamba che continuerà con il clavicembano, doveranno essere tocchi ad imitatione delle passioni de' l'orattione.

La voce del Testo doverà essere chiara, ferma et di buona pronuntià alquante discontra da gli istromenti atiò meglio sià intesa nel oratione. Non doverà far gorghe ne trilli in altro loco, che solamente nel canto della stanza che incomencia la Notte. Il rimanente porterà le pronuntie a similitudine delle passioni del oratione.

In tal maniera (gia dodeci anni) fu rappresentato nel Palazzo dell' Illmo. et Eccmo. Sig. Girolamo Mocenigo, mio particolar Signore. Con ogni compitezza per essere cavaliere di bonissimo e delicato gusto. In tempo però de Carnevale per passatempo di veglie. Alla presenza di tutta la nibiltà laquale resto mossa del affetto di copassione in maniera che quasi fù per gettar lacrime et ne diede applause per esser stato canto di genere non piu visto ne udito."

(147) For Opera in Venice see: Galvani, *Teatri Musicali di Venezia.* Goldschmidt, *op. cit.* Prunières, *l'Opéra Italien,* chap. i. Romain Rolland, *op. cit. ;* Kretzchmar, *op. cit.*

(148) De Saint-Didier, *La Ville et la République de Venise. De l'Opéra.*

(149) Cf. the curious Passacaglia by Luigi Rossi which I have published (Senart), with its series of sevenths and its extraordinary final cadence.

(150) *Les véridiques avantures de Ch. Dassoucy, Revue de Paris,* October 1922.

(151) It is not, however, excluded that the work was written to be performed at Vienna. Monteverdi was on excellent terms with the Austrian sovereigns. The *Selva Morale* of 1641 is dedicated to the Empress Eleanora di Gonzaga, and the 1638 edition of the Madrigals to the Emperor. It was discovered in the Library of Vienna by Ambros and Kiesewetter, attentively studied in 1904 by Dr. H. Goldschmidt, and published in 1922 in the collection of the *Denkmale in Osterreich.* There is no doubt that they are authentic.

(152) In his preface, Badoaro does not conceal Monteverdi's part in the elaboration of the poem. " I have left out the ideas and maxims having no connection with the subject of the poem, and have applied myself above all to rendering emotion, as is desired by Signor Monteverdi, to please whom I have changed and omitted many things I had first written." Yet Monteverdi did what he liked even with the text which had been written according to his directions. Whole scenes were omitted, speeches cut, words changed. The libretto was divided into five acts. He reduced it to three. He brought the drama to an abrupt conclusion with the love-duet of Ulysses and Penelope, suppressing all the subsequent verbiage.

(153) Cf. the interesting work by Dr. Haas, author of the new edition of the *Ritorno d'Ulisse, Studien zur Musikwissenschaft,* 14. Vienna, 1922.

(154) This is not the only passage which recalls the *Combattimento.* A

little later, when Ulysses describes his proposed attack upon the suitors, the rapid runs in contrary motion and the melody constructed upon the notes of the common chord are reminiscent of similar passages of the celebrated warrior madrigals.

(155) *Encyclopédie Lavignac*, II. 707.

(156) It has been published by Van den Borren in the supplement of the *Revue Musicale* (Paris) for July 1922.

(157) Since every music-lover should possess the score of the *Incoronazione*, it seemed unnecessary to make frequent quotations from the musical text. See Goldschmidt's edition, *Studien sur Italienischen Opera* (II) and Vincent d'Indy's selections (*Schola Cantorum*). Van den Borren is at present preparing a complete and handy edition of this masterpiece.

(158) Letter of September 10, 1627.

(159) Monteverdi carried on a lengthy correspondence with the Duke of Modena; his letters have unfortunately disappeared from the archives. There exist only the drafts of two letters addressed to Monteverdi by the Duke of Modena to thank him for two madrigals. The first is dated March 24.

"*Il madrigale che V.S. mi ha mandato è piaciuto sommamente a tutti quel li che l'hanno sentito, ond'elle ha molto ben compensata quella poca tardanza, che a lei ha dato fastidio con la leggiadria e finezza della composizione, et ha corrisposto pienamente al concetto che cammina del suo valore. Io poi, che sono stato sempre partialissimo delle cose sue, mi sono hora tanto piu confermato in questa dispositione che ho fatto intiera esperienza e con mio particolare gusto del suo veritiero talento et della sua amorevolezza. Staro attendendo ch' ella mi raddoppii il godimento e l'obbligo con l'altro madrigale et che possa insieme avisarmi di star bene di salute, essendomi grandemente rincres ciuto del male ch'ella ha havuto, et della briga che io le ho data in tale congiuntura. Intanto ringraziandola quanto devo della prontezza che ha mostrata nel sodisfare al mio desiderio me le offero contutto l'animo. . . .*"

In the second, dated July 4, 1624, the Duke thanks him for sending further compositions, regrets to hear he has been unwell, and says that he is awaiting with great interest two other Madrigals and some *Canzonette a tre voci* which Monteverdi is to send him.

On April 7, 1623, the Prince of Modena requests his correspondent, Alberto Colombo, to give him news of Monteverdi and to add his opinion of the *castrato* Luca Salvadori of Pistoia and of a Brescian organist who has published some madrigals.

On May 11, 1623, the prince writes to the lutanist, Bellerofonte Castaldo, that he has had Monteverdi's madrigals sung "*con molta mia ricomandatione perche mi piacquero assaissimo come io sapeva che non potre essere di manco per l'eccellenza del autore, la qual appresso di me è in quella stima maggiore che puo.*" He asks for further compositions by Monteverdi. (*Archivio di Stato. Modena. Minute di lettere ducali.*)

(160) Letters of December 13th, 1619, January 5th and February 28th, 1620 (Arch. Orsini, Rome). These letters were discovered by M. Ferdinand Boyer, who has been kind enough to send me a copy of them.

(161) Published by Masolli at Rome in 1627.

(162) Letters of March 15th, August 23rd, September 19th, 1625, February 15th and 24th, March 29th, 1626.

(163) Cf. Bertolotti, *op. cit.*, and Monteverdi's letters.

(164) Letters of November 5th, 1615, and July 27th, 1616.

(165) In 1622, Monteverdi offered the Duchess a monkey as a token of gratitude (letter of April 15th, 1622).

(166) Cf. Davari, pp. 51, 99.

(167) Letter to Marigliani, September 1st, 1627.

(168) Letters LII and LIII. It is not known to whom these letters were addressed, but it seems likely that it was G. B. Doni, celebrated for his theoretical works, and for his research in ancient music, and inventor of the *Lira Barberina*. As he had long been Secretary of the Holy College and courtier of Pope Urban VIII, he must have held some ecclesiastical office which justifies Monteverdi's use of the formula " Reverendissimo." It might also be the Duke of Bracciano, Paolo Giordano Orsini, with whom Monteverdi was in correspondence in 1615. A passionate lover of music, he had, as Mandova tells us, invented new instruments. " *Musican, toto pectore adoravit et in ea ita valuit ut novi instrumenti inventor ab omnibus commendetur cui Rosidrae nomen dedita Rosa, quam propria in Parma gestat Ursina Domus.*" The supposition that the letters were addressed to Doni seems preferable.

(169) Anatole France, *La vie en fleurs*, p. 201.

(170) André Pirro, *Schutz*, p. 78.

(171) Romain Rolland, *l'Opéra en Europe,* p. 109.

(172) Carkwright, " An English Pupil of Monteverdi," *Musical Antiquary*.

(173) This air, on the subject of *Alcide Ingrato*, apparently extracted from an opera, is to be found in a precious manuscript collection once the property of Filippo del Noro, and now preserved in the *Liceo Musicale* of Bologna.

(174) Library of the *Liceo Musicale*, Bologna. Saraceni uses all Monteverdi's methods, particularly the *stile concitato*.

(175) The Italian text is quoted by Sonneck, Volume I of the *Catalogue of Opera Librettos*, p. 1112.—(Washington, 1914.)

(176) The foreign ambassadors communicate the news to their governments. The Florentine President, Francesco Maria-Zati, writes to Gondi, Secretary of State, on December 5th, 1643. " *Mori l'ultimo di del passato il famoso musico Monteverde da Cremona ed il seguente giorno dalla mazione milanese con pompa funebre le furono celebrate l'esequie con l'intervento di quasi tutti i Musici della Città. Vaca per questa morte il luogo di maestro della Cappella di San Marco, preteso ad straordinari emulazione da molti virtuosi di Venezia ma intanto s'intende che questi SSri procurano un soggetto forestiero.*"—Arch. de Florence, *Mediceo* 3022, f. 573.

Mgr. Casimiri tells me that he has had in his hands a letter written from Venice to Carissimi, offering him Monteverdi's place, and giving interesting details of the latter's death, I have been unable to procure a copy of this document.

CATALOGUE OF MONTEVERDI'S WORKS.

Note.—As Vogel has published in the appendix of his study of Monteverdi a detailed catalogue of his works, with an alphabetic list of all the madrigals and motets published in the various collections, the reader is referred to that list, to Eitner's *Quellen lexicon*, and to Vogel's *Bibliothek der Vokalmusik Italiens.*

The present list contains only the indication of the first edition of each collection, without details of its contents. For the general bibliography of the collections, see Vogel.

1583. *Madrigali Spirituali a quattro voci porsi in Musica da Claudio Monteverde Cremonese, Discepolo del Signor Marc' Antonio Ingegnieri.* Brescia, Sabbio, in 4to (bass part only).

1584. *Canzonnette a tre voci. Libro Primo.* Venezia, Amadino.

1587. *Madrigali a cinque voci. Libro Primo.* Venezia, Gardano.

1590. *Il Secondo libro de Madrigali a cinque voci.* Venezia, Gardano.

1592. *Il Terzo libro de Madrigali a cinque voci.* Venezia, Amadino.

1603. *Il Quarto libro de Madrigali a cinque voci.* Venezia, Amadino.

1605. *Il Quinto libro de Madrigali a cinque voci . . . col basso continuo, per il Clavicembano, Chitaronne od altro simile istromento.* Venezia, Amadino.

1607. *Scherzi Musicali a tre voci di Claudio Monteverde Raccolti da Giulio Cesare Monteverde suo fratello con la Dichiarazione di una lettera che si ritrova stampata nel quinto libro de suoi Madrigali.* Venezia, Amadino.

1609. *L'Orfeo, favola in musica da Claudio Monteverde reppresentata in Mantova l'anno 1617.* Venezia, Amadino in fol.

1610. *Sanctissimae Virgini Missa senis vocibus ac Vesperae pluribus de cantandae con nonnullis sacris concentibus, ad Sacella sive Principum cubicula accomodata.* Venetiis, apud Amadinum, in 4to.

1614. *Il Sesto libro de Madrigali a cinque voci con un dialogo a sette con il suo basso continuo per poterli concertare nel Clavicembano et altri stromenti.* Venezia, Amadino.

1619. *Concerto settimo libro de Madrigali a 1, 2, 3, 4 et sei voci con altri generi da canti.* Venezia, Bart. Magni.

1623. *Lamento d'Ariana del Sigr. Claudio Monteverde et con due lettere amorose in genere rappresentative.* Venezia, Magni, in 4to.

1632. *Scherzi Musicali cioe Arie et Madrigali in stile recitativo con una Ciaccona, a 1, a 2, voci.* Venezie, Magni.

1638. *Madrigali guerrieri et amorosi con alcuni opuscoli in genere reppresentative che saranno per brevi episodii fra i canti senza gesto, Libro Ottavo.* Venezia, Aless. Vincenti.

1640. *Selva Morale e Spirituale.* Venezia, Magni.

1650. *Messa a quattro voci et salmi a una, due, tre, quattro, cinque, sei, sette, et otto voci, Concertati, e Parte da Cappella et con le Letanie della B.V.* Venezia, Vincenti.

1651. *Madrigali e Canzonetti a due e tre voci.* Venezia, Vincenti.

PRINCIPAL UNPUBLISHED WORKS.*

* For the Bibliography of the old copies of Monteverdi's works, see Eitner and Vogel.

1641. *Il Ritorno d'Ulisse in Patria.* Favolo di Badoaro, Biblio. de Vienne.

1642. *L'Incoronazione di Poppea, opera di Busenello.* Bibl. San Marco Venice.

COMPLETE LIST OF MONTEVERDI'S CORRESPONDENCE.

Except where otherwise stated, the originals of these letters are preserved at Mantua (*Archivio Gonzaga, Autografi, Lettere del Monteverdi*). As the names of those to whom they were addressed have in almost all cases disappeared, they are given here conjecturally, and with great reserve.

The letters reproduced in the following pages are indicated by Roman numerals placed in the right-hand margin. Those indicated by an asterisk have already been published in the original text by Davari.

1.* 1601. November 28th.   From Mantua to Duke Vincenzo Gonzaga.
(He applies for the post of *Maestro di Cappella e di Camera* rendered vacant by the death of Benedetto Pallavicini.)

2. 1604. October 27th.   From Mantua to the Duke.   I

3.   December.   From Cremona to the Duke.   II

4. 1607. July 28th.   From Cremona to the Ducal Secretary Annibale Iberti.
(Immediately after the Duke's departure he went to Cremona to see his father. In spite of his bad state of health, he has set to music the sonnet which the Duke sent him.)

5. 1608. November 26th.   From   Cremona   to   Annibale Chieppio.   III

6.* December 2nd.   From Cremona to the same.   IV

7. 1609. August 24th.   From Cremona to Count Alessandro Striggio.   V

8.   September 10th.   From Cremona to the same.   VI

9. 1610. June 9th.   From Mantua to the same.   VII

10.   December 28th.   From Mantua to Cardinal Ferdinando, Mantuan Ambassador to Rome.   VIII

11.* 1611. March 26th.   From Mantua to Duke Vincenzo Gonzaga.
(He proposes the engagement of a musician who plays the flute, the cornet, the trombone and the bassoon to take the *quinta pars* in wind-instrument concerts.

He will present him at Easter. He sends the Duke the
Dixit a 8 which he ordered, and two motets for 2
and 5 voices.)

12. June 22nd. From Mantua to Cardinal Ferdinando
Gonzaga.   IX

13. 1613. October 12th. From Venice to Alessandro Striggio.   X
(Unpublished in the original, translated by L.
Schneider.)

14. 1615. January 28th. From Venice to the same.
(President Sordi has conveyed to him the Duke's
invitation to go to Mantua immediately. He is
going to ask leave from the Procurators, since nothing
special retains him at St. Mark's.)
[Unpublished; the paper is corroded by damp, and
the letter is only partially legible].

15. February 11th. From Venice to the same.   XI
16. August 22nd. From Venice to Duke Ferdinando Gonzaga.
(He begs him to use his influence with the *Presidente
del Magistrato* to get payment of the pension of one
hundred crowns granted him by the late Duke
Vincenzo).

17. November 6th. From Venice to Alessandro Striggio.   XII
18.* November 21st. From Venice to the same.
(He has received the Duke's command for the composition of a ballet, but would be glad to know precisely what he requires. He explains his ideas on the
way in which the ballet *Tirsi e Clori* is to be performed.)

19. 1616. July 27th. From Venice to the Duke of Mantua.   XIII
20.* December 9th. From Venice to Alessandro Striggio.   XIV
21. December 29th. From Venice to the same.   XV
22. December 31st. From Venice to the same.
(He insists on having the names of the singers who are to
take part in *Le Nozze di Tetide*.)

23. 1617. January 6th. From Venice to the same.   XVI
(Erroneously classified with the letters of 1611.)

24*. January 14th. From Venice to the same.
(He regrets that the Duke should have abandoned the
idea of producing *Le Nozze di Tetide*, for the score is
well advanced. There is no time to be lost if
another opera and interludes are required for Easter.)

25. January 20th. From Venice to the same.   XVII

26.   February 4th. From Venice to the same.
(He has obtained the Procurators' leave of absence
for ten to fifteen days to go to Mantua but, having
heard that the Duke has already left for Florence,
he prefers to await further instructions in Venice.)

27.   February 18th. From Venice to the same.
(He leaves the matter in the Duke's hands and awaits
his orders.)

28.   November 28th. From Venice to the same.
(He is glad to hear that the Duke has received the
ballet, and is pleased with the fragments he has had
performed.)

29*. 1618. April 21st. From Venice to Prince Vincenzo Gonzaga.
(He excuses the delay in sending the music for the
Andromeda, but he has been much occupied with
the Easter ceremonies, and has to write, by Ascension
Day, some motets and a cantata for the ceremony of
the Marriage of the Doge with the Adriatic. He
would be glad to know the cast of the *Andromeda*.)

30.*   July 21st. From Venice to the same.
(He sends fragments of the *Andromeda*. He has been
delayed by headaches caused by extreme heat following on the heavy rains. He asks for details as to the
composition of the choruses and the orchestra.)

31. 1619. February 9th. From Venice to Alessandro Striggio.   XVIII

32.   March 7th. From Venice to Marigliani (?).   XIX

33.   March 22nd. From Venice to Prince Vincenzo Gonzaga.
(He excuses himself for not having set to music Marigliani's verses. He has been overwhelmed with work.
" Saturday never comes but I sigh to see it so soon
here.")

34.*   October 19th. From Venice to Alessandro Striggio.
(He hopes to leave shortly for Mantua. He will
present his new book of Madrigals to the Duchess,
to whom it is dedicated. He hopes to be able to hand
over to Striggio the music of his 9th Eclogue.)

35.   December 13th. From Venice to Alessandro Striggio.
(His departure has been postponed but he is awaiting
the Duchess's return in order to give her the work
which is dedicated to her.)

36.   December 13th. From Venice to the Duke of Bracciano at Rome.
(Expressions of respect. He has given the manuscript
to the printer and has got from him a motto, which
he is sending to the Duke.—*Archivio Orsini, Corri-
spondenza di Paolo Giordano II. Busta 163. F⁰ 306.*)

37. 1620.   January 5th. From Venice to the same.
            (He has handed over the money to the printer, who will
            do his best.—*Busta* 164. *F°* 348).

38.*   January 9th. From Venice to Alessandro Striggio.
            (He sends him the *Lamento di Apollo*, and asks him
            to write a second verse, for the cheerful love-song
            which follows. He is working at the music of Marig-
            liani's *Andromeda*, which Prince Vincenzo wishes
            to produce at the Carnival. The time allowed him
            seems very short, and he fears that the music will not
            be good. He hopes that the Duke will postpone the
            performance of *Andromeda* and will give Striggio's
            ballet.)

39.   January 16th. From Venice to the same.
            (He sends the beginning of the ballet. The *Andro-
            meda* is nearly finished and he thinks he will cer-
            tainly be able to get to Mantua for the performances.)

40.   February 1st. From Venice to the same.
            (He is working on the ballet. The *Lamento di Apollo*
            has been successfully sung in Venice. He has given
            up the idea of coming to Mantua, as he does not
            wish to kill himself with fatigue in attempting to
            get through the necessary number of rehearsals of
            the *Andromeda* in time.)

41.*   February 8th. From Venice to the same.
            (He is going to send him the end of the Eclogue, and
            asks him to present the Duchess with the Madrigals
            he has dedicated to her. He hopes that Striggio
            will use his influence with the Duke in connection
            with the grant that was made him by the late Duke.
            He has two sons, citizens of Mantua, who are studying
            law and medicine, and is in great need of help.)

42.*   February 15th. From Venice to the same.
            (He sends him the song of the River Peneus, and the
            rest of the ballet.)

43.*   February 15th. From Venice to Ercole Marigliani.
            (He sends the song for eight voices which has been
            asked for.)

44.   February 22nd. From Venice to Alessandro Striggio.   XX

45.   February 29th. From Venice to the same.
            (He pleads his state of health and press of work as
            excuse for not having been able to go to Mantua.
            He would be glad to obtain from the Duke the con-
            version into a grant of land of the pension bequeathed
            to him by the late Duke.)

46. February 29th.   From Venice to the Duke of Bracciano.
     (He thanks him for the kindness done him.   He will
     take the first occasion of sending the books to Rome.
     —*Archivio Orsini, Corrisp. Paolo Orsini. II. B.* 164,
     F⁰ 62.)

47. March 8th.   From Venice to Alessandro Striggio.   XXI
48.* March 13th.   From Venice to the same.   XXII
49. March 17th.   From Venice to the same.
     (He has received the Duke's command for a copy of the
     Arianna, which he sends.   He would be glad to obey
     the Duke's orders to go to Mantua before Easter,
     but he does not think he will get leave.   He is con-
     ducting music three times a week in the Oratory
     of the Primiciero of St. Mark's, and is very busy.)

50.* March 21st.   From Venice to Alessandro Striggio.
     (He sends fragments of the *Arianna*.   He hopes to
     go to Mantua for the rehearsals.   He insists that
     he must have proper payment of the grant made to
     him by the late Duke.)
     [Published partially by Davari.]

51. March 28th.   From Venice to the Duke of Mantua.
     (He sends him part of the *Arianna*, the rest will follow
     by the next post.   Protestations of devotion and
     allusions to the favour he expects from the Duke.)

52. April 4th.   From Venice to the Duchess of Mantua.
     (He thanks her for the gold necklace she has given him
     as a reward for the Madrigals.)

53. April 4th.   From Venice to Alessandro Striggio.   XXIII
54. April 18th.   From Venice to the same.
     (He begs him to use his influence to get payment of his
     pension.)

55. May 10th.   From Venice to the same.   XXIV
56. July 11th.   From Venice to the same.   XXV
57. July 19th.   From Venice to the same.   XXVI
58. July 24th.   From Venice to the same.   XXVII

59. September 22nd.   From Mantua to a Secretary.
     (The Duke, whom he has just seen at Goito, has
     promised to pay him his pension in advance.   He
     asks the Secretary to hand over the money to Signor
     Paolo Anselmi.)

60. October 9th.   From Venice to Alessandro Striggio.
     (He missed Striggio in Mantua, and thanks him for
     what he has done about the pension.   He has at
     last obtained the advances he wanted.)

61.		October 21st. From Venice to the same.	XXVIII
62.		October 31st. From Venice to the same.	

(He had scarcely written to the Duke to ask him to allow D. Francesco Dognazzi to come to Venice when the latter informed him that he could not obtain leave on account of press of work. This makes him still more grateful to Striggio for the favour he has obtained.)

63. 1621. February 26th. From Venice to the same.
(He will do as Striggio orders, and leaves the matter entirely in his hands.)

64. March 5th. From Venice to the same.
(He expresses his pleasure in carrying out Striggio's orders. He will send the compositions to Marigliani.)

65. March 17th. From Venice to Marigliani.
(He thought that the compositions in recitative style (*certi canti rappresentativi*) which had been ordered from him were not required before September. That is the reason why he has sent none of them yet. He is, moreover, much occupied with the composition of the Mass and motets which are to be sung in Florence as a requiem for the Grand Duke of Tuscany.)

66. August 7th. From Venice to the Duchess of Mantua. XXIX

67. September 10th. From Venice to Marigliani. XXX

68. November 27th. From Venice to the Duchess of Mantua. XXXI

69. 1622. February 26th. From Venice to the same.
(He thanks her for having helped his son Massimiliano to enter at the College of the Cardinal di Montalto at Bologna.)

70. April 15th. From Venice to the same. XXXII

71. October 1. From Venice to Alessandro Striggio. XXXIII

72. November 19th. From Venice to the same.
(Signor Giustiniani has been to thank him for having obtained the loan of the Duke of Mantua's company of actors for Venice.)

73. December 3rd. From Venice to the same. XXXIV

74. December 10th. From Venice to the same.
(He has not been able yet to show Striggio's favourable reply to Signor Giustiniani, but he wishes to express his thanks without delay.)

75. December 31st. From Venice to the same. XXXV

76. 1623. January 23rd. From Venice to the same.
(He is complying with the Duke of Mantua's wishes, and has not written to the organist Ottavio Barani.)
77. February 10th. From Venice to the same.   XXXVI
78. March 11th. From Venice to the same.
(He thanks Striggio for having conveyed his excuses to the Duke. He is better, but his health is not yet quite restored.)
79. June 4th. From Venice to the same.
(Signor Donati will accompany Signora Adriana and Signor Muzio to Mantua, in compliance with the Duke's orders.)
80. 1624. March 2nd. From Venice to the Duke of Mantua.   XXXVII
81. 1625. March 15th. From Venice to Ercole Marigliani.   XXXVIII
82. August 23rd. From Venice to the same.   XXXIX
83. September 19th. From Venice to the same.
(He thanks him for having taken an interest in his lawsuit, which he hopes will soon lead to a definite decision. He is sending a Murano vase which he has ordered for Marigliani.)
84. November 22nd. From Venice to the same.
(He sees that his adversary is persisting in the lawsuit. He begs Marigliani to use his influence, and gives some details of the affair, which disgusts him thoroughly.)
85. 1626. February 15th. From Venice to the same.
[This letter is illegible owing to a large tear. It concerns the despatch of a chemical product which Marigliani desires, doubtless for his alchemy.]
86. February 24th. From Venice to the same.   XL
87. March 19th. From Venice to Alessandro Striggio.
(Letter of introduction for his son, who wishes to settle in Mantua as doctor of medicine.)
88. March 28th. From Venice to Marigliani.   XLI
89. 1627. January 2nd. From Venice to Alessandro Striggio.
(Campagnola has told him of Striggio's wish that he should set his verses to music. Protestations of devotion.)
90. March 20th. From Venice to Alessandro Striggio.
(He thanks him for having obtained a month's advance on his pension for his son Massimiliano.)
91. May 1st. From Venice to Alessandro Striggio.
(He will gladly compose the opera which the Duke desires, but he insists on having plenty of time and a good libretto. It is easy to write interludes

quickly, but not an opera, if one does not wish to
fall ill over it. He has just set to music the *Armida*
stanzas from Tasso, and has finished the *Combattimento*. He is thinking, too, of writing a short opera
to a libretto by Strozzi, *La Finta Pazza Licori*. If
the Duke wants some church music, he can send some.)

92 *   May 7th. From Venice to Alessandro Striggio.   XLII
93.*   May 22nd. From Venice to the same.
(He hopes that Striggio will soon be cured of his gout.
He has received the Duke's orders to set *La Finta
Pazza* to music. He is going to ask Strozzi to
introduce some scene-changes, and some new characters. Signor Giacomo Rapalini is prepared to enter
the Duke's service, but upon certain conditions.
Monteverdi asks the exact range of voice of Signora
Margherita, who is to play the principal part in the
opera.)

94.*   May 24th. From Venice to the same.
(He is waiting for Strozzi to return to set to work. He
wishes that each appearance of the pretended madwoman should be accompanied by some new and
striking musical effect, etc.)

95*.   June 5th. From Venice to the same.
(Strozzi is back. He is going to recast his libretto in
accordance with the new circumstances which have
arisen, and will contrive a part for all the *virtuosi* of
the Court. Strozzi has told him that the Duke of
Tuscany had thought of commissioning Monteverdi
to write an opera, but that in the end he employed
Marco da Gagliano.)

96.*   June 13th. From Venice to the same.
(Strozzi has not yet returned the libretto, but he is at
work on it. He indicates that it may be possible
to engage a singer, aged twenty-four years, who
has a well-trained bass voice.)

97.*   June 20th. From Venice to the same.
(He insists upon the excellence of the singer of whom
he has already spoken. Strozzi is going to give him
the libretto which he has divided into five acts,
and Monteverdi hopes to send parts of the score to
Mantua in a fortnight's time.)

98.*   July 3rd. From Venice to the same.
(His work has been interrupted by a cold which has
caused a violent inflammation of his right eye. The
young singer has asked the Procurators for his
release, in order to go to Mantua.)

99.*   July 10th. From Venice to the same.
              (He sends the first act of the libretto of *La Finta Pazza Licori*. There will be a ballet in each act, all different and all extraordinary. He wishes to imitate in his music the actions of the characters, etc.)

100.*   July 24th. From Venice to the same.
              (He has been very busy. On Saturday, which is post day, he was occupied from five to eight o'clock with chamber music at the English Ambassador's house, then he went to the church of the Carmine for vespers and arrived home very late. He is working at the opera. He gives a technical criticism of the voice of the young singer engaged by the Duke.)

101.*   July 31st. From Venice to the same.
              (He excuses the delay in the despatch of the *Finta Pazza*, which he is having copied.)

102.*   August 17th. From Venice to the Duke of Mantua.
              (Same subject.)

103.*   August 28th. From Venice to Count Striggio.
              (The copier has been ill. He sends the first three acts.)

104.*   September 10th. From Venice to the same.
              (He sends the end of *La Finta Pazza Licori*. Marquis Bentivoglio has asked Monteverdi to compose interludes for the marriage of the Duke of Parma to verses of his composition. He has agreed, and finds the task easy, for the verses are principally monologues. He is anxious to obtain a canonicate at Cremona, as that will assure him of a place of retirement for his old age, and hopes the Duke will use his influence with the Emperor to obtain it.)

105.*   September 10th. From Venice to Ercole Marigliani.   XLIII
106.*   September 10th. From Venice to the Marquis Bentivoglio at Parma.   XLIV
              [Published by Florimo, I, 115, with the date September 10th, 1617. The original is in the Conservatorium of Naples.]

107.*   September 18th. From Venice to Count Striggio.
              (He shares his opinion of the *Finta Pazza*, although the whole thing may pass off well, thanks to the variety of the music. He has not finished the *Aminta*, for which he requires another two months' work. He entrusts the affair of the canonicate to Striggio's prudence.)

108.*   September 25th.   From Venice to Count Striggio.
          (He is working at the interludes for Parma. He
          thinks that he will like the *Armida*, which he has
          just finished.)

109.*   September 25th.   From Venice to Marquis Bentivoglio.   XLV
          [Published by Tierset. *Lettres de Musiciens*, p. 63.
          Translated into French by Weckerlin, J. G. Prud-
          homme, Tierset, etc. The original is in the Library
          of the Paris Conservatoire.]

110.*   October 2nd.   From Venice to Count Striggio.
          (He is going to send off the little work which Striggio
          has asked for.)

111.*   October 30th.   From Parma to Marquis Bentivoglio.
          (He has been through Modena with Gorretti. He
          has finished the interlude of *Bradamante*, and is
          working at the third interlude and at the tourna-
          ment. He asks to be back in Venice for Christmas.)
          [The original is in the *Liceo Musicale* at Bologna.
          Published by Caffi, II. p. 171.]

112.*   November 8th. From Parma to one of the Procurators.
          (The rulers of Parma would like him to stay till the
          end of the month and return immediately after
          Christmas. They have written to ask this favour from
          the Procurators.)
          [Published by Caffi, I. p. 243. The original is in the
          Liceo Musicale at Bologna.]

113.   December 18th.   From Venice to Count Striggio.   XLVI

114. 1628.   January 1st.   From Venice to Ercole Marigliani.   XLVII

115.   January 9th.   From Venice to the same.   XLVIII

116.   February 4.   From Parma to Marquis Alessandro
          Striggio.   XLIX

117.   July 1st.   From Venice to the same.   L

118.   July 8th.   From Venice to the same.   LI

119. 1630.   February 23rd.   From Venice to the same.
          (He is going to set to music the words which have
          been sent to him. He has been delayed by the
          composition of religious music for the Sisters of
          San Lorenzo.)
          [Original at Cologne, Heyer Museum.]

120. 1633.   October 22nd.   From Venice to G. B. Doni (?).   LII

121. 1634.   February 2nd.   From Venice to the same.   LIII
          [The originals of these two letters are at the Florence
          Conservatorium of Music. They have been
          published by Vogel.]

SELECTED LETTERS FROM
MONTEVERDI'S CORRESPONDENCE

[Anno 1604]

I. Al Sereni.mo S. Duca di Mantova. Casal Monferrato.

Seren.mo Sig.re et Padron. mio Coll.mo

*Per ultima provigione pur mi convien ricorrere alla infinita bontà de l'A.
S. S. perchè sia quella finalmente che cometta il voler suo circa delle paghe
concessimi dalla sua gratia. Vengo però a piedi suoi con quella maggior humiltà
ch'io posso a supplicarla dignarsi di movere il sguardo non al ardire mio (forse)
circa questo scrivere ma si bene al molto bisogno causa ch'io scriva non al Signor
Presidente che moltissime volte ha datto la commissione del si amorevolissimante
et creatamente, ma si bene al Belintento che mai l'ha voluta eseguire, se non
quando a lui e piaciuto et all'hora che si è indotto a questo effetto, mi è bisognato
quasi usar termine d'haver l'obligo a lui et non alla infinita bontà di S. A. S.
che fa gratie anco a servitore di poco merito per sua infinita bontate come son
io presso al molto risguardo del grande merito de l'A. S. S. doperando elli che è
il più anco mala creanza verso di me quando non ha voluto darmi tal pagamento;
questa scrittura mia ad altro fine non viene inanti a piedi suoi che per supplicare
l'A. S. S. dignarsi di cometter ch'io habbia paghe tali che assendono alla somma
di cinque mesi nel qual termine si trova ancora la Sig.ra Claudia, et mio messere
et questa somma cresce anco nel più non vi veggendo per lè altre futture speranze
di poterle havere senza commissione particolare di V. A. S., senza il qual fondamento tutta la fabrica mia resterà cadente et ruinosa, poichè di giorno in giorno
mi va sovravegnendo danni, et non ho con che ripararli, non ho doperato nondimeno per haver tali pagamenti almeno di un mese solo, se non di tutti, che
preghiere humiltà, et creanze, mattina e sera, in virtù del qual uffitio, ho
perso et vado perdendo quasi tutto il tempo de li miei studij che devo spendere
per gusto et bisogno di V. A. S. trovandomi in tal carico come sono da lei agratiato
et non posso nondimeno haver nulla, s'io son degno di ricevere questa particolar
gratia dalla bontà infinita di V. A. S. ch'ià chieggo supplicarla con quel maggior affetto di core ch'io so et posso a concedermela, la quale sarà di un comando
che sia pagato non solo, ma maggiormente mi sarà di somma gratia ogni volta
che io non sia pagato per mano di quel Belintenti, perchè son sicuro che V. A. S.
non mi potrebbe dare altri fuorche lui che non doperasse verso di me qualche
sodisfationi almeno di parole se non di fatti, almeno di honore se non di effetti,
almeno una volta se non sempre et non so io per qual causa ciò va usando questo*

231

*verso di me, la qual gratia sua se si estendesse sopra li datij di Viadana integral-
mente resteressimo soddisfatissimi; et assicurato dalla infinita bontà di V.
A. S.; et dalli molti altri signalati favori, et gratie fattemi spero anco di questo
che ho chiesto all' A. S. S. di restarne agratiato in virtù delle quali gratie et
favori, io non potendo altro, pregherò N. S. per la conservatione longa di S. A. S.
alla quale m'inchino et humilissimamente li faccio riverenza. Da Mantova
il 27 ottobre 1604.*

D. V. A. S.

Humilissimo et obblig.mo Ser.re

Claudio Monteverdi.

II. Al Duca di Mantova.

Seren.mo mio Sig.re et Pad.n Coll.mo

*Dieci giorni fa dal corriere hebbi l'ultima lettera di V. A. S., che mi coman-
dava che dovessi fare due entrate l'una per le stelle che hanno a seguitare la
luna, et l'altra per li pastori che hanno a seguitare Endimione, et duoi balletti
parimente, l'uno per dette stelle solamente, et l'altro per le stelle et pastori insieme, così con un desiderio ardentissimo di ubbidire et servire prontissimamente
alli comandi del A. V. S. sicome sempre ho hauto et ho fatto, et haverò sin ch'io
mora et farò sempre, mi posi per fare prima quello delle stelle, ma non trovando
nella instrutione quante di numero hanno ad essere nel ballarlo, volendolo fare
intercalato come mi pare che sarebbe statto novo, bello, et gustevole, cioè facendo
sonare prima da tutti li instrumenti un aria allegra et corta, et danzata da tutte
le stelle parimente, di poi in un subito le cinque viole da brazzo pigliando un
aria diversa dalla detta, fermandosi li altri instrumenti, ballandola solamente due
stelle, restando le altre, et nel fine di detta partita a dover di novo ripigliar la
prima aria con tutti li instrumenti et stelle seguitando questo ordine sino che
havessero ballato a due a due tutte le dette stelle; ma non havendo hauto il
detto numero, et questo essendo di necessario il saperlo (piacendolo però alla
A. V. S. in tal maniera d'inventione intercalata come ho detto) per tanto sino
ch'io lo sappia ho tralasciato il farlo, et per saperlo ho scritto a Mons. Gio.
Batta ballarino, atiò per mezzo di mio fratello me ne dia il numero preciso,
et fra tanto ho fatto quello delli pastori et stelle il quale hora invio a V. A. S.;
l'ho fatto si, Seren.mo Mio Sig.re, con quel buon affetto solito, et pronta volontà
di servirlo che ho sempre hauto et sempre havero, ma non già con la obidienza
delle forze mie solite et pronte al mio volere che ho per lo passato haute che ancora
si trovano indebolite dalle fatiche passate et fatiche in tal maniera, che ne per
medicine, ne per star a dieta, ne per tralasciar li studij sono ritornate nel loro-
primo vigore, ben inqualche parte si; spero nondimeno nel Signore di ricuperarle
le quali haute se piacerà a Sua Divina Maesta, supplicherò l'A. V. S. all'hora*

che per l'amor di Dio, non mi vogli mai più caricare ne di tanto d'affari in una volta, ne di tanta brevità di tempo che certamente, il mio gran desiderio di servirla et la molta fatica, immediatamente me tirerebbero alla brevità della mia vita, la quale pur se vivendo più longamente potrà servire all'A. V. S. et giovare i miei poveri filioli.

Si che Ser.mo Sig.re se l'A. V. S. non si trovasse da me hora servita, ne nel bello ne nel presto come forse aspettava, et come era desiderio mio di fare, come parimenti ho sempre desiderato, non incolpi la bona mia volontà, ne l'animo mio, poichè sempre et questo et quella haveranno a somma gratia et a sommo favore che l'A. S. V. si degni di comandarle, alla quale inchinandomi li faccio humilissima riverenza et li prego da N. S. ogni compita felicita. Da Cremona il dicembre 1604.

D. V. Altezza Ser.ma

Humiliss.mo et devot.mo servitore
Claudio Monteverdi.

[Anno 1608]

III. Al Conte Annibale Chieppio (?)

Ill.mo et Reveren.mo Sig. mio et patron Coll.mo

Non men pronto che desideroso di servire a V. S. Ill.ma et Rev.ma subbito che fu gionto il staffiere, cominciai mandar ad esecutione il suo comandamento della compositione che li mando; Et si bene con verità posso dire che stando la indispositione mia della quale non sono ancora risolto per le fatiche li giorni passati costi haute, V. S. Ill.ma non resterà così servita conforme al desiderio mio; non dimeno sarà per benignità sua agradito il buon animo mio assicurandola che maggior favore non potrò ricevere che servir sempre a V. S. Ill.ma et Rev.ma alla quale per fine facendole humilissima riverenza; li prego da N. S. quel contento che a tanto principe si conviene. Di Cremona li 26 novembre 1608.

D. V. S. Ill.ma et Rev.ma

Humilissimo et Divot.mo Servit.re
Claudio Monteverdi.

IV. Al Sig.r Alessandro Striggio.

Ill.mo Sig. et Pron. Oss.mo

Hoggi che è l'ultimo di Novembre ho ricevuto una lettera di V. S. Ill.ma dalla quale ho inteso il comando di S. A. S. ma atiò me ne venga quanto prima a Mantova. Sig. Chieppio Ill. mo, se per venire a faticarmi di bel novo cos comanda, io dico che se non riposo intorno al faticarmi nelle musiche teatrali, al sicuro breve sarà la vita mia, poichè per le fatiche passate così grandi, ho acquistato un dolore di testa et un prurito così potente et rabbioso per la vita che nè per cauteri che m'habbia fatto fare, nè per purghe pigliate per boca, nè per salassi et altri rimedii potenti mi son potuto ancora risolvere, bene in parte sì, et il S. r padre atribuisce la causa del dolore di testa a li studii grandi, et del prurito, all'aria di Mantova, che m'è contraria, et dubita che solamente l'aria, fra poco di tempo sarebbe la mia morte. Hor pensa V. S. Ill.ma la gionta de li studi che farebbero se per venire a ricever gratie et favori dalla bontà et benignità di S. A. S.ma così comanda. Io dico a V. S. Ill.ma che la fortuna mia hauta a Mantova per 19 anni continui m'ha datto occasione di chiamarla inimica a me et non amica, perchè se dal S.mo S.r Duca m'ha favorito d'esser gratiato di poterlo servire in Ongheria, m'ha disfavorito con farmi havere una gionta di spese che la povera casa nostra quasi ancora ne sente di quel viaggio. Se m'ha fatto chiamare nel servitio di S. A. S.ma in Fiandra m'è stata contraria anco in quella occasione di far che la Sig.a Claudia stando à Cremona portasse spesa alla casa nostra con serva et servitore, ancora non havendo lei all'hora da S. A. S.ma che 47 lire al mese oltre alli denari che mi diede il Sig. Padre dietro; se mi diede occasione che il S.mo Sg.r Duca all'hora mi cressesse la provigione dalli 12 scudi et mezzo di moneta di Mant.a sino alli 25 scudi al mese mi fu inimica anco in far che il detto Sig.r Duca dopo si risolvesse mandarmi a dire per il Sig.r D.n Federico Follini che in tal cresimonia s'intendeva che facessi le spese al Sig.r Campagnolo, all'hora putto, et perchè non volsi tal briga mi convenne lasciar adietro 5 scudi al mese per le dette spese, così restai con li 20 scudi che mi ritrovo, Se mi favori in far che il S.r Duca l'anno passato mi adimandasse per servitio delle musiche delle nozze mi fu inimica anco in quell'occasione con farmi far una quasi impossibile fatica, et di più mi fece patire di freddo, de vestiti, de servitute, et quasi de magnare con perdita della provigione della S.ra Claudia, et aquisto di grande malattia senza essere punto agratiato da S. A. S. ma di qualche favore in pubblico, che ben sa V. Ill. S. che li favori de' principi grandi alli servitori giovano, et nel honore, et nel utile in occasione di foresterie in particolare, Se mi feci havere un vestito da S. A. S.ma per comparire nel tempo delle nozze mi feci anco questo danno che me lo feci havere di un drappo che era di seta et bavella lavorato, senza gioppone, senza calzetti et cinte et senza fodera di cendalo per il ferarolo, per lo che spesi io di mia borsa 20 scudi di moneta di Mantova. Se mi ha fatto favore in farmi havere occasioni tante et tante d'essere adimandato da S. A. S. ma mi ha anco fatto questo danno, che il S.r Duca sempre m'ha parlato per faticarmi et non mai per portarmi qualche allegrezza d'utile.Et se finalmente (per non essere più longo) m'ha favorito in farmi credere d'havere da S. A. S.ma una pentione de 100 scudi di moneta di Mant.a sopra al capitanato della piazza, m'ha disfavorito poi anco che finite le nozze più non sono stati li 100 scudi, ma solamente 70, con perdita della adimandata occasione et con perdita delli denari delli mesi scorsi, quasi forse meravigliandosi che fossero troppi li 100 scudi, li quali poi aggionti alli 20 che mi trovo havere, facevano 22 ducatoni in circa al mese, quali poi quando li havessi hauti che mi haverei avanzato per servitio de li miei poveri filioli? Haverìa potuto affaticarsi assai in avanzare 500 scudi l'anno d'entrata senza la provigione ordinaria Oratio della Viola se altro non havesse havuto che li detti al mese; haverìa parimente potuto affaticarsi bene Luca Marenzo in avanzarsene altre tanti; parimente Filippo di Monte; il Palestina che lasciò a filioli suoi per mille scudi et passa d'entrata; haverìa potuto affaticarsi bene il Luzzasco et il Fiorini ad avanzarsi per 300 scudi d'entrata per uno, poi lasciati a' filioli loro. Et finalm'te per non dir più, haverìa potuto affaticarsi per avanzare Franceschino Rovighi sette milla scudi come ha fatto se altro non havesse havuto che li detti, li quali apena bastano in far le spese ad un patrone et servitore et vestirlo; non so poi io ad havere duoi filioli agiunti come mi trovo. Sicchè Ill.mo S.r s'ho da cavare la conclusione dalle premesse, dirò che mai ho da ricevere gratie nè favori a Mantova, ma più tosto sperare (venendo) di haver da la mia mala fortuna l'ultimo crollo. So benissimo che il S.mo S.r Duca è di buonissima intentione verso di me, et so che è principe liberalissimo, ma io sono troppo sfortunato a Mantoa, et V. S. Ill.ma lo creda da questa ragione, che so che molto bene S. A. S.ma, morta la Sig.ra Claudia, fece risolutione di lasciarmi la provigione sua, ma gionto io a Mantoa, subito cangiò pensiero, così non diede tal commissione per mia disgratia, per lo chè sin hora vengo ad haver perso passa 200 scudi, et ogni giorno vado perdendo. Fece anco risolutione, come ho detto di sopra, di darmi li 25 scudi al mese, ecco che subito cangiò pensiero et per mia disgratia me ne calarono 5. Sicchè Ill.mo S.re all'aperta si conosce la mia mala fortuna essere a Mantova. Che vuole V. S. Ill.ma di più chiaro? Dare 200 scudi a Mes.r Marco de Galliani che si può dire che nulla fece, et a me che feci quello che feci, niente! Per tanto conoscendomi et ammalato et sfortunato a Mantova, supplico il S.r Chieppio Ill.mo che per l'amor di Dio mi vogli far havere una bona licenza da S. A. S., che conosco da questa ne nascerà ogni mio bene. Il S.r Don Federico Follini mi promise per mezzo d'una sua dimandandomi da Cremona l'anno passato a Mantoa per le fatiche delle nozze, mi promise dico, quello che V. S. Ill.ma può vedere in questa sua che l'invìo, et poi alla fine nulla è stato, o se pure ho havuto, ho havuto mille et cinquecento versi da mettere in musica. Caro Sig.re mi aiuti ad havere bona licenza che mi pare che questo sii il meglio d'ogni cosa, perchè muterò aria, fatiche et fortuna, et chi sa, che alla peggio che posso altro che restar povero come sono? Il venirmene a Mantoa per havere la licenza con bona gratia di S. A. quando altro non vogli, tanto farò, assicurando V. S. Ill. che sempre per mio Sig.re et padrone predicherò quella A. S.ma ovunque sarò et lo riconoscerò con mie povere orationi presso la M.tà di Dio sempre, altro non potrò.

In quanto poi a considerare a le gratie et a favori ricevuti tanti et tanti dall'Ill.mo. Sig. Chieppio, sappia certo che non penso intorno a tal capitolo, mai che non arosisca in aricordarmi d'esserle stato tanto noioso, ma ove non ponno giungere le forze mie deboli agiungerà almen l'animo et la voce mia in

*predicare le infinite sue cortesie et in restar perpetuamente obligato a V. S. Ill.,
alla quale per fine faciole riverenza et le bacio le mani. Da Cremona il 2 dicembre
1608.
Di V. S. Ill. Ser.re Ob.mo sempre,*

Claudio Monteverdi.

V. Al Medesimo.

Ill.mo mio Signore et Patron Osser.mo

*Ho ricevuto una lettera di V. S. Ill.ma ed insieme certe parole da mettersi
in musica di comissione di S. A. S., et la riceuta fu eri che fu al 23 del presente,
quanto prima mi porrò a comporle et finite ne darò ragualio a V. S. Ill.ma opurre
le porterò io a Mantova perchè in breve voglio essere al servitio; queste ho pensato prima di farle ad una voce sola, et se poi S. A. S. comandera che riporti
quel aria a cinque, tanto faro, altro non mi occorre dire a V. S. Ill.ma se non che
l'Orfeo speroche dimane che sarà alli 25 mio fratello riceverà la copia finita
di stampare dal stampatore che glie la manderà per il corriere di Venetia che
gionge apunto dimani; et subbito hauta ne farà legare una et la donerà a l'A.
S. del Sig. Principe, et donandogliela supplico V. S. Ill.ma a compagnarla di
parole presso quella Altezza S. che significano il molto che desidero nel animo
mio di mostrarli quanto li sono devotissimo et humilissimo Servitore et che dono
poco a S. A. S. (che molto merita) per mancamento di fortuna si, ma non già
per difetto d'animo; Con questa occasione mi farà anco gratia di far sapere
al detto Seren.mo Signore Principe che io ho parlato a questi sonatori di cornetto
et tromboni come mi diede commissione ch'io facessi, et che mi hanno risposto
che verano a servire S. A. S. ma questi due capi l'uno che vorrebbero essere aiutati,
da S. A. S. di lettere di favore presso il Conte di Fontes overo a chi si aspetta
atiò possano scodere certe paghe che avanzano dopochè il Conte di Fontes è nel
stato di Milano, et atiò V. S. Ill.ma intenda questi li avanzano perchè sonano
nel castello di Cremona, et l'altro capitolo è che il padre et duoi filioli li quali
sonano di tutti li ustrimenti da fiato vorebbero dodici scudi al mese per cadauno,
a questo di longo mi sono opposto et li ho detto che se S. A. S. giongesse alli otto,
che mi pare che sarebbero sodisfatti; a questo non hanno ne detto nè di si nè di
nò, li duoi altri perchè non sono così sofficienti come questi tre creddo che si
haverebbero con manco salario, sonano uniti et prontamente, et dà ballo et di
musica perchè ogni giorno si esercitano, io starò aspettando di questo risposta
et quello che comanderà S. A. S. tanto farò nè passerò più oltre del suo comandamento, et con questo io finisco facendo riverenza a V. S. Ill.ma et pregarla che
mi mantenghi nelle sue gratie. Da Cremona il 24 agosto 1609.
D. V. S. Ill.ma.*

*Servitor di core
Claudio Monteverdi.*

VI. Al Medesimo.

Ill.mo Mio Sig.re et Padron Osser.mo

A li 9 del presente hebbi una di V. S. Ill.ma la quale mi comette che io non afferma quelli suonatori da fiato senza novo avviso, ma che ben li vada mantenendo con qualche speranza, tanto ho fatto et tanto haverei fatto senz'altro avviso tuttavia più sicuramente lo faro havendolo di comandamento; li dissi tre giorni fa a questi tali, se il Sig.r Comendatore o Castellano, sapesse che vi voleste partire vi darebbe egli licenza; rispose che non solamente non li darebbe licenza ma l'impedirebbe ogni via perchè non si potessero partire; et sè nascesse il caso come vi partireste, risposero andaressimo senza dir altro, più oltre non tratai, et V. S. Ill.ma ha inteso anco circa del loro difficile partirsi.

Alli 4 del presente hebbi ancò una lettera del Seren.mo Sig.r. Prencipe scrittami da Maderno, questa contiene che m'informi di un certo Galeazzo Sirena compositore et suonatore d'organo se venirebbe a servire S. A. S., et che provisione vorebbe, et che li faccia intendere alla detta Serenissima Altezza la sufficienza sua et intelligenza, et perchè il detto Galeazzo lo conosco benissimo anzi ogni giorno mi viene a trovare a casa che per tanto lo conosco intrinsicamente, di longo riceuta la comissione feci l'ufficio il quale di subbito mi rispose che la mente sua non era d'andare a servire prencipe, ma che desiderava andare a stare a Milano per maestro di capella della Scala come ben certi cantori milanesi gli havevano promesso di farle havere tal loco, perchè con quella occasione dice che haveria guadagnato in insegnare, in far musiche per la città, in comporre per le monache, et in far fare chitarri et clavicembali da vendere, che per ciò per tal mezzo haveria sperato di diventar ricco in breve tempo, al che risposi che desiderava che pensasse un poco sopra a quello gli havevo detto, et che se poi non havesse voluto andare a servire quell'Altezza che almeno mi havesse detto che scusa dovevo pigliare, sichè dopo più volte havendolo visto et mai non mi havendo risolto: ho pensato per bene scrivere a V. S. Ill.ma chi è questo tale atiò possa informare S. A. S.ma che volendo aspettare che mi risponda et all'hora scrivere a S. A. S. dubbito che stando tardi S. A. non creda che sia negligente nel far quanto mi comanda. Pertanto dicco a V. S. Ill.ma questo Galeazzo essere uno di età di trentasette anni, povero, con moglie et filioli, con padre che lavora per lavorente nelle carozze, et scranne da poggio, con madre molto più povera che tutto il giorno li convien filare nel molino; questo ha ingegno universale et ove si aplica non fa male, si pose in far un salterio lo fece assai bene, si pose infar un chitarone lo fece ancor lui assai bene, et parimente un clavicimbano et molte altre cose manuali, nella musica è intendente si, ma di sua opinione, et vole che quello che riesse dal suo ingegno sia il più bello dell'arte et se altri non si tosto lo dicono lui è il primo, del suo non ho udito che di due messe a otto de l'una li chirie et la gloria, et de l'altra tutta eccetto il Sanctus et l'Agnus che più non haveva composto, et un credo di un altra a quattro, un dixit a dodici, et certe canzoni da sonarsi con le viole overo ustrimenti da fiato a quattro

*voci, queste assai comodamente ben tirate nel arte, et di qualche inventione
nova, ma le messe et dixit, sono di uno stile ricco d'armonia si, ma dificoltoso
da cantarsi, poichè va cazzando certe parti et interumpimenti che tosto affaticano
et affannano i cantanti, ma da ben a credere che si accomodarebbe anco a quantc
cerca S. A. S. ma perchè non ne ho sentito di tal genere del suo non voglio darne
il parere, perchè avanti che havesse cognitione di teatri mi dò a credere che
gli vorebbe a lui non poca fatica, havendo speso gli anni suoi intorno ali generi
di canto ecclesiastici, et parvà in quelli anco dura fatica ad incontrare nelle
proprie perchè è di sua testa; et conoscendolo et nella povertate et nella opinione
di suo pensiero esser molto ricco, et non essendo sicuro che dia la intera sodisfatione a S. A. S. li dissi perchè so che vui vorreste essere ben pagato,
atiò sappia S. A. S. in chi ha da spendere tali dinari, a vui sarà poco il far
quanto comandarà la detta Sereniss. Altezza, per tanto se vorete andar a
stare a Mantova in prova per tre mesi, et ivi mostrar il valor vostro farò
che vi sarà datto stanza, servitute, da magnare, et anco qualche cortesia dopo,
et così traterete l'acordio vui, et a questo rispose che non vole, et io sogiunsi
voi non havete in stampa cosa alcuna sopra de la quale se ne possa dar il giuditio
del vostro valore, ne volete anco venire in prova, nè havete fatto mai canti teatrali, et come si potrà venire in cognitione di questo senza esperienza alcuna,
di maniera come V. S. Ill.ma ha visto e così fatto, ha non poca di persuasione
ne ha troppo modo di farsi voler bene alli cantori che questi da Cremona non
vogliono cantarle sotto, ben lo stimano si, et volontieri dice male del terzo. Circa
poi del sonar l'organo per la cognitione del contrapunto suona, ma non già per
bontà di mano chè lui non ha mano da far tirate nè grappoli, ne accenti, ne altri
adornamenti; et lui confessa non farne professione, se bene suona un organo in
Santo Agostino qui di Cremona, ma questo lo fa per essere povero. Mi adimando
dopo dui o tre giorni che li dissi se sarebbe andato a servire S. A. S. se il Sereniss.
Sig. Prencipe lo voleva per maestro di capella suo o per altro, a questo li risposi che non sapevo la mente sua; sicchè Sig.r Striggio mio Sig.re mi è parso
da scriverne a V. S. Ill.ma quattro parole sopra di ciò che mi mettono l'animo
in sospensione perchè di ciò il sig.r Prencipe è padrone di far quanto piace et
pare all'Altezza S.ma pigliando o lui o altri per maestro di capella (se pure
tal titolo li vol dare che non lo sò) mancando il Sereniss.mo Sig.r Ducca et che
volesse Idio benedetto che io restassi dopo, et havendo maestro di capella il Sig.r
Prencipe, che vorrebbe che facessi io handarmene all'hora poi da Mantova!
Desidero da V. S. Ill.ma essere favorito di sapere con quel destro modo che so che
meglio sarà fare lei che io dire, se S. A. S. ha tal intentione atiò sappi che fare,
mi perdoni s'io son statto troppo lungo ma incolpi la mia ignoranza che non
mi ha lasciato imparare a dir conciso, et a questo li resto servitore di core, et
li bacio le mani pregandola che mi mantenghi nelle gratie sue facendole sapere
che presto sarò a Mantova. Da Cremona il 10 settembre 1609.
    Di V. S. Ill.ma servitore di core*

Claudio Monteverdi.

VII. Al Duca di Mantova.

Seren.mo Sig.re et padron mio Coll.mo

Da Messer Pandolfo me statto commesso da parte de l'A. S. S. ch'io senta
un certo contralto venuto da Modena desideroso egli di servire all'A. S. S.
così di longo l'ho condotto in Santo Pietro et l'ho fatto cantare un motetto nell'organo,
et ho udito una bella voce gagliarda et longa, et cantando in sena giongerà benissimo senza discomodo in tutti li lochi cosa che non poteva cosi bene il Brandini,
ha trillo assai bono, et honesta gorgia et canta assai sicuro la sua parte ne motetti,
et spero che non dispiacerà all' A. S. S. Ha qualche diffettuzzi, come a dire s'in-
gorga un poco tal volta la vocale quasi nella maniera di Messer Pandolfo, et
talvolta se la manda nel naso et ancora la lassia sdrussilare tra denti che non fa
intelligible quella parola et non percotte bene la gorgia come bisognerebbe, ne
la rindolcisse a certi altri lochi, ma tutte queste cose io sono di certa opinione
che subbito avertito il tutto si leverebbe; non l'ho potuto sentire ne madregali
poi che era già in pronto per partire et venire alli comandi de l'A. S. S. di maniera
che in quello che l'ho udito, ne do relatione all'A. S. S., et perchè altro non mi
ha comandato, io qui finirò la lettera con far humilissima riverenza all' A.
S. S. et pregar N. S. che largamente conservir in quella bona sanità et nella
gratia sua l'A. V. S. da Manto il 9 giugno 1610.

D. V. A. Ser.ma

Humiliss.mo et obblig.mo Ser.re
Claudio Monteverdi.

VIII. Al Cardinale Ferdinando Gonzaga (?)

Ill.mo mio Sig.re et padron Coll.mo

Con questa mia vengo pregando da Dio con ogni affetto di core che dia il
buon capo d'anno a V. S. Ill. l'ottimo mezzo et il miglior fine ad ogni suo Ill.mo
pensiero et a me sempre occasione di merito nella gratia di V. S. Ill.ma con
la quale son sicurissimo havere quella allegrezza ch'io spero havanti ch'io mora
con il vedere mio filiolo nel seminario Romano con benefitio da chiesa che li paghi
la donzena, essendo io povero, et senza la quale nulla potrei sperare da Roma
in aiuto di Franceschino già fatto pretino per vivere et morire in tale vocatione
sotto alla protetione et servitore humilissimo di V. S. Ill.ma essendo vasallo della
Ser.ma Casa Gonzaga nato da padre et madre servitori di lungo tempo delle
Altezze Vostre Seren.me et da matrimonio fatto con particolar consenso del
Ser.mo Sig.r Ducca Vincenzo; che se Roma con il favore di V. S. Ill.ma non
lo aiutasse, resterebbe egli et un altro fratello suo poveri si che apena potrebbono

*andarsene in capo del anno con pane et vino, mancandoli io. Cercherò qualche
benefitio semplice o altro che possa portar pensione sufficiente per ottenere la
gratia di questo bisogno da Sua Santità se V. S. Ill.ma si degnera volerli favorire
lui et io insieme (come spero dalla infinita bonta sua, o presso a Sua Santità
o presso a Monsignor Ill.mo Dattario che in altra maniera temendo di haverla
fastidita troppo quando fui a Roma non oserei di bel novo dimandarli gratia
alcuna. Avanti mi partissi da Roma udi la Signora. Ippolita molto ben cantare
a Firenze la Sig.ra filiola del Signor Giulio Romano molto ben cantare et sonare
di leutto chitaronato et clavicembano, ma a Mantoa la Sig.ra Adriana benissimo cantare, benissimo sonare et benissimo parlare ho udito, sino quando tace
et acorda, ha parte da essere mirate et lodate degnamente fui forzato assicurar
la quanto Ill.mi Sig.ri Cardinali Mont'Alto et Perretti l'honoravano et sti-
mavano et maggiormente anco quanto V. S. Ill.ma in risposta della qual lode
di V. S. Ill.ma disse la Sig.ra Hippolita ha parti più degne di me presso la
gratia di questo Sig.re che non ho io, che ben ho udito le lodi infinite che li da;
sopra a questo mi affaticai molto per farla credere lo contrario, ma mi pare
che non ottenni il fine che io desideravo, poichè soggiunse se il Sig.r Cardinale
Gonzaga mi tenesse nel concetto delle vostre ragioni, mi haverebbe fatta degna
di qualche sua bella aria, atiò la potessi cantare caro signore, me ne faccia degno
di una atiò la possa sgnannare con questo argomento, con la qual occasione la
prego anco a committere al Sig.r Sante mi mandi la cantata nelli duoi chitaroni
promessami da V. S. Ill.ma atiò la possa fare udire a Sua Altezza Seren.ma
convenire di sera nella sala de Specchi, che del tutto glie ne resterò obblig.mo
servitore, et qui per fine li faccio humilissima riverenza et li bacio le mani.
Da Mantoa il 28 dicem.bre* 1610.

    D. V. S. Ill.ma.

Humiliss.mo et obblig.mo Ser.re

Claudio Monteverdi.

[ANNO 1611]

IX. AL CARDINALE FERDINANDO GONZAGA.

    Ill.mo et Rever.mo mio Sig.re et Padron Coll.mo

    *Hor hora ho riceuto la carissima lettera da V. S. Ill.ma con insieme li duoi
bellissimi Madrigali in musica, et questa et quelli, ho letto et riletto, cantati
et ricantati, fra me di subito baciati et ribaciata, con estrema consolazione,
vedendo in quello quanto sia grande la amorevolezza di V. S. Ill.ma verso un
suo minimo servitore come son io che nulla merita; ogni venere di sera si fa
musica nella sala de specchi, viene a cantare in concerto la Sig.ra Arianna,
et così fatta forza, et particolar gratia da alle compositioni aportando col fatto
diletto al senso, che quasi novo teatro divien quel loco, et creddo che non si finirà*

*il carnevale de concerti, che sarà di bisogno che il Sereniss.mo Ducca facci stare
guardia all'entrata, che giuro a V. S. Ill.ma che questo Venere passato ad udire
non solamente il Seren.mo Sig.r Ducca et Seren.ma Sig.a Duchessa, la Sig.a
Donna Isabella di Sant'Martino, Sig.re Marchese et Marchesa di Solfarino,
Sig.ri Dame et Cavaglieri di tutta la corte vi erano ma più di cento signori
altri de la Città ancora, con tal bella occasione farò sonare li chitaroni ali casa-
leschi nel organo di legno il qual è soavissimo, et così cantera la Sig.a Andriana
et D. Gio. Batt.a il Madregale bellissimo* Ahi che morire mi sento, *et l'altro
madregale nel l'organo solamente, dimani partirò le dette compositioni pre-
sentandole alla Sig.a Andriana et so quanto le saranno care, ne voglio dirle il
nome dell'Autore sino a tanto che ella non le haverà cantate et de la riuscita
del tutto ne darò ragguaglio a V. S. Ill. Non mancherò di attendere a Franceschino mio filiolo et servitore humilissimo di V. S. Ill.ma atiò impari tre virtù
l'una il servire a Dio con ogni diligenza et timore, l'altra le lettere, et terza
un poco di musica che sino a quest'hora mi pare che faccia assai bene et trillo
et gorgia atiò con il mezzo de la gratia di V. S. Ill.ma possa ottenere da Dio
et da Sua Santita la gratia che ogni ora nelle mie deboli orationi li prego. Io
non so Ill.mo Signore se sarei troppo ardito se la supplicassi hora, essendo vacato
il Vescoato di Novara qual'è di rendita 8000 scudi che si degnasse di intercedere
qui sopra la pensione per il detto filiolo che li pagasse la donzena, che sarebbe
alla meno cento scuti d'oro, se fossi troppo presto in fastidirla mi perdoni per
l'amor di Dio, ma se anco potessi ricevere la gratia, o quanto contento al animo
sentirei mi parrebbe di haver aquistato tutto l'oro del mondo, caro Signore, se
è possibile per sua infinita gratia mi aiuti, et risguarda più alla sua infinita
gentilezza in farmi favore, che alli miei meriti, che so benissimo ch'altro non
ho in me, che quello che nasce dalla sua infinita bonta, et a V. S. Ill.ma me
l'inchino et li faccio humilissima riverenza, et li prego da N. S. ogni compita
felicità. Da Mantova il 22 giugno 1611.*

   D. V. S. Ill.ma et Reveren.ma

   Humiliss.mo et obblig.mo Ser.re

   Claudio Monteverdi.

X. Al Consigliere Alessandro Striggio.

   Ill.mo mio Sig.re et padron Coll.mo

*Vengo a far saper a V. S. Ill.ma come ritrovandomi in compagnia del coriero
di Mantova partendomi con esso lui per Venetia, a Sanguanato non nel proprio
loco ma se bene lontano da esso duoi miglia, da tre forfanti fora usciti fossimo
svaligiati in cotal maniera, al improviso da un campo quale metteva capo sopra
la strada corente usci fuora duoi di chiera brunotta con poca barba et mezzani*

di statura, con un scioppo per uno da ruota longo con giu il cane, et l'uno di questi venendo da la banda mia per impaurirmi con il sciopo et l'altro mettendo le mani nella brilia a cavalli quali andasevano piano senza replica alcuna ne tirorno in un campo, et me facendomi inginochiare subbito smontato che fui et dimandandomi la borsa da uno de detti duoi che havevano li schiopi, et l'altro intorno al coriere dimandandole le valigi et tirate giù dalla carrozza da esso coriere ad una ad una gliele aperse et esso assassino pigliando ciò che li pareva et da esso coriere prontamente dandole il tutto et io pur tuttavia stando in ginochione così tenuto da quel altro che haveva l'archebugio; pigliorno in tal maniera ciò che a loro parvero, il terzo de tre assasini che haveva un spedo in mano et che haveva fatto la spia et tuttavia facendola tendendo che non venisse gente dalla strada; quando hebbero ben bene rivoltato tutte le robbe, mi venne quello che cercava le robbe del coriere a torno a me et mi disse ch'io mi spogliassi che voleva vedere se io havevo altri denari, ma certificato che io non ne havevo, andò intorno alla mia serva per far il simile et essa aiutandosi con diverse preghiere scongiuri et pianti fece si che la lassio stare, di poi tornando alle robbe et alle valigie, fece un fagotto delle migliori et de le più belle, et nel cercare per coprirsi trovò il mio feraiolo di rassa longo novissimo che all'hora a Cremona me lo havevo fatto et disse al coriere mettimi questo feraiolo, et esso assasino vedendo che gli era longo disse damene un altro, così pigliò quello di mio filiolo ma trovandolo troppo corto, disse all'hora il coriere, e sig.i di quel povero prettino donate glielo et egli si contento trovo ancora la veste di detto putto et fece il simile, et ancora de le robbe della serva il coriere gliele chiese in dono con molte preghiere così glie le dono. Del resto fecero un fagotto grande et lo presero a bazzolo et portorno via; poi noi pigliassimo li avanzi et se ne andassimo al' hosteria, alla mattina sequente dessemo la quarella a Sanguaneto, poi si partissimo, io molto sconsolato et giongessimo a Este; si pigliò una barca per Padoa la quale ne tenne tutta la notte di giobia et quasi tutto il venere insabiati, niuno curandosi che passasse avanti finalmente su le venti hore a bona pioggia et vento sopra un burchio scoperto non vi essendo in poppa che vogasse che il nostro coriere il quale fece una bona fatica vogando giongessimo a Padova che apena ad una hora di notte potessimo entràre dentro, alla mattina del sabato levandosi a bon hora per partirsi per Venetia stessimo più di due hore di giorno a partirsi, nel qual mentre che stessimo in Padova il coriere mettendosi un braccio al collo dicendo che ciò era nato per quell'occasione de .... quando fu svaligiato, et io sapendo che nulla fu tocco ne anco cercato adosso al carociere, io rimasi un altro, il qual atto di esso coriere diede da sospettare a tutti che erano con noi che prima l'havevano visto senza male alcuno; et vi fu nella barca di Padova che ci disse al coriere che inventione è questa fratello et volendo soggiungere altre parole (diro forse in burla) egli si parti da tal ragionamento; così giongessimo egli giocando et ridendo in barca alle 24. del sabato in Venetia che poi vi stette se non due hore et riparti per Mantoa; questo e statto il negotio di ponto; et perchè qui da me e statto questo altro coriere di Mantoa a lamentarsi meco con dire che ha inteso che ho sospettato del coriere passato, gli ho

risposto che nulla ho sospettato et che io l'ho per homo da bene, ma e ben vero
che ha fatto quel tal atto con mettersi quel braccio al collo il sabato mattina per
l'occasione scorsa del mercore passato di sera, et non fu chi lo tocasse, et esso
navigò tutto il venere; Io vengo a far sapere a V. S. Ill.ma che nulla ho sos-
pettato in questo homo che se mi fosse andato nell'animo tal pensiere di subbito
no haveria datto ragualio a V. S. Ill.ma dico bene che di questo atto che fece il
detto coriere con mettersi il braccio al collo diede da pensare al giudiciosissimo
parere di V. S. Ill.ma che quanto a me nulla penso et nulla cerco se non da la
mano di Dio. Io Ill.mo Sig.re li certifico che mi hanno rubato per passa cento
ducati venetiani tra robbe et denari dal sig.r Presidente hebbi gratia quando
fui a Mantoa d'havere un semestre et ne avanzo ancora un altro gia tre mesi
sono maturo; io li ho narato la mia disgratia grande se lei mi volesse agratiar
presso esso Sig.r Presidente d'una parola di favore benche sappia che la genti-
lezza del Sig.r Presidente sia molta, io la riceverei a somma gratia che signore
ne tengo infinitamente bisogno; et qui facendo una humilissima riverenza a
V. S. Ill.ma io li prego da Dio ogni vera felicita. Da Venetia il 12 ottobre 1613.
D. V. S. Ill.ma

Humiliss.mo et obblig.mo Ser.re

Claudio Monteverdi.

XI. Al Medesimo.

Ill.mo mio singolar Sig.re et Padron Coll.mo

Hoggi che ne habbiamo 11 del mese quasi su le 27 hore la lettera di V. S. Ill.ma
mi è statta datta dal dispensatore de le lettere de la posta; la quale ritorna
a Mantova all'hora prima di notte di questo stesso giorno, si che a ragione di
dover esser all'ordine per venire sicome mi comanda, mi bisogneria esser stato
con li stivali in piedi (come si suol dire ad essere a tempo de la barca del cor-
riere; et adesso di poi patire una mala notte causa di poi di qualche malatia
mia; oltre che il tempo statto gran pezzo bono, si è cangiato in pioggia in maniera
che appena si può uscire di casa; oltre che la lettera di V. S. Ill.ma mi fa una
certa dolce istanza per la quale et per le ragioni sovradette ho preso ardire di
non mettermi così affanato in viaggio, si per veder ciò che farà il tempo, si
per potermene andar a Padova di giorno aspettando colà il corriere con mia
comodità, come anco per haver occasione di veder di farmi prolongare un poco
di più la licenza (come V. S. Ill.ma anco mi scrive ch'io procura) et realmente
non pensano ne anche al futuro ordinario essere al ordine, come ben si piacera
al Sig.re sarò pronto ad ogni hora, poichè a dir il vero a V. S. Ill.ma stando
l'andata di S. A. S. a Fiorenza mi credevo che ella al sicuro havesse ad havermi
a comandare in Venetia et non in Mantoa, cioè che mi havesse da favorire a
mandarmi la favola; la qual gratia se potesse V. S. Ill.ma farlami essendo
che in un istesso tempo schiverei le strade cattive, non dubiterei de fora usciti,

et potrei servire anco Santo Marco, poichè avvicinandosi la settimana santa, nel qual tempo si fanno molte fontioni presente la Seren.ma Sig.ria che in essa settimana viene in chiesa perciò mi saria di molta mia comodità prego V. S. Ill.ma non argomentare che ciò che ho detto naschi da animo non pronto di non ubbidire alli comandi suoi perchè realmente mi conosco desiderosissimo di far cosa sempre che sij di gusto all'A. S. sua, tanto più questa trattandosi di compositione fatta per mano di quel Seren.mo Signore. Ma la supplico realmente a credere quanto ho detto di sopra essere la pura verità; ho posto sotto avanti a li occhi di V. S. Ill.ma il tutto, atiò per questo altro ordinario comandandomi possa lei credere che senza altra replica faro quanto mi accennerà, che se risolvesse di mandar l'opera, prometto a V. S. Ill.ma di affaticarmi intorno adessa più di quello penserà, mandandole di settimana in settimana per il coriere quello che di giorno in giorno anderò facendo; et qui facendole a V. S. Ill.ma humilissima riverenza da Dio N. L. li prego il colmo d'ogni sua felicità. Da Venetia le 11 febraio 1615.

D. V. S. Ill.ma

Obblig.mo Serv.re
Claudio Monteverdi.

XII. Al Segretario del Duca di Mantova.

Ill. mio Sig.re et padron Coll.mo

Spinto da le molte spese che mi convien fare per servitio de li miei duoi filioli desiderando che imparano lettere et si levino nel timor di Dio et honor del mondo che per quesii rispetti tanto necessarii sempre mi e convenuto mantenerli con il loro maestro in casa mia che tra li uni et l'altro mi sono costati passa ducento ducati al anno et ritrovandomene trecente da Santo Marco et cento dalla gratia della donatione che si degno concedermi la felice memoria del Ser.mo Sig.r Ducca Vincenzo, li quali cento non potendoli havere, et havendone molto bisogno, feci ricorso con una mia alla infinita bonta del A. Ser.ma del Sig.r Duca Ferdinando, già un mese fa overo più; et hebbi risposta dal Sig.r Cognato mio Capuzzino; V. S. Ill.ma non solamente haver in mano la lettera mia ma anco una autorita dalla benignita di questa Seren. Altezza di potermi consolare non solamente de li cento scudi ch'io havanzo dalla Camera Ducale per livelli scorsi, ma di farmi havere il fondo dal quale ne possi cavare comodamente questa annua entrata; Quando udij dal Sig.r Cognato mio V. S. Ill.ma haver hauto tal comissione, restane sicura che di subbito me ne corsi a ringratiar Dio di cotanto segnalato favore et tutto mi rallegrai, sapendo quanto V. S. Ill.ma mi sia sempre statta mia protettrice et fautrice. Io non staro a dirle le mie fatiche passate le quali ne sento spesso hor alla testa hor alla vita mia per il pattir grande ch'io feci nell'Arianna ne staro a dirle li duoi filioli aquistati in Mantova che pur ne fu cagione del Matrimonio mio il Sig.r Ducca Vincenzo; ne che mi sia partito da quella Seren.ma Corte cosi disgraziamente che per Dio altro non portai via che venticinque scudi dopo il corso de 21 anni, ne insomma staro racontando altro a V. S. Ill.ma perchè so che del tutto e benissimo informata; dirò solamente et con infinita preghiera che si vogli degnare a far si ch'io resti consolato di questo benedetto fondo dal quale ne possi trarre queli benedetti cento scudi, si per godere segno delle mie fatiche et de la gratia della gloriosa memoria del Sig.r Ducca Vincenzo, et dell'aiuto per giovare a miei poveri filioli; come anco per mostrare alli presenti Sig.ri Musici che servono la presente Ser.ma Altezza che so molto bene che sono et favoriti et honorati, che anco erano tali chi ha servito il Ser.mo Sig.r Ducca Vincenzo; caro Sig.re Ill.mo la prego per l'amor di Dio vogli in ciò giovarmi che in un istesso giovera a miei filioli, al honor mio et al anima, et alla splendidezza del Sig.r Ducca Vincenzo che purre comanda Idio che la mercede non sia tenuta dalla sera alla matina al povero servitore et la città di Venetia et altre ancora pur vederanno ch'io sono in parte meritato, dove si stupiscono ora che nulla vedeno, non so che mi dire altro, se non rimettermi alla bonta di V. S. Ill.ma dalla quale spero ogni consolatione mia, per lo che io non manco ne mancherò ne me, ne miei poveri filioli di pregar Dio per il colmo d'ogni sua esaltatione et il fine dogni suo honorato desiderio, et qui facendole humil riverenza li baccio le mani. Da Venetia il 5 novem. 1615.

D. V. S. Ill.ma

Obblig.mo Ser.re
Claudio Monteverdi.

[ANNO 1616]

XIII. AL DUCA DI MANTOVA.

Sereniss.mo Sig.re e Padron Coll.mo

Il grandissimo bisogno nel qual mi trovo hora Seren.mo Sig.re dovendo necessariamente provedere la povera mia casa di pane vino e altri molti, impoverito principalmente dalla carica de filioli acquistati costi in Mantova a quali per la pericolosa libertà costà in Venetia son necessitato mantenerli un maestro et altre si per il caro vivere che qua si ritrova, mi sprona a supplicarla, con quel magnifico affetto d'animo ch'io posso et humiltà ch'io devo farmi gratia commettere che sij dato in mano a mio Suocero almeno li denari di tre semestri passati ch'io dalla Tesoreria avanzo; Sperando poi nell'innata bonta sua d'essere nella prima occasione gratiato in riccompensa della longa servitu prestata a questa Seren.ma Casa del capitale di questi denari come per benignita singolare dell'A. V. S. s'è dignata rispondere in tal modo a mio Cognato Capuzzino qual sapendole mie calamitose necessità fu spinto presentar per carita a V. A. caldissime preci e intanto pregarò sempre Nostro Sig.re che conceda all'A. V.

felicissimo stato, e a me presti gratia d'esser da lei per minimo servitore mai sempre conosciuto e con tal fine facio a V. A. S.ma humilissima riverenza. Di Venetia a 27 luglio 1616.

    D. Vostra Ser.ma Altezza.

                    Humiliss.mo et devotiss.mo Ser.re

                       Claudio Monteverdi.

XIV. AL CONSIGLIERE ALESSANDRO STRIGGIO.

Ill.mo mio Sig.re et Padron Coll.mo.

Ho ricevuto con ogni allegrezza d'animo dal Sig.r Carlo Torri la lettera di V. S. Ill.ma et librettino contenente la favola marittima delle nozze di Tetide. V. S. Ill.ma mi scrive che lei me la manda atiò la vegga diligentemente et dopo glie ne scriva il parer mio dovendosi porre in musica per servirsene nelle future nozze di S. A. S. ma. Io Ill. mo S. che altro non desidero che valere in qualche cosa per servitio di S. A. S. altro non dirò per prima risposta che prontamente offerirmi a quanto S. A. S.ma sempre si degnerà comandarmi et sempre senza replica honorare et reverire tutto che S. A. S.ma comanderà. Sichè se l'A. S. S. ma aprobasse questa, questa per conseguenza sarebbe et bell.ma et molto a mio gusto, ma se lei mi agiunge ch'io dica, io sono ad ubedire alli comandi di V. S. Ill.ma con ogni reverenza et prontezza; intendendo che il mio dire sia un niente come persona che vaglia poco in tutto, et persona che honora sempre ogni virtuoso, in particolare il presente Sig.r poeta che non so il nome, et tanto più quanto che questa professione della poesia non è mia. Dirò dunque con ogni riverenza per ubidirla perchè così comanda, dirò. Dico prima in genere che la musica vol essere padrona del aria et non solamente dell'acqua, volio dire in mio linguaggio che li concerti descritti in tal favola son tutti bassi et vicini alla terra, manca- mento grandissimo alle belle armonie, poi che le armonie saranno poste ne' fiati più grossi dell'aria della terra, faticosi da essere da tutti uditi et dentro alla scena da essere concertate, et di questo ne lascio la sentenza al suo finiss.mo gusto et intelligent.mo, che per tal diffetto in loco d'un chitarone ce ne vorà tre, in loco d'un Arpa ce ne vorebbe tre, et va discorendo, et in loco d'una voce delicata del cantore ce ne vorrebbe una sforzata; oltre di ciò la imitatione propria del parlare dovrebbe a mio giuditio essere appoggiata sopra ad ustrimenti da fiato più tosto che sopra ad ustrimenti da corde et dilicati, poichè le armonie de tritoni et altri dei marini crederò che siano sopra a tromboni et cornette et non sopra a cettere o clavicenbani et arpe, poichè questa operatione essendo maritima per conseguenza è fuori della città; et Platone insegna che cithara debet esse in civita, et thibia in agris. Sichè, o che le delicate saranno inproprie, o le proprie non delicate. Oltre di ciò ho visto li interlocutori essere Venti, Amo- retti, Zeffiretti et Sirene, et per conseguenza molti soprani faranno di bisogno;

et s'aggiunge di più che li venti hanno a cantare, cioè li Zeffiri et li Boreali; come caro Sig.re potrò io imitare il parlar de' venti se non parlano? Et come potrò io con il mezzo loro movere li affetti? Mosse l'Arianna per essere donna, et mosse parimente Orfeo per esser homo, et non vento. Le armonie imittano loro medesime et non con l'oratione et li strepiti de' venti, et il bellar delle pecore, il nitrir de' cavalli et va discorendo, ma non imitano il parlar de' venti che non si trovi. Li balli poi che per entro a tal favola sono sparsi non hanno piedi da ballo; la favola tutta poi, quanto alla mia non poca ignoranza, non sento che ponto mi mova, et con difficoltà anco la intendo, nè sento che lei mi porta con ordine naturale ad un fine che mi mova. L'Arianna mi porta ad un giusto lamento et l'Orfeo ad una giusta preghiera, ma questa non so a qual fine; sichè, che vole V. S. Ill.ma che la musica possa in questa? Tuttavia il tutto sarà sempre da me acettato con ogni riverenza et honore quando che così S. A. S.ma comandasse et gustasse, poichè è padrona di mi senza altra replica, et quando S. A. S.ma comandasse che si facesse in musica, vedendo che in questa più deitati che altro parlano, le quali piace udire le deitate cantar di garbo, direi che le Sirene, le tre signore sorelle cioè S.ra Adriana et altre le potrebbono cantare, et altresi comporsele. Così il Sig. Rasi la sua parte, così il S.r. D. Francesco parimente et va discorendo ne li altri Sig.ri. Et qui imitare il Sig.r Cardinal Montalto che fece una comedia che ogni sogetto che in essa interveniva si compose la sua parte. Che se fosse cosa questa che ben desse ad un sol fine, come Arianna et l'Orfeo ben si ci vorebbe anco una sola mano, cioè che tendesse al parlar cantando, et non come questa al cantar parlando, et la considero anco in questo pensamento troppo longa in ciascheduna parte nel parlare, dalle sirene in poi et certa altra ragionatezza.

... Mi scusi caro Sig.re se troppo ho detto, non per detraere cosa alcuna, ma per desiderio di ubedire alli suoi comandamenti, che havendola da porre in musica, se così mi fosse comandato, possa V. S. Ill.ma considerare li miei pensamenti; Mi tenghi la supplicco con ogni affetto devotissimo et humiliss.mo Servitore a quella Seren.ma Altezza alla quale faccio humilissima riverenza et a V. S. Ill.ma bacio con ogni affetto le mani et li prego da Dio il colmo d'ogni felicità da Venetia il 9 dicembre 1616.

D. V. S. Ill.ma alla quale auguro con ogni affetto le bone feste.

Humiliss.mo Ser.re et obblig.mo

Claudio Monteverdi.

XV. Al Medesimo.

Ill.mo mio Sig.re et Padron Coll.mo

Mi perdoni V. S. Ill.ma se non ho procurato con mie lettere di sapere da V. S. Ill.ma la risposta de la mia che già venti giorni sono io inviai a V. S.

Ill.ma per risposta de la gentilissima sua quale insieme fu acompagnata con la favola Marittima de le Nozze di Thetide per intendere da lei ciò che intorno ad essa io mi dovevo fare havendo V. S. Ill.ma scritto nella sua che avanti io mi facessi altro dovessi scriverliene a lei il mio parere. Questa tardanza mia e divenuta dalla fatica fatta della Messa della Notte di Natale, che tra il comporla et rescriverla mi e convenuto spendere tutto il mese di Dicembre quasi senza intentione alcuno ; hora che per gratia del Sig.re mie ne trovo libero et il tutto passato honoratamente me ne vengo con questa di novo a V. S. Ill.ma dicendole che mi honori di farmi sapere ciò che desidera che facci l'A. S. S. che trovandomi disoccupato, poichè passato tal fatica de la Notte et giorno di Natale per un pezzo mi staro senza haver che fare in Santo Marco perciò comincero a far qualche cosetta intorno a detta favola se così comandera ne altro faro per sino a nova comissione di V. S. Ill.ma io l'ho ritornata a riguardare più minutamente et diligentemente et quanto a me li veggo molti soprani far di bisogno, et molti tenori, pochissimi dialogi et que pochi parlano et non cantano di vaghezze insieme, cantar a cori altri non vi sono che li Argonauti nella nave, et questo sara il più vago et il più galiardo et si risolvera poi in sei voci et sei istromenti, vi sono bensi li Zefiretti et li Venti Boreali ; ma questi non so come habbino a cantare, ma ben so che soffiano e sibillano, et aponto Virgilio parlando de venti adopera questo verbo sibillare, quale aponto imita nel pronunciarlo l'effetto del vento ; Vi sono altri duoi cori, l'uno de Nereidi et l'altro di Tritoni, ma questi pare a me che andcrebbono concertati sopra ad ustrimenti da fiato, che se dovesse essere così, adimando a V. S. Ill.ma che diletto ne riuscira al senso et perchè V. S. Ill.ma possa ancora lei diligentemente veder questa veritate. Mando a V. S. Ill.ma sopra alla presente carta qui inclusa l'ordine de le sene come stanno sopra a detta favola poste atio mi favorisca di dirmi il parer suo ; Il tutto pero stara benissimo che dipendera da la mente di S. A. S. alla quale prontamente et me l'inchino et me l'esibisco humilissimo servitore. Staro dunque aspettando risposta da V. S. Ill.ma et quanto si degnera comandarmi, fra tanto che qui humilmente li bacio le mani et pregole con ogni affetto di core il compimento d'ogni suo honoratissimo pensiero, da Venetia il 29 dicembre 1616.

D. V. S. Ill.ma

Obblig.mo et Devotiss.mo Ser.re
Claudio Monteverdi.

XVI. AL MEDESIMO.

Ill.mo mio Sig.re et Padron Coll.mo

La carissima lettera di V. S. Ill.ma hora da me riceuta insieme con la carta che mi dinota li personaggi che hanno ad operare nella favola di Tetide, m'ha recato chiarezza molta nel far cosa che possi essere a proposito secondo il gusto di V. S. Ill.ma che so che insieme anco sara di gusto di S. A. S. al quale desidero con ogni affetto far cosa che li agrada; Io Ill.mo Sig.re che all'hor scrissi la prima lettera in riposta della prima sua confesso che la favola mandatami da lei, non havendo sopra di se altra intitolatione che questa Le Nozze di Tetide, favola marittima; confesso dicco, che ella fosse cosa da essere cantata et rapresentata in musica come fu l'Arianna. Ma dopo intesi dalla passata di V. S. Ill.ma che ha da servire per intermedij de la comedia grande. Sicome in quel senso primo io me la credevo cosa di poco rilievo così per lo contrario in questo seconda me la creddo degna cosa et nobilissima. Manca però al mio parere per conclusione del tutto dopo l'ultimo verso che dice

Torni sereno il ciel, tranquillo il mare

manca dicco una canzonetta in lode de Seren.mi Prencipi sposi l'armonia de la quale possa essere udita in cielo, et in terra de la sena et alla quale possano nobili ballarini far nobil danza che cosi nobil chiusa mi par convenire a cosi nobile vista proposta et insieme se si potesse acomodare a metro di ballo li versi che le Nereidi haveranno a cantare al tempo de quali si potesse far ballare con legiadro modo esperti ballarini mi par che sarebbe cosa molto più propria; Ho un poco di oppositione contro alli tre canti de le tre Sirene, et è questa che dubito se haveranno a cantar tutte tre separatamente che troppo lunga riuscirà l'opera ali ascoltanti, et con poca differenza, poichè tra l'una et l'altra farà de bisogno sinfonia che tramezzi, tirate che sostentino il parlare et trilli, et in genere riuscirà una certa similitudine, che perciò giudicherei anco per variatione del tutto che interzatamente li duoi primi madregaletti, hor da una et hor da due voci insieme fossero cantati, ed il terzo da tutte tre insieme. La parte di Venere parte prima che vien dopo il pianto di Peleo et prima ad essere udita nel cantar di garbo cioè in tirate et trilli haverei giudicato per bene che dovesse essere cantata forsi anco dalla Sig.ra Adriana come voce forte, et dalle due altre sue Sig.re sorelle servita per risposta di eco stando che l'oratione ha dentro questo verso: E sfavillin d'Amor li scogli e l'onde = ma prima preparando li animi de li ascoltanti con una sinfonia di ustrimenti, contenente se fosse possibile mezza la sena perchè prevegono avanti questi duoi versi di Peleo dopo fatto il pianto

Ma qual per l'aria sento
Celeste soavissimo concento!

Et creddo chi la Sig.ra Adriana haverebbe tempo di transvestirsi, o pure ad una de le tre altre Sig.re. Sino a quest'hora io mi vo credendo che sarà in essere da cento et cinquanta et forsi più versi, et creddo che questa altra settimana non sarà fuori che se piacerà al Signore tutti li soliloqui saranno fatti, cioè quelli che parlano, mi ponerò poi dietro a quelli che cantano di garbo; piacia a Dio che si come mi ho desiderosissimo animo di far cosa che sij di gusto a questo Seren.mo Sig.re che così anco l'effetto mi rieschi, atiò li effetti mi servono per veri testimoni presso alla gratia di S. A. S. che tanto bramo et riverisco, et alla

quale in ogni stato et loco sempre me li dicherò per humilissimo servitore non meno restando obblig.mo Servitore a V. S. Ill.ma che si va degnando mantenermi vivo in quella con li suoi gentilissimi costumi et honoratiss.me maniere, et qui facendo humilissima riverenza a V. S. Ill.ma pregole da Dio con ogni caldo affetto il colmo d'ogni sua vera esaltatione. Da Venetia il 6 gennaio 1617.
    D. V. S. Ill.ma

Obblig.mo et Devotiss.mo Servitore

Claudio Monteverdi.

XVII. Al Medesimo.

Ill.mo mio Sig.re et padron Coll.mo

Mi havisa V. S. Ill.ma del stabillimento del matrimonio di S. A. S. con Toscana dal quale horamo ne havera da nascere la sicura risolutione del far qualche cosa in musica per questa Pasqua, come ben a questo fine lei mi mandera nova favola da porre in musica; se questo rispetto del servire al A. S. del Sig. Ducca di Mantoa mio antico Signore non mi teneva in Venetia al sicuro me ne transferivo sino a Fiorenza, invitato da una lettera caloratissima del Sig.r Ottavio Rinuzzini che mi havisa con la bella occasione del Seren.mo Sig.r Ducca di Mantoa vogliami transferire a Firenze che non solamente sarò ben visto da tutta quella nobilta ma da lo stesso Seren.mo Gran Ducca; che oltre alle presenti nozze di Mantoa ancora altre se ne sperano che perciò haverei non poco gusto quasi quasi significandomi che sarei statto inpiegato in qualche fatica musicale et mi havisa le nozze con il Seren.mo di Mantoa essersi conclusi con grandissimo applauso di tutta la città di Firenze che nostro Sig.re sij quello che anco così sempre li facci caminare per gusto del Ser.mo Sig.r Ducca di Mantoa et di tutte le città sue che così con ogni affetto desiderero sempre bene et lielo pregherò da Dio a quella Seren.ma Casa. Staro dunque aspettando quanto V. S. Ill.ma mi comandera havertendola, che il presto con il bene insieme non conviene. Voglio dire se ella stara tardi non si lamentera di me se non havero fatto et io haverei con il tempo potuto et creduto. Mandando in questa vece il mio prontissimo animo a supplire per me et devotissimo il quale anco hora con il medesimo rispetto fa riverenza a V. S. Ill. et li prega da Dio ogni esaltatione et felicita. Da Venetia il 20 gennaio 1617.
    D. V. S. Ill.ma

Ser.re Humiliss.mo et aff.mo

Claudio Monteverdi.

XVIII. AL MEDESIMO.

Ill.mo mio Sig.re et padron Coll.mo

Et la passata et la presente lettere di V. S. Ill.ma ho ricevuto ma ben si con questa differenza, che io essendo andato ad acompagnare Francesco mio filiolo primo a Bologna passate che furno le prime feste di Natale con occasione di levarlo da Padoa per levarlo dal bon tempo che l'Ill.mo Sig.r Abbate Morosini li somministrava per il mezzo de la sua gentilezza per godere d'un poco del cantare del putto, qual alla fine mi sarebbe riuscito più tosto bon cantore con li altri agionti, come sarebbe a dire (ma e meglio ch'io me li taccia) che mezzano dottore, et purre il mio pensiere vorebbe che fosse in questo secondo bono, et nel primo mediocremente, et per adornamento, si che per causa di giovare al putto come ben ho fatto, et a la mia sodisfatione; me ne andai dico ad acomodarlo in Bologna in dozina de Padri de Servi nel qual convento vi si legge quotidianamente et si disputa; et ivi son statto per tal acidente da 15 giorni, si che tra l'andare, tornare et stare, appena posso dire d'essere gionto in Venetia nel cui mio arrivo la detta prima di V. S. Ill.ma mi fu consegnata; et se questa presente seconda hor hora dalla posta riceuta non havessi hauto, come debitore ch'io ero in rispondere alla humanissima lettera di V. S. Ill.ma per questo presente coriere che si ritorna, havevo determinato far sapere a V. S. Ill. quanto anco al presente ho a lei di sopra narato; Spero come gentiliss.ma acetterà la mia vera scusa per legittima; assicurandola certo che se a tempo io havessi hauto la prima lettera et che io non fossi stato da urgenti necessita impedito di già haverei mandato ad effetto quanto si e dignata comandarmi. Ma poichè V. S. Ill.ma si contenta haver il ballo per questa Pascha, siano sicura d'haverlo, ne farei questo così gran mancamento apresso di me di non far tutto ch'io possa per servirla per mantenermi tanto suo Servitore con li effetti quanto faccio professione d'esserle et in voce et in iscritto. Dio N. S. conceda il colmo d'ogni compita felicita a V. S. Ill.ma alla quale per fine faciole riverenza et li bacio le honorate mani da Venetia il 9 febraio 1619.

D. V. S. Ill.ma

Ser.re devotissimo

Claudio Monteverdi.

XIX. AL SEGRETARIO DUCALE ERCOLE MARIGLIANI (?)

Ill. mio Sig.re et padron Coll.mo

Poichè V. S. Ill.ma mi concede gratia di un poco di tempo in scrivere la musica sopra alle bellissime parole di V. S. Ill.ma accetterò il favore, per li

*affari della settimana santa ch'io havero in Santo Marco et per le feste ancora,
che certamente non sono pochi al maestro di capella in tali tempi, oltre che
potrei ancora star meglio di sanita di quello che al presente mi ritrovo, et sto
aspettando il bon tempo per far un poco di una purghetta, così il Sig.
Medico mi ha consigliato allora poi mi trovero libero et sano se piacera a Dio, che
saran due cause da tre levate qual non m'impediranno ricevere il favore di
servire a V. S. Ill'ma che tanto bramo, et alla quale sono tanto tenuto et obligato, che per fine facio humiliss.ma riverenza pregandole da N. S. ogni
compita felicità. Da Venetia il 7 marzo 1619.*

    D. V. S. Ill.ma

Ser.re di vero core
Claudio Monteverdi.

[Anno 1620]

XX. Al Conte Alessandro Striggio.

    Ill.mo mio Sig.re et padron Coll.mo

*Ho ricevuto la carissima lettera di V. S. Ill.ma ma così tardi dal coriere
che apena ho potuto haver tempo da scrivere la presente in risposta, non che
per mettermi al ordine, et manco per pigliar licenza dal Seren.mo et Sig.ri
Ecc.mi Procuratori miei padroni come e di necessario sempre fare, che sa bene
V. S. Ill.ma che chi è servo convien vivere sotto ubidienza; oltre che di sanità
potrei anco star meglio, perchè non poco ho faticato questo carnevale; si che
me ne piange il core non poter ubidire a suoi comandi più per mostrar effetti
che li sono ubidiente servitore; che sperare al presente sicurezza d'effetto di
quel ch'io bramo, che è il poter una volta godere certamente quelle terre che il
Ser.mo Sig.r Ducca Vincenzo si degno promettermi in donatione, poichè dal
singolar ufficio che per me si e degnata fare presso il Ser.mo dico ufficio tale che
mi terra per sin ch'io vivo obligato a V. S. Ill.ma ho visto sicome il solito bona
speranza di futuro V. S. Ill.ma havervi tratto; ma non già come ho sempre
bramato e come tutta via bramo, potere havere il presente; poichè le formate
sue parole sono queste cioè; e se bene non cavai all'hora risolutione presi tuttavia
grande speranza, che venendo ella in qua questo Carnevale sia per ottenere lo
intento; risposta Sig.r Ill.mo che sempre per mia disgratia da la Sereniss.ma
Casa Gonzaga ho hauto, perche sempre ho ottenuto il futturo ma non già il
presente onde che ne resto così impaurito, che se mi fosse statto concesso dal
tempo et da la sanita il poter ubidire alli presenti comandi di V. S. Ill.ma io
son di certo che sarei ritornato, con le solite speranze in maniera; et haverei
riportato come feci anche la passata volta sospitione di cangiar padrone poichè
fu messo in pensiero qui al Ser.mo che io ero venuto a Mantova per muttar
servitio, ne durai poca fatica in levarle tal suspetto; mi fara dunque gratia*

V. S. Ill.ma perdonarmi se non vengo di lungo al ubidienza de suoi comandi, per l'impedimenti detti, et poichè si è degnata honorarmi di promessa di presentare a nome mio a Madama Ser.ma li miei madregali; ecco li inviati a mio suocero qual li vera a portare a V. S. Ill.ma et la servira sino da Madama; et la supplico a far mia scusa sopra le ragioni de li impedimenti di sopra narateli et farli fede ch'io le vivo honoratiss.mo et devotiss.mo servitore, et mi racomando nel mio genotio, alla infinita bonta del A. S. sua. Ecco la sinfonia per amore; et l'altra per la entrata se in altro mi conosce bono V. S. Ill.ma per l'amor di Dio mi facci degno de suoi honorati comandi che maggior favore non potro ricevere dalla buona mia fortuna; et qui basandole con tutto l'affetto del core le mani da Dio li prego il colmo d'ogni felicità. Da Venetia il 22 febraio 1620.

D. V. S. Ill.ma

Ser.re obblig.mo

Claudio Monteverdi.

XXI. AL MEDESIMO.

Ill.mo mio Sig.re e padron Coll.mo

Havero tanto obligo a V. S. Ill.ma in vitta mia che se io spendessi si può dire il sangue mi conosco certamente che non pagherei il debito, pregherò Dio per sempre che colà dove non potranno le debil forze mie voglia sua Divina Maesta entrar in mio aiuto. La carissima lettera di V. S. Ill.ma mi è pervenuta tardi alle mani, si che mi fara gratia darmi tempo persino al venturo ordinario ch'io possa pensare sopra al secondo capo di essa, se ben sia certissimo che passando per le mani di V. S. Ill.ma non potrebbe havere se non fine di mio meglio et di mia quiete nulla di meno mi sara favore sommo che ella si contenti per l'ordinario che viene de la risposta; supplicandola pero, che tal proposta fattami dalla infinita bonta di S. A. S. o riussendo o no l'effetto, nulla sia penetrata da qual si voglia cantore ne sonatore ne da altro de la professione musica di S. A. S. facendola certa che non tantosto l'haverebbero intesa quanto anco di subbito l'haverebbero qui a Venetia publicata, et tutto riuscirebbe a danno mio; Et questa fu una de le principal cause che nulla volsi trattare di detto negotio con il Sig.r D. Francesco Dognazzi di quando a questo novembre passato si trovo qui in Venetia, con questo segnalato favore di farmi da parte di S. A. S. che fu medesimamente l'offerirmi il servitio, ma egli per essere de la professione per conseguenza poteva haver passione ne così ritenente in se il tutto che non passo troppo dopo la sua partita che mi pervenne al orecchia, che era sparso voce che tornavo a Mantoa ma di più già un mese fa lasciandomi intendere che ritornate le loro Altezze da Casale volevo portarle a presentar li detti miei libri; Il Sig. Ill. Premicerio filiolo del Ecc.mo Sig.r Procuratore mio Sig. de Cà Cornari ', mi disse questo vostro andare di Mantova, si crede sia per andarle

*a stare. Et questo forsi e statto uno de migliori capi che mi ha tenuto a non portar
in persona detti libri perchè caro Sig.re mi deve essere più cara la sostanza
che l'acidente, Hor che il negotio si trova in mano di V. S. Ill.ma che a tutte
le qualita che si aspetta al trattare tutto con mio utile, et senza alcuno mio
danno, perciò nel venturo ordinario, dirolle il pensier mio, cercando di poggiarlo
sopra a così fatto giusto, che quando non riuscisse spererò che non sia per aportarmi
ponto di danno ne al presente mio servitio, ne apresso alla gratia di S. A. S.
la quale honoro et riverisco quanto ogni mio bene maggiore che possa havere
a questo mondo; Ho inteso la riuscita che ha fatto quelle mie deboli notte, aiutate
protette et solevate dal molto et infinito merito delle bellissime parole di V. S.
Ill.ma non men ammirate et honorate da questi Sig.ri Ill.mi di quello che da
me hora son predicate, et lo dico di vero et real core, et non meno solevate alla
gratia di S. A. S. altrettanto dalla infinita bonta di V. S. Ill.ma che però con
ragione li dovero anco essere per sempre obligato che nel modo di sopra ho narato
a V. S. Ill.ma alla quale facio humil riverenza et da Dio li prego con ogni caldo
affetto il colmo d'ogni felicita aspettando ricevere dalla larga mano di lei
per quanto si e degnata promettermi nella sua per lo venturo ordinario. Da
Venetia li 8 marzo 1620.*

D. V. S. Ill.ma

Oblig.mo Ser.re
Claudio Monteverdi.

XXII. Al Medesimo.

Ill.mo mio Sig.re et Pat.ne Coll.mo

*Vengo a rispondere al capo secondo de la lettera di S.V.Ill. ma sopra al
quale pigliai tempo di risposta sino al presente ordinario. Dico dunque a V.S.
Ill.ma per prima cosa che l'honore singolare che ha fatto S.A.S. alla persona
mia in farmi questa singolar gratia di offerirmi di bel novo il servitio suo mi è
stato così grato al animo et di così fatto favore che mi confesso non haver lingua
che possa esprimere così signalata gratia, essendo che gli anni miei spesi di
mia gioventù a quel S.mo servitio hannomi così fattamente radicato nel cuore
una memoria di obligo et di benevolenza et di riverenza verso quella S.ma casa
che sino che haverò vita pregherò Dio per quella, et li bramerò quella maggior
felicità che servitore a quella inchinato et obligato possa augurarle et bramarle.
Et certam.te che se io non havessi altro riguardo che a me medesimo solo, s'as-
sicuri V.S.Ill. che sarei sforzato a volare s'io potessi, non che correre alli comandi di S.A.S. senza altro pensamento ne altra pretentione, ma havendo et
questa S.ma Repub.ca et filioli che mi sforzano a pensar seconda cosa per tanto
sopra a questi duoi capi mi concederà ch'io possa far un poco di discorso credendo
anco aiuto parimente dalla bontà di V.S.Ill. sopra a ciò sapendo quanto nella*

prudenza ella molto vaglia et nel carità fraterna. Metterò dunque in considera-
tione a V.S.Ill. come che questa S.ma Republica mai a qual altro per avanti
mio antecessore o sij stato Adriano o Cipriano, o Zarlino od altro, ha datto
che ducento ducati di salario et a me ne da 400, favore che non deve così di
leggero da me essere passato senza non poca consideratione, poichè Ill. S.re questa
S.ma S.ia non innova una cosa senza una ben pesata consideratione, onde che
(torno) questa particolar gratia deve da me essere molto ben risguardata, nè
dopo fattami non se ne sono mai pentiti anzi mi hanno honorato et mi honorano
tuttavia in così fatta guisa che in capella non si accetta cantore che prima
non piglino il parere del M.ro di capella, ne vogliono altra relatione di cause
di cantori che quella del M.ro di capella, nè accettano, nè organisti ne Vice
M,ro se non hanno il parere et la relatione da esso M.ro di capella, nè vi è
Gentilhomo che non mi stimi et honori, et quando vado a far qualche musica o
sia da camera o chiesa, giuro a V.S.Ill. che tutta la città corre. Il servitio
poi è dolcissimo poichè tutta la capella è sottoposta al ponto, eccetto il M.ro
di capella, anzi che in man sue sta il far pontare et dispontare il cantore, il
dar licenza o no, et se non va in capella non vi è chi altro dichi; et la provigion
sua è certa sin alla morte, nè la disturba morte nè di Procuratori nè di Principe
et sempre con il servire fedeliss.te et con riverenza sta pretendendo maggior-
mente, et non per lo contrario, et li denari de le sue paghe se a suo tempo non
le va a pigliare li vengono sino a casa portate; et questo è il primo rispetto in
quanto al essentiale, vi è mo l'accidentale, che è, che di stravagante con mio
comodo guadagno fuori di S. Marco, pregato et ripregato da Sig.ri Guardiani
di scole, da 200 ducati al anno, perchè chi puo havere il M.ro di capella in far
le loro musiche, oltre al pagamente di trenta, anco di 40 et sino a 50 ducati,
per dui vespri et una messa, non mancano di pigliarlo, et li rendono anco gratie
di belle parole dopo. Hor V.S.Ill. pesa mo con la bilanza del suo purgatissimo
giuditio quel tanto che ella mi ha offerto a nome di S.A.S.ma, et vegga se con
vero et real fondamento potrei fare il cambio o no, et per prima consideri di
gratia V.S.Ill. che danno mi darebbe nella reputatione presso questi Ill.mi
Sig.ri, et a S.A. medesima s'io consentissi che questi presenti dinari ch'io mi
ritrovo in mia vita si cambiassero in quelli della Thesoreria di Mantoa, che
mancano alla morte del Principe o a suo minimo disgusto, lasciandone di più
450 di Mantova ch'io mi trovo havere da questa Thesoreria di Venetia, per
venirne a pigliare 300 come haveva quel S.r Santi. Che cosa con ragione contro
di me non direbbero questi Sig.ri? È vero che ella mi agionge ancora di più
da parte di S.A.S. 150 scudi di terre quali saranno libere mie, ma a questo
rispondo, che non occore che il S.mo mi dona quello che è mio, non saranno 150
ma si bene 50, poichè li 100 di già mi deve S.A., onde non occorre mettere in
conto quello che di già un altra volta da me con sudore et infinita fatica aquistato;
si che non sarebbero in tutto che 350, et qui me ne ritrovo 450 et 200 altri di
straordinario. Perciò vegga V.S.Ill. che il mondo senza altro direbbe contro
di me molto, et se non fossero altri, che cosa non direbbe una Adriana, un suo
fratello, un Campagnolo, un D.n Passano, che sono sino ad hora molto et molto

più riconosciuti et meritati? Et che vergogna non haverei io di loro vedendoli stati meritati più di me? La città poi di Venetia? Lo lascio considerare a V.S. Ill. Fu miglior partito che mi offerse S.A.S. per bocca del S.r Campagnolo, di quando mi trovai nella morte del S.r Santi a Mantova, alloggiato in casa di detto S. Campagnolo che fu 300 scudi d'entrata di terre, 200 de quali havessero da intendersi miei sino alla morte et 100 per pagamento del mio livello o donatione et perchè dissi di non voler haver che fare con la Tesoreria, me ne offerse altre 200 di pensione, che in tutto venevano ad essere da 600 di Mantoa, et hora vorrebbe S.A.S. che mi rivolvessi a manco di gran lunga, con andar dal S.r Thesoriere ogni dì a suplicarlo che me dasse il mio? Dio me ne guardi. Non ho in vita mia patito maggior affitione di animo di quella di quando mi bisognava andar a dimandare il mio quasi per l'amor di Dio al S.r Thesoriere, mi contenterei piuttosto andar cercando che tornar a simile impertinenza. Prego V.S.Ill. a perdonarmi s'io parlo liberamente, et si compiacia per questa volta et per amor mio, che li sono servitore di vero core, di ascoltarmi con la parte della sua infinita umanità, no con la parte de' suoi singolari meriti. Il S.r Ecc.mo Procuratore Landi quando insieme con li altri S.ri Ecc.mi forno col crescermi 100 altri ducati, disse quel S.re le formate parole: S.r Ecc.mo collega, chi vole il servitore honorato bisogna anco tratarlo honoratem.te. Si che se il S.r duca ha pensiero che mi habbia a vivere honoratamente, è il giusto che in tal maniera mi tratti, se anche non lo supplico a non scomodarmi, poichè stò honoratamente et V.S.Ill. se ne informi. Tacio il capo de filioli, perchè parlando con V.S.Ill. che è ancora lei padre di famiglia, sa benessimo che risguardo bisogna che habbi un padre che ha desiderio, et che deve per legge di natura havere per honore di se medesimo, et de la casa che resta adietro. La conclusione mia Ill. S.re è questa, che in quanto a Claudio, di già si mette in tutto et per tutto al volere et comando di S.A.S. in quanto mo con li rispetti detti considerato, non può con honor suo mutare se non muta in meglio, atiò potesse licentiarsi da questi Ecc.mi S.ri con sua real sodisfatione, essendo stato da essi S.ri così honorato et favorito, per non essere anco burlato da chi con poco merito ha meritato molto, et non essere biasimato nè dal mondo nè da filioli. Et ben potrebbe S.A.S. con sua comodità, hora essendo passato a miglior vita il S.r Ill. Vescovo di Mantoa con pensione sodisfare et con un poco più di terre, senza mettere il Monteverdi alli disgusti di Thesoreria, et alla incertezza di quella. Quattro cento scudi di Mantoa insomma di pensione et 300 di terre sarebbero pochi S.A.S, et a Claudio il suo vero et real riposo, et che forse adimanda impossibilitate? Adimanda insomma anco di manco di quello haveva una Adriana et forse di una Settimia, et adimanda quello che di presente si trova. Altro non vi scorge di diferenza che quel poco di stabile, che pure è il dovere che lassi qualche cosetta a filioli, et se li lascierà di quello donato dalla S.ma Casa Gonzaga anco sarà ad honore perpetuo di quella per haver aiutato un servitore di cotanti anni, ne forse anco sprezzato da Principi. Et se questo troppo a S.A.S. mì honori di farmi segnare le mie poche terre, che io me ne starò nel capitale, poichè li 400 ducati che qui mi trovo sono come pensione, et S.A.S. haverà il

servitore bell'è pagato, che se si degnarà comandarle, vedrà che per servire, di bella mezza notte si leverà dal letto par far maggiormente l'ubedienza. Mi perdoni V.S.Ill. s'io son stato troppo longo altro non mi resta di presente che non le viscere del core ringratiar V.S.Ill. del singolar favore fattomi in haver presentato li miei madrigali a quella S.ma Sig.ra, et son certo che per l'honoratis.mo mezzo di V.S.Ill. saranno stati molto più acessi et grati Dio agionga per me dove io non posso in felicitar la honoratissima persona di V.S. Ill.mo alla quale con tutto l'affetto del core nel l'inchino e bacio le mani... Da Venetia il 13 marzo 1620.
D.V.S. Ill.ma

S.re Ob.mo.
Claudio Monteverdi.

XXIII. Al Medesimo.

Ill.mo mio Sig.re et padron Coll.mo

Io non so se haverò fatto bene o no ad haver scritta la presente a Madama Seren.ma in ringratiamento di così signalato favore che si è degnata farmi me nè il mezzo della particolar petitione di V. S. Ill.ma con lo havermi mandato a donare quella bella collana per il coriere ; mi farà gratia V.S. Ill.ma darliene una occhiata et quando che ella giudica essere a proposito supplicare V.S. Ill.ma farla tirare et presentargliela ; quando che nò, supplico degnarsi di complire con la sua conpitezza al mio bisogno, ringratiandone l'A.S.S da parte mia, con quel maggior affetto che può.

Supplico anco V. S. Ill.ma far il simile ufficio verso il Ser.mo Sig.r Duca mio Singolar Signore ; come principal mittore di così signalata gratia.

Invio a V. S. Ill.ma il rimanente dell'Arianna, se più havessi hauto tempo più diligentemente sarebbe statta da me revista et forsi anco di gran lunga migliorata ; non mancherò alla giornata di far qualche cosa in tal genere di canto rapresentativo, et più volontieri se ella maggiormente con suoi bellissimi versi me ne farà degno, per mostrar segni di questo animo mio quanto brama mantenersi nella gratia di quell'A. S., et quanto brama essere favorito da le singola virtù di V. S. Ill.ma.

Non posso più di quel che io sono essere obbligato a V.S. Ill.ma per li singolari favori che per sua nobil mano ogni giorno vado ricevendo et perchè molto più eccedono le gratie al mio merito perciò, in quel ch'io non posso io prego Dio che per me complisca in meritare V. S. Ill.ma in ogni compito et felicità alla quale con ogni riverenza bacio le mani. Da Venetia il 4 aprile 1620.
D. V. S. Ill.ma

Ser.re obblig.mo
Claudio Monteverdi.

XXIV. Al Medesimo.

Ill.mo mio Sig.re et padron Coll.mo

Infiniti favori vado ricevendo dalla larga mano di V. S. Ill.ma ogni momento, cosi tanto più ogni giorno vado anch'io conoscendomi obligato alle nobili maniere di V. S. Ill.ma potessi io far andar dal pari l'effetto con l'affetto, che forsi sarei più degno de comandi di V. S. Ill.ma di quel ch'io mi sono, ma la fortuna mi va tormentando con questo bel modo mentre che mi fa degno de favori et non di merito. Ho ricevuto una benignissima risposta alla lettera mia dalla infinita bontà di Madama Ser.ma che bastava sola questa singolar gratia a farmele perpetuo servitore per forza, non che altro riconoscimento; ma non son così poco conoscitore del vero ch'io non sappia che la maggior parte del credito mio presso la gratia di S. A. S. nasce dalla singolar protetione di V. S. Ill.ma che perciò non men, devo restarne obligato a V. S. Ill.ma per riconoscimento di favore, di quello devo a S. A. S. per riconoscimento di padronanza. Vorò molto più sperare per l'avenire apoggiato sopra la gratia di S. A. S. et quella di V. S. Ill.ma di quello la fatte per lo passato in credere d'esserne fatto degno di quel poco di fondo ch'io mi pretendo. Per gratia non per merito dalla gran mano del Ser.mo Sig.re Ducca di Mantoa altretanto benigno Sig.re quanto giusto, et uno sperare una volta avanti mi mora poter godere di quella gratia che la benignità del Serenissimo Sig.r Ducca Vincenzo che sia in gloria mi fece virtuosa risolutione è stata quella del Ser.mo Sig.r Ducca che ha fatto in lasciar che l'Arianna et parimente quell'altra compositione del Sig.r Zeferino, non siano poste in sena in così poco tempo perchè realmente il presto è nemico troppo a tali ationi essendo che il senso dell'udito e troppo comune et troppo delicato, tanto più al sindicato dove habbi da entrare le presenze de Gran Prencipi pari suoi et con molta prudenza Madama Ser.ma ha terminato nel balletto perchè basta la presenza di gran soggetto a dar il bisogno a simil feste; ma ne l'altre non va così. Che puoi habbi datto occasione al Sig.r Zazzarini che anch' egli si possa mostrare servitore di merito de la gratia di S. A. S. ha tutti li requesiti che ella mi scrive non tanto, ma la dolce et virtuosa emulazione darà occasione maggiore di far altra cosa ali altri per mettersi in gratia che senza la cognitione de la via non si può arrivare a porto determinato, l'affetto però di V. S. Ill.ma che ella mi va mostrando per tutte le vie l'assicuro che mi va infinitamente più stringendo nel nodo de la servitù.

S'io sono anco ardito in accettar la gratia tanto a me bisognevole al presente per servitio de filioli più che per me; che ella per sua spontanea volontà mi offerisce in questa gentilissima sua lettera, qual' è che mio suocero si lassi vedere da Sua Sig.ria Ill. che procurerà che li sia pagato quel mio bollettino che tiene egli in mano al presente, incolpi il mio molto bisogno et la sua gentil natura, che l'uno ma fatto ardito et l'altro spinto, et non l'ardir mio proprio perchè non sapevo pur troppo d'haverla discomodata. Verà dunque mio suocero da lei et li perdoni il discomodo. Et con questo facendo a V. S. Ill. humiliss.ma

riverenza da Dio prego con il più vivo del core a V. S. Ill.ma ogni vero contento.
Da Venetia il 19 maggio 1620.
    D. V. S. Ill.ma

Ser.re obblig.mo
Claudio Monteverdi.

XXV. Al Medesimo.

Ill.mo mio Sig.re et padron Coll.mo

Hora che sono passate le mie fatiche di Santo Marco ne mi verranno a ri-trovare per sino ad ogni Santi trovandomi in tale poca di libertà non tanto mai spinto anco dal bisogno accidentalmente natomi che è statto, che Francesco mio filiolo di età di venti anni credendo tra un anno o poco più vederlo dottorato in legge inaspettatamente ha fatto risolutione in Bologna andar frate de la Religione de padri Carmelitani Scalzi riformati; per lo che tra il viaggio nel andar a Milano et ne li abbiti da frate mi ha fatto un debito adosso di più di cinquanta scudi havevo perciò et per l'occasione et per il bisogno fatto riso-lutione di venirmene a Mantova per veder d'havere da la bontà di S.A.S. que pochi denari ch'io mi avanzo; ma avanti la mia venuta già otto giorni sono ne diedi prima parte a mio suocero, et egli havendomi scritto in questa presente posta essere stato da V. S. Ill.ma; et lui haverli accennato che senza che mi scomodassi, et che venissi a patire per il viaggio in questi caldi, che havendoli hora di comissione di S. A. S. da pagare la musica che m'haverebbe honorato di far opera che il mio bollettino anco fosse pagato, et credendo più tosto che il detto mio messere ciò havesse detto perchè sa che qui meco si trova Massimigliano verso il quale temo che poco affetto li porta perchè è putto che sa il suo che dubi-tando non lo conducesse meco havesse d'haver disgusto; sferzato dal bisogno detto di sopra, non ho potuto di meno che non scriver la presente a V.S. Ill.ma supplicandola che mi honori di accennarmi se senza che mi venghi a Mantova potrò essere agratiato di tali denari, in questo presente mese, che se sarà così, mi fermerò, se non anche per non perdere la comodità del poter venire, piglierei la congiuntura del mio tempo libero et venerei a supplicare S.A.S. così sforzato in verità dal mio molto bisogno sperando che dovendoli io adoperare per aiutar quel putto che e andatto a così santa vita, et questo altro alli studi ambidui sudditi suoi, non mi mancherebbe di così giusta gratia. So d'essere et essere maggiormente stato importuno a V.S. Ill.ma per li tanti travagli che gli ho datto, ma assicuro V.S. Ill. che arrossito per li ditti, mi sarà levato l'ardire d'importunarla, ancora che sia sicurissimo che la sua gentilezza mai manche-rebbe del suo naturale verso ad ogni uno specialmente verso me che mi ha datto V.S. Ill. tanti segni d'essere sicuro della honorata gratia sua; nella quale prego Dio che sempre mi mantenghi et che insieme feliciti et conservi la persona di

V.S. Ill.ma alla quale per fine faccio humil riverenza et bacio le mani. Da Venetia li 11 luglio 1620.
D. V. S. Ill.ma

Ser.re Devot.mo et oblig.mo
Claudio Monteverdi.

XXVI. Al Medesimo.

Ill.mo mio Sig.re et Padron Coll.mo

Se V. S. Ill.ma non sarà quella che mi honori de suoi bramati comandi, confesserami a lei (così sarà forza) sempre avvinto d'un nodo indissolubile di infinito obligo per così segnalata et a me importante gratia; che ella mi ha ottenuto appresso alla gratia di S. A. S. Ma come potrei anco all'hora adimandarmi slegato se li comandi di V. S. Ill.ma m'apporterebbero et favori et honori; Iscusa V. S. Ill.ma questo povero animo mio che più vorrebbe di quello che non può; non li sarà però distolto mai d'alcuno la conoscenza d'esserle servitore di vero core; Se havessi saputo d'incontrar nel gusto di S. A. S. in qualche piccola parte et parimenti in quello di V.S. Ill.ma creddami al certo che di già 15 giorni fa sarei venuto volando a Mantova. Ma la mia buona fortuna così non mi ha voluto acompagnare, mi resterò non tanto perchè l'occasione (come ella ben mi accenna) non sarebbe più in pronto, quanto che mi s'aggionge il bisogno di servire a questa Seren.ma Repubblica dimani che sarà alli 20 del presente alla chiesa del Salvatore, giorno celebrato da questa Ser.ma Repubblica in memoria d'una gratia ricevuta dalla man di Dio, che fu la liberatione de la città da una crudel peste; Ho tocco a mio suocero del favore particolare che V. S. Ill.ma mi ha fatto presso S. A. S. non so se egli pctrà restare che non si lassi vedere da lei, per essere indrizzato di quanto doveva fare atiò si possa godere de la bramata gratia; iscussando il mio bisogno, et il desiderio grande che ha il povero homo in farmi servitio, se forsi in tal lasiarsi vedere a V. S. Ill.ma aportasse qualche mira che del tutto maggiormente ne terrò infinito obbligo alla cortese natura di V. S. Ill.ma alla quale con ogni affetto di core pregole da Dio il colmo d'ogni felicità mentre che li faccio riverenza et li bacio le mani. Da Venetia il 19 luglio 1620.
D. V. S. Ill.

Serv.re obblig.mo
Claudio Monteverdi.

XXVII. Al Medesimo.

Ill. mio Sig.re et Padron Coll.mo

Piaccia a Dio ch'io mi sia nato servitore di quel merito in servirla, ch'ella è nata a me padrone in sempre favorirmi et honorarmi, quando ch'io mi penso haver pur troppo ricevuto da la cortesissima sua mano, in haver ricevuto la comissione tanto da me desiderata di que pochì denari per potermene servire nel bisogno urgente de miei filioli che non manca con la pressa del tempo darmene ogni diligente aricordo, ecco che mi agionge V. S. Ill.ma novo avviso di novo favore, che è statto che queste deboli notte mie ch'anno servito ben con grand'animosi ma con debole forze, alla bellissima egloga di V.S. Ill.ma di bel novo siano statte et da S. A. S. et da V. S. Ill.ma doppiamente honorate et lodate, giudica lei che obbligo deve esser questo mio, verso V. S. Ill.ma. Ma se in altro non potrò, cercherò di pregar Dio con ogni affetto che entri in mio soccorso, a prestar ogni gratia et felicità alla honoratissima et gentilissima persona di V. S. Ill.ma alla quale faccio humilissima riverenza. Ho scritto al Sig. Iacomo mio suocero, che si lassi vedere da V. S. Ill.ma si come ella me ne ha comesso, et se per accaso V. S. Ill.ma restasse da la sua solecitudine forse qualche poco noiata, incolpa et la gentilezza di lei che così ha comandato et il mio molto bisogno che così mi sprona. Da Venetia il 24 luglio 1620.

D. V. S. Ill.ma

Ser.re obblig.mo
Claudio Monteverdi.

XXVIII. Al Medesimo.

Ill.mo mio Sig.re et padron Coll.mo

Desiderano li Sig.ri Milanesi oltre modo haver il Sig.r D. Francesco Dognazzi per honorar maggiormente la loro festa di Santo Carlo che sarà alli 4 del venturo, ma più di loro io, poichè mi hanno pregato ad haver tal carica, et desiderandomi far honore per questo oltre la preghiera di questi Signori agiongo la mia con ogni caldo effetto, supplicando V. S. Ill.ma se acadesse l'occasione presso la bona mente di S. A. S. di qualche preghiera per lasciarlo venire, vogliami anco in questo obligare (se più posso essere obligato alli infiniti favori riceuti da V. S. Ill.ma) di facilitare tal strada atiò esso Sig. D. Francesco possa venire a Venetia per otto giorni et non per più qual allogiarà in casa mia. Caro Sig.re Ill.mo mi perdoni di cotanto incomodo, che se non fosse negotio che mi premesse certamente che non ardirei tanto perchè s'io facessi il fascio di tutti li incomodi datti a V. S. Ill.ma et che bene li mirassi abrugerei di vergogna, ma il bisogno non mi fa veder al presente tanto, solamente che so di certo d'essere a V. S. Ill.

servitore perpetuamente obligato qual con ogni riverenza bacia le mani a V.
S. Ill.ma et da Dio pregole ogni felicità. Da Venetia il 21 ottobre.
D. V. S. Ill.
Sigr. Ill. Conte Alessandro Striggio.

Ser.re oblig.mo
Claudio Monteverdi.

_____

[Anno 1621]
XXIX. Alla Duchessa di Mantova.

Ser.ma Sig.ra et padrona Coll.ma

Trovomi Madama Ser.ma un filiolo di età da 16 anni e mezzo suddito et hu-
milissimo servo di V. A. S. quale hora è uscito dal seminario di Bologna, per
haver in questo finito il corso del humanità et Ret.ca. Vorrei che camminasse
alle altre scienze per dottorarsi in medicina; Egli e statto sotto sempre ad ubi-
dienza di precettori che l'hanno mantenuto, et nel timor di Dio, et nella buona
continuatione de studi; pensando io alla sua vivezza et alla libertà licentiosa
de scolari; per mezzo de la quale cadono molte volte in male compagnie che poi
li distolgono dal dritto camino con molto dolore de padri et perdita grandissima
de detti filioli, per rimediare a questo gran danno che potrebbe nascere, ho pen-
sato che un loco nel Collegio del Sig. Ill.mo Cardinal Mont'Alto che ha in Bo-
logna sarebbe ogni quiete mia et salute del filiolo ma senza una principal mano
in aiuto mio in così gran bisogno, non sarebbe possibile che potessi ottenere così
segnalata gratia, perciò sapendo quanto V. A. S. sij per natura Prencipessa piena
d'infinita humanità verso ogni uno, in particolare a suoi riverenti suddditi come
e questo povero filiolo et servitore benchè minimi come son io; Ho per questo
preso ardire di supplicare V. A. S. con il più vivo del core come faccio et con
ogni più humil riverenza ch'io posso atiò si degni scrivere in raccomandatione
d'un tal loco per detto filiolo in detto collegio di Bologna al detto Sig.r Ill.mo
Cardinal Mont'Alto per poter ricevere così alta gratia, et se di presente tutti
li lochi si trovassero pieni, il primo vacante anche sarebbe a tempo. Supplico
l'A. S. Vostra a perdonarmi il troppo ardire, mentre che con ogni più profonda
riverenza me l'inchino, et li prego con tutto l'affetto del animo mio ogni più
compita felicità. Da Venetia li 7 agosto 1621.
D. V. A. Ser.me

Humiliss.mo et obblig.mo Ser.re
Claudio Monteverdi.

_____

XXX. Al Segretario Ducale Ercole Marigliani.

Molto Ill. mio Sig.re et padron Osser.mo

Invio a V. S. per lo presente ordinario parte del terzo intermedio in musica il rimanente spererò se piacerà a Dio mandarlo per lo venturo, li daffari hauti nella passata et parte de la presente settimana mi hanno tenuto il potere ma non già il volere prontissimo chio tengo in servirla del che la prego a farmi degno di scusa. Ho hauto haviso da Bologna come di già il Sig.r Ill.mo Cardinal Mont'Alto ha riceuto con particolar gusto la preghiera di Madama Seren.ma et mi vien scritto che tengono di fermo che resterò favorito de la gratia, et la risposta si crede sarà o per il presente a futuro ordinario senz'altro; hauta prego V. S. farmi favore de la bona dispositione di esso Sig. Ill.mo atiò mi possa vivere consolato; Ho datto la nova che ho riceuto al putto, et ne ha sentito tanto contento, ancora si trova in stato di doversi poco ralegrare, perchè già otto giorni fa si pose in letto con grandissima febre, et sei giorni fa l'incominciorno a saltar fuori le nuvole, et hora si trova nel colmo, tuttavia però si spera ogni bona riuscita in breve se piacerà a Dio, perchè sono venute alla superfitie molto bene, si che di dentro si sente a star bene et spero che li habbino a servire per una bonissima purga; Altro non mi resta che baciar le mani a V. S. con il maggior affetto del core, et pregarò da Dio ogni felicità, da Venetia li 10 Settem.re 1621.

D. V. S. Ill.ma

Ser.re obblig.mo
Claudio Monteverdi.

XXXI. Alla Duchessa di Mantova.

Seren.ma Sig.ra et padrona Coll.ma

Per la passata inviai al Sig.r Marigliani la licenza in musica de li intermedi che V. A. Ser.ma si degnò comandarmi, et chiesi nova occasione per dovermi affaticare, mi rispose Sua Sig.ria non voler altro al presente. Vengo pertanto con questa mia a piedi di V. A. Ser.ma a ringratiarla con il più interno del core, dell' honore riceuto dal detto comando di V.A. Ser.ma offerendomeli per humilissimo Ser.re, se occorresse concertarli tali detti intermedi et nella variatione de ustrimenti, sinfonie, et proprietate de voci, ne mancherei insieme offerire alla infinita humanità di V.A.S. una messa solenne in musica quando che ciò gustasse di agradire, et quando ch'el' A. S. V. altro non comandi la supplico con ogni più humil riverenza ch'io so et posso dignarsi di tenermi nel numero de più humili si, ma ben devoti et riverenti Serv.ri di V. A. S., alla quale con ogni più profonda riverenza ch'io so et posso humilmente me l'inchino,

*et da Dio con il più vivo del core pregoli ogni più compita felicità. Da Venetia
li 27 novembre* 1621.
   D. V. A. Ser.ma

> *Humiliss.mo et oblig.mo. Ser.re*
> *Claudio Monteverdi.*

[ANNO 1622]

XXXII. ALLA MEDESIMA.

Ser.ma Sig.ra et padrona Coll.ma

*Il padre Reverendo frate Cesare mio cognato venuto da Alessandria di Egitto,
havendomi donato un simiottino qual da molti gentil' homini è stato lodato per
la non così usata vista del pelo; ho per questo preso ardire di venire a piedi
del A. V. S. con ogni più riverente affetto supplicandola si vogli degnare di
agradirlo; so che doverebbe assai essere più bello, per sodisfare maggiormente al
nobilissimo gusto dell'A. V. Ser.ma, ma sperando nella infinita humanità sua,
spererò insieme che mi honorerà di agradire in sua vece il riverente animo mio,
qual con ogni maggior caldezza d'affetto prega Dio che sempre feliciti l'A.
V. S., et con ogni riverenza maggiore se l'inchina. Da Venetia li* 15 *aprile* 1622.
   D. V. A. Ser.ma.

> *Humiliss.mo et oblig.mo Ser.re*
> *Claudio Monteverdi.*

XXXIII. AL CONTE ALESSANDRO STRIGGIO.

Ill.mo mio Sig.re et padron Coll.mo

*Il Sig.r Ill.mo Giustiniano Gentil' homo di molta autorità in questa Serenis-
sima Republica et molto mio Signore tre giorni fa mi venne aposta a ritrovare
a casa in compagnia di molti altri Sig.i Ill.mi a nararmi come che non pochi
giorni fa fece scrivere et scrisse al Sig.re Lelio Andreini comico ació si dispo-
nesse con la Sig.ra Florinda insieme et tutta la compagnia sua a venire a
Venetia a recitar comedie nel suo loco publico, intendendo però che il Serenissimo non se ne volesse prevalere che in tal caso s'intendeva nulla voler trattare; hebbe per riposta che era prontissimo tanto più che il sig. Ducca di già
si era lassiato intendere non se ne voler prevalere, mancava solamente che
Arlechino dicesse di sì, senza il quale per non perdere di riputatione dovendo
recitare in loco, ove recitarà anco Fritelino (però in altra stanza) non con-
sentiva venire così; questo Sig. Ill.mo fece scrivere a detto Arlechino et hebbe
per risposta che quando S. A. S. non lo havesse adoperato et che insieme li havesse*

concesso bona licenza che sarebbe venuto intendendo però ancora lui quando però li fosse venuto un tal dottore Gratiano che hora si trova in Savoia ; Et mentre questo Sig.re va vedendo con il negotiamento di mettere il tutto a segno, Ecco il Sig.r Lelio che li scrive una lettera che in quanto alla persona sua è prontissima a servirla, et che se li condona servitore humilissimo ma che fa sapere però a Sua Sig.ria Ill.ma come che la Sig.ra Florinda non vol recitare, et che egli ha fatto pensiero di farsi istrione solo in altre compagnie ancora per duoi anni ; et non più capo di compagnia vedendo cotanti sinistri acadere et disturbi nel voler reggere compagnia ; per la qual lettera havendo concluso questo Sig.r Ill.mo il detto negotio essere quasi a terna ; sapendo quanto sia io servit.re humilissmo a quella Sereniss. Altezza et a V. S. Ill.ma mi ha caldamente pregato con insieme quelli altri Sig.ri che erano in sua compagnia, che voglia con una mia (ogni volta però che S. A. S. non sii per prevalersene) pregar instantemente V. S. Ill.ma a disporre questo Sig. Lelio atiò favorischi questo Signore, il quale Sig.r Lelio se si volesse iscusare sopra al mancamento de le parti di sua compagnia, questo Sig.r li offerisse et Gratiano et Zanni, et Dottore, et ogni altra parte che potesse mancare. Vengo pertanto a supplicar V. S. Ill.ma anzi per dir meglio vengo a pregare la infinita gentilezza di V. S. Ill.ma che mi honori di pregar V. S. Ill.ma si vogli degnare passar quest'ufficio di preghiera con il detto Sig.r Lelio atiò si disponghi venire a favorire questo Sig.r Ill.mo che lo ritrovara pieno di cortesie verso la persona di esso Sig.r Lelio, et con donativi et pagamento di viaggio et altro, et che meni anco la Sig.ra Florinda et altri che a lui parerà et non volendo mette in consideratione ad esso signor Lelio che per le sue speranze di già con lettere dattele sarà restato et di cercar altra compagnia et che il suo teatro resterà per lui di non far comedia disgusto qual egli si potrà immaginare. L'autorità di V. S. Ill.ma so sarà quella che acomoderà il tutto in bene, et io ne resterò per sempre obbligatissimo a V. S. Ill.ma di così bramato favore qual so appreso di questi Sig.ri Ill.mi mi farà conoscere quanto ella tien cara a presso la sua gratia la mia servitù. Non guardi la supplico al mio debole merito, ma mi scusi lei nella sua gentilezza dignandosi di far adimandar esso Sig.r Lelio. disponendolo con la dolcezza del suo favore, et qui facendole humil riverenza da Dio li prego con tutto l'affetto ogni più bramata felicità. Da Venetia li 21 ottobre 1622.

D. V. S. Ill.ma

Ser.re Devotissimo et obblig.mo

Claudio Monteverdi.

XXXIV. Al Medesimo.

Ill.mo mio Sig.re et padron Coll.mo

L'Ill.mo Signor Giustiniani mio Sig.re e venuto a posta a ritrovarmi in camera proppria questa mattina che ne habiamo 3 del presente a nararmi una certa gelosietta che tiene per causa di dubitatione che Fritellino non si sij affaticato con qualche sue arti per restar solo a Venetia (se ben poco piaciuto) atiò s'intorbidi la venuta, aspettata però molto da tutta la città, de li Comici di Mantoa, essendo che tarda; et maggiormente havendo inteso, il Dottore Gratiano essere statto di gusto tale a S. A. S, che l'ha riconosciuto di un donativo di cento scudi spesa in vita et altro sicuro tratenimento che però incontrandosi tal congiontura di gusto non vorebbe che l'arte del detto Fritellino potesse haver fatto incontro. Dal altro canto havendo di già visto la lettera di V. S. Ill.ma che si degno mandarmi in risposta che assicurava la venuta de detti Comici con bona sodisfatione del Ser.mo et di presente non havendo visto lettere dal coriere portate di niun de detti comici, che però fa sperare che venghino, si è per tanto datto a credere di ricevere il bramato favore. Merita certamente questo Sig.r Ill.mo che S. A. S. in ciò lo consoli, poichè mi credda V. S. Ill.ma che non ha mancato di adoperarsi con ogni diligenza et affetto atiò anco S. A. S. restasse gustata nel haver le parti mandate per empire il bisogno de la compagnia, non solamente s'adoperò in far che venissero quelle prime parti, et maggiormente in far risolvere Franceschina, ma intorno al dottore quale non volendo dire di sì per la via di dolci et instante preghiere, si rosolse per contrario muttar le preghiere in minazze per lo che bisogno che il detto dottore montasse seco in gondola et lo condusse ale baffeterie con pensiero di farvelo condure per forza ma il dottore havendo giurato a Sua Sig.ria Ill.ma che sarebbe venuto sì contento a farlo compagnare solamente per questo essersi Sua Sig.ria Ill.ma con così caldo affetto adoperata et per la promessa che V. S. Ill.ma li fece nella sua promessa in risposta alla mia et per non haver visto lettere in contrario nel presente dispaccio vivi sua Sig.re Ill.ma con bonissima speranza, tuttavia perchè troppo desidera questo favore mi ha di novo comandato sua Sig.ria Ill.ma che torni a pregare V. S. Ill.ma atiò in evento di bisogno lo vogli favorire et quando anco (come creddo) havessero da venire senza altro incomodo di V. S. Ill.ma prega però a volerlo far restar consolato con aviso novo de la certa venuta, la quale anco sarebbe a tempo se fra dieci o quindici giorni fosse come spera. Mi ha soggionto esso Sig.r Ill.mo che se potesse scrivere a V. S. Ill.ma poichè sa bene che questi signori non ponno scrivere a Ministri di Prencipi senza licenza, che di già haverebbe mostrato l'obligo a V. S. Ill.ma che li deve. Et qui di bel novo ripregando la gentilezza di V. S. Ill.ma al favore bramato essendo il Sig.r Ill.mo Giustiniani molto mio Sig.re a Lei le resto et resterò per sempre obbligatiss.mo Ser.re, Et qui facendo riverenza a V. S. Ill. da Dio N. S. le prego il colmo d'ogni maggior felicità. Da Venetia li 3 dicembre 1622.

D. V. S. Ill.ma

Ser.re Devotiss.mo et oblig.mo

Claudio Monteverdi.

XXXV. Al Medesimo.

Ill.mo mio Sig.re et padron Coll.mo

Riceuto che ho dal presente coriere due di V. S. Ill.ma presenti vi era che attendeva quanto ella si degnava scrivere il fattore del Sig.r Ill.mo Giustiniani, le quali subbito lette et datte al detto fattore da portarle a vedere al detto Sig. Ill.mo mi è ritornato alla camera con le dette lettere, et mi ha imposto ch'io scriva a V. S. Ill.ma a nome del Sig.r Ill.mo Giustiniani, che si conosce a lei cotanto obligato come se propriamente havesse ricevuto il favore in effetto, et lo supplica a comandarle se in qualche cosa lo conosce bono in servire et con la vita et con la robba a V. S. Ill.ma, Quanto di novo ricerca dalla gentilezza di V. S. Ill.ma e che havendo inteso che a Mantova si ritrova una compagnia di comici spagnoli, che se con tal bella congiuntura con quel destro modo che sapera usare V. S. Ill.ma si potesse havere lo intento gustandosi forsi S. A. S. de li detti spagnoli più che de li Italiani sarebbe sempre a tempo il favore, desiderando però che il tutto sij fatto con il gusto di V. S. Ill.ma altretanto et maggiormente di più resto a V. S. Ill.ma obligato poichè si è degnata mostrar in carta che non sdegna amare la persona mia anchor che debole a questo mondo per lo che sarò sempre tenuto pregar Dio che feliciti et conservi la persona di V. S. Ill.ma et me che facci degno di meriti de comandi di V. S. Ill.ma atiò con li effetti possa mostrarmi degno servitore di Lei.

Sig.r Ill. già un mese et mezzo fa passò a miglior vita un organista di Santo Marco et poco dopo la detta morte scrissemi il Sig.r Ottavio Bergnani lamentandosi meco che non l'havessi havisato di cotal vacanza per poter adimandar il loco. Li risposi Sig.r Bergnani caro amo V. S. con ogni affetto, ma l'essere V. S. servitore di quel prencipe tanto mio padrone et Sig.re mai haverei pensato non che tentato di servirle tal cosa, che sarebbe statto un desiderar che ella si partisse da questa servitù la quale con tanto riverisco et amo. Mi farà gratia dunque V. S. trattarmi d'ogni altra cosa fuorche di questo. Il negotio così si tacque, ma quando mi creddo che nulla sia, ecco non heri l'altro vengo adimandato in procuratia da Sig.r Procuratori ridotti così gionto di lungo fanno leggere una lettera del Sig.r Bergnani hauta non so d'onde che procura d'haver detto loco che tuttavia sta vacando la quale finita mi adimandò se tal soggetto e bono li rispondo di sì, mi soggiongono che li scriva una lettera da parte de le loro Ecc.ze che li farà a piacere lassiarsi udire, che l'assicurano che se sarà tale quale si offerisce che non faranno torto alla sua virtù, ci sono però anco cinque altri che chieggono detto loco si che sarà necessario il concorso. Io pensando fra me che tal lettera senza prima darne parte a V. S. Ill.ma atiò ne dia parte a sua A. S. ancora potrebbe molto pregiudicarmi a la gratia di S. A. S. la quale stimo et stimerò sinch'io vivo per infiniti rispetti; per tal fondamento ho narato il negotio a V. S. Ill.ma supplicandola ad accenarmi per lo venturo ordinario quello potrò fare con bona gratia di S. A. S., stando che egli accenna nella sua lettera che con bona gratia di S. A. potrebbe venire a servire in Santo Marco, l'ho voluto poner in mano a V.S. Ill.ma perchè so che riuscirà il tutto secre-

tamente, et senza mio disgusto. Et qui facendo a V. S. Ill. humil riverenza da Dio N. S. li prego il felice bon capo d'anno. Da Venetia li 31 dicembre 1622.

D. V. S. Ill.ma

Ser.re oblig.mo

Claudio Monteverdi.

___

XXXVI. AL MEDESIMO.

[ANNO 1623]

Ill.mo mio Sig.re et padron Coll.mo

Il Serenissimo Sig.r Ducca mio Singolar Sig.re si è degnato di farmi intendere per bocca del Sig.r Bergamaschino qual è hora ritornato da Mantoa per Venetia che haverebbe gusto che per l'ordinario venturo mi trovassi in Mantova con condur insieme meco duoi soprani et duoi chitaronisti. Vengo con questa mia a supplicarla si vogli degnare di far sapere a S. A. S. che realmente mi trovo da una dissesa che per causa di purga feci a questo principio di ottobre prossimo passato collatami dalla testa per le spalle et tutta la vita così mal trattato che è necessario che mi facci vestire non potendo io per dolore de mani braccia et piedi quasi aiutarmi, è vero che pare che dij segno di principio di giovamento, nulladimeno però mi trovo più su la parte del male che del bene oltre di ciò mi ci è giunto da tre giorni in qua anco una rilassatione di corpo che non mi lascia quetare, con tutto ciò mettendo insieme il disgusto dell'animo ch'io sento del non poter venire per causa del mal detto, più tosto mi offende questo non potere che il mal stesso; son però tanto desideroso che se niente mi da tempo per il futuro procaccio il male vo credendo d'essere tanto ardito aiutato dal desiderio di servire al A. S. sua, che spero mi mettero in viaggio ma quando che non venghi mi credda V. S. Ill.ma che saro astretto dal male a restare contro ogni mia volià et perciò ne supplico V. S. Ill.ma per l'amor di Dio, quando nasesse il caso come vo più tosto credendo di si che di no porgere questa vera et real scusa al A. S. sua; In quanto al condur soprani mi credda V. S. Ill.ma che non ci è cosa al proposito, ne meno chi soni di chitarone sopra alla parte se non ordinariamente, che però secondo il parer mio non porterebbe la spesa a condur di qui gente ordinaria. Istrumenti da fiato ben si ve ne sono et boni. et se de questi V. S. Ill.ma mi acennera qualche cosa spererei mandarli cosa honestamente bona et circa al bisogno de chitaroni per cosa ordinaria creddo che l'A. S. sua potrebbe restare sodisfatta a Verona per conseguenza con manco spesa ancora; caro padrone V. S. Ill.ma mi scusi di cotanto discomodo, et mi perdoni, li vivo et vivero perpetuamente servitore obblig.mo con pregar Dio che sempre feliciti et conservi la persona di V. S. Ill. alla quale bacio con ogni affetto le mani. Da Venetia li 10 febraro 1623.

D. V. S. Ill.ma

Ser.re obblig.mo

Claudio Monteverdi.

XXXVII. AL DUCA DI MANTOVA.

Ser.mo mio Sig.re Singolar et padron Coll.mo

Vengo a rendere a V. A. S. quelle maggior gratie che mai riverentemente posso con tutto l'animo et tutto il core, del particolar honore che si è degnata farmi, che e statto l'havermi honorato de comandi suoi, quali sempre stimerò mandatemi da la man di Dio per mio maggior honore et fortuna che possi ricevere. Al presente Sere.mo Sig.re qui in Venetia non si trova sogetto al proposito, mi corre però questo acidente per mano di un padre del ordine di Santo Stefano di Venetia cantore di Santo Marco che dieci giorni fa mi disse havere un fratello al servitio del Sig.r Ill.mo Arcivescovo di Salisburgh di età giovanile, castrato, di assai bella voce, et comoda gorgia, et trillo, ma per non esi essere a quel servitio chi lo possa migliorare nella virtute haverebbero a piacere che venesse a stantiare in Venetia quando li fosse occasione di qualche utile; li risposi che lo facesse venire che non haverei mancato di giovarle apresso a Padroni et anche conqualche avertimenti in questa mane apunto avanti ricevessi il Comando di V. A. S. in capella mi ha detto haver scritto, che se ne venga. Hora ch'io so quanto debbo adoperarmi per gusto di V. A. S. non mancherò diligentemente informarmene meglio, et se sarà a proposito non mancherò solecitar il negotio atiò possa mostrar con li effetti oltre il prontissimo animo mio quanto bramo d'esser servitore all'Altezza Vostra Sereniss.ma ne firmandomi in questo solo, non mancherò di investigar altrove altra occasione la quale se mi si rapresenterà subbito ne darò parte a V. A. S. Creddo che il Sig.r Campagnolo come quello che è statto in quelle bande ne poterebbe forsi dar conto all'A. V. S.; alli giorni passati intesi che in Ferrara ve ne era uno che serviva a que' Sig.ri nel Spirito Santo assai di bella voce et boni garbi il quale daseva non ordinaria sodisfatione. Il Sere.mo Sig.r Prencipe di Modona cominciandosi a dilettar di musica come fa, et questo Sig.re non manca di haverne ma con faticare trova per tal fondamento. Non do tutta la credenza a quelli che mi hanno detto di questo di Ferrara, non ho però voluto restare di acenarne a V. A. S. atiò a Dio piacesse potesse essere servita come bramo, et qui faciendo a V. A. S. humilissima et profonda riverenza supplicandola con ogni instanza d'affetto a conservarmi in quella parte di gratia che sol donare a più minimi si ma a più veri et reali servitori dell'A. V. S. alla quale pregole da Dio con il più vivo del core il colmo d'ogni maggior felicità. Da Venetia li 2 marzo 1624.

D. V. S. Ill.ma

Humilissimo et oblig.mo Ser.re

Claudio Monteverdi.

[Anno 1625]

XXXVIII. Al Segretario ducale Ercole Marigliani.

Ill.mo mio Sig.re et padron Coll.mo

Non potei ringratiar per la passata la infinita bontà di V. S. Ill.ma come era di mio debito, poichè oltre il mio merito si era degnata assicurarmi dela sua gratia nel accidente di uno certo mio disturbo che mi trovo in Mantova per certa lite non voluta da me ne pensata; ma il molto daffare hauto et che ho tuttavia in servire et in chiesa et alla camera quest'Altezza di Pollonia mi ha levato l'haver potuto pagar in questa picciola parte almeno il molto debito che ho et haverò per sempre a V. S. Ill.ma prego a perdonarmi, sicome la prego ancora a farmi gratia ch'io possa per lo venturo ordinario informarla del detto mio negotio per supplicarla vedute le mie ragioni che almen si quieti il negotio senza mio danno havendo hauto la parte tutto che voleva da me. Et con tal fine, facendo riverenza humilissima a V. S. Ill.ma da Dio N. S. li prego ogni conforto et bene. Da Venetia li 15 marzo 1625.

D. V. S. Ill.ma

Servitor Obblig.mo
Claudio Monteverdi.

XXXIX. Al Medesimo.

Molto Ill.re mio Sig.re et padron Osser.mo

Ho ricevuto la gentilissima lettera di V. S. Molto Ill.ma piena d'una singolar affetione verso di me che nulla vaglio, nella quale mi promette degnarsi di parlare con il Belli per una volta finir con dolce accordo quello che mi ha noiato, si che mille volte mi pento haver mai lassiato principiare, non per altro maggior fondamento che per levarmi dal litigare qual mi è così in disgusto che se havessi ragione non so se volessi principiare simili intrichi, mai più; Mi scrisse V. S. Molt. Ill.re nella passata come che haveva ella parlato al Sig.r Dottore de la parte, et che haveva detto che io mi ero contentanto nullare quel Istromento di transaccione affatto, non so se ciò, dissi, ma se lo dissi bisognava che fossi ubriaco che altro, poichè il Sig. Prencipe comette che in tre giorni io vegga il tutto, et come haverei tanto giuditio a metter in lunga lite quello che altro non bramavo che finirlo per partirmi per Venetia. Di più non facevo se non quello voleva il mio procuratore. Dunque havendomi consigliato al litigare mi consigliava al mio peggio et tanto più havendomi consigliato a far cosa contro di me et per conseguenza o che era ignorante verso di me o vitioso. Hor su sij la cosa come si voglia supplico il Sig.r Marigliano mio Signore a farmi gratia di accomodar la cosa con quel modo che meglio saprà operare lei che io dire; et mi perdoni la prego con le viscere del core a perdonarmi assicurandola che il tutto sarà legato nel mio core con un nodo perpetuo di obligo.

Mi è statto donato le presente bevande che nella detta canevetina invio a V. S. Molto Ill.e mi farà gratia accettar il tutto per amor mio per segno almeno di quel obligo che gli devo, so che la proportione al molto il poco non arriva, ma ci rimetta della sua solita gentilezza che il tutto caminerà benissimo.

Cerca al vaso per calcinar l'oro con il Saturno mi ha detto il Sig.r Piscina et il Sig.r Medico de Santi, amboduvi sogetti grandi in tal arte, che si piglia un vaso come un orinale di terra; apure una pignatella, et si luttano bene atiò stijno salde al foco, in fondo del uno de quali vasi vi si mette piombo honestamente, più tosto tendente al molto che al poco atiò caminano assai fumi. Poi si piglia del filo di ferro suttile et si batte un Cechino facendolo venire alquanto sottile, et si fura il vaso verso la cima in quattro lochi et in mezzo vi si pona il detto cecchino apiccato da quattro parti acomodato in quadro che sia in aria. Poi sopra al detto vaso se li pone il suo coperchio di terra et si luta con il vaso atiò stij saldo et ben turi la bocca del detto vaso, et nella cima del detto coperchio si fa un buco picciolo poi si da foco sotto al detto vaso facendo bollire il detto saturno, così li fumi vanno circolando intorno al detto cechino, et lo calcinano in maniera che si può prestare il qual viene così sottile che e quasi impalpabile; Si può anche ataccare un filo solo a la cima del coperchio et nel detto filo di rame, metterle il detto cechino et duoi et più secundo piaura ma pero alquanto lontani l'uno dal altro, così in tal modo si calcina l'oro con il saturno et non in altro meglio di questo. Il vaso sarà come per esempio questo.

Quel filo che perpendicularmente nel mezzo del zechino potrà star solo senza gli quattro fili opure potra atacarlo con li quattro fili senza quello che pende; faccia uno lei.

Io poi gli notifico come saperò fare il mercurio del vulgo che si converta in aqua chiara, et se bene sarà in aqua non però perderà l'essere mercurio; et il suo peso perchè ho provato pigliarne una goccia et lo posta sopra un cucchiaro di ottone et fregatolo, et è divenuto tutto tinto in color d'argento; de la qual aqua retificata spererò far qualche cosa degna essendo che solve l'argento galiardemente. Et qui facendo riverenza con tutto il core a V. S. Molto Ill.r da Dio gli prego il colmo d'ogni maggior felicità. Da Venetia gli 23 agosto 1625.

D. V. S. Molto Ill.re

Ser.re obblig.mo

Claudio Monteverdi.

XL. AL MEDESIMO.

[ANNO 1626]

Molto Ill.re Ill.mo mio Sig.re et padron Osser.mo

Ho sentito sommo a piacere del gusto che ella la hauto nel ricevere il mercurio vergine mandato come ella mi comise, staro su l'avertito se poterò haverne altro per completamente servire alla sua voluntà quando però altro gli ne facesse bisogno. Ho inteso dopo quanto m'impone cioè che operi in maniera con un tal Sig.r Medico per havendo lui il modo come fa a far un certo mercurio agiacciato me adoperarò et dimanderò diligentemente qual possi essere questo sig.r Medico et farò ogni opera per servire a V. S. Conosco un tal Sig.r Medico De Santi di pelo rosso qual si diletta molto d'investigare la pietra filosofica quando che questo non sij, altri non conosco che mi possa insegnare quanto V. S. mi comanda per lo venturo ordinario potro forsi meglio sodisfarla che al presente perciò mi havera per iscusato hora. Et qui facendole riverenza con tutto l'affetto da Dio N. S. gli prego ogni felicità. Da Venetia gli 24 febraro 1626.

D. V. S. Molto Ill.re

Ser.re obblig.mo

Claudio Monteverdi.

XLI. AL MEDESIMO.

Molto Ill.re mio Sig.re et padron Oss.mo

Sto sollecitando il mercurio da un sogetto assai inteligente per inviarlo quanto prima V. S. Molto Ill.re ma però anche non me l'ha potuto dare spero per l'ordinario venturo mandarlo, ho voluto raguagliarla di questo atiò sapia che gli comandi di V. S. Molto Ill.re mi vivono nel core. Scrissi quattro lettere l'una al Seren.ma padrone et l'altra alla Seren.ma padrona, et terza al Sig. Don

Vincenzo Seren.mo et la quarta al Sig.r Ill.mo Conte Alessandro Striggio mio Sig.re ; supplica il Signor Marigliani mio Sig.re occorendo al filiolo introdutione honorarlo de la sua gratia che di tal favore ne terro perpetuo obligo a V. S. Molto Ill.re per sempre come di infiniti altri che faccio ; Mi scrive nelle sue hora solecitar gli circoli ne studi et andar ad udire Astrologia da un tal Sig.r padre Giesuitta scritte et similmente tendere alli consulti, seguitando continuamente il servire al Signor Ecc.mo Bertoletti, et servire parimente il Sig.r Conte Bruschi mio Sig.re. Sto aspettando insieme che mi havisa Massimigliano l'haver hauto tre bollettini ch'io avanzo da la Camera Ducale et che speranza terrà in haver detti denari, cinquanta scudi de quali mi son contentato che se ne servi per il suo vitto, et mi son fermato il cor nel corpo non consentire che ritorni a Venetia per fina a tanto che non habbi stabilito di far altra vita et altro profitto di quello ha fatto, spero però in Dio che mi fara honore perchè so che ha giuditio et honore. Et voglio sperare che quando il Seren.mo havera conosciuto un giorno quello che sa il filiolo forse che non sdegnera in concederle la sua bona gratia qual bramo con l'anima stessa che Dio lo facci degno ; Et qui facendo riverenza al molto illustre mio Sig.r Marigliani da Dio insieme gli prego con tutto l'affetto del core il colmo d'ogni sua compita felicità dandole nova come che hora son dietro a far foco sotto ad un orinale di vetro con sopra il suo capello per cavarne un non so che per far di poi un non so che piacia a Dio che possi allegramente poi esplicare al mio Sig.r Marigliani questo non so che. Da Venetia gli 28 marzo 1626.

    D. V. S. Molto Ill.re

Ser.re obblig.mo per sempre
Claudio Monteverdi.

XLII. AL CONTE ALESSANDRO STRIGGIO.

Ill.mo mio Sig.re et padrone Coll.mo

Invio a V. S. Ill.ma la finta pazza Licori del Sig.r Strozzi come mi ha co-mandato nella gentil.ma di lei, non fatta per anco in musica, non stampata, nè mai recitata in scena, poichè subito fatta dal Autore, egli stesso di lungo me ne diede di propria mano la copia, che fu la presente. Se il detto Sig.r Giulio saperà che dovesse essere in gusto di S. A. Ser.ma son sicuriss.mo che con prontiss.mo affetto et effetto la porrà in ordine, diviso in tre atti, o come piacerà a S.A.S.ma, bramando egli oltre modo di vederla da me fatta in musica, godendo di vedere vestito con le mie deboli note gli suoi honorat.mi componimenti, che veramente, et nella bellezza del verso, et nella inventione, io l'ho provato in atto di grand.mo soggetto et prontis.mo ; sichè se gustasse tal inventione a V. S. Ill.ma non guardi nella presentanea sua dicitione, perchè sò di certo ridurà l'autore alla compita sodisfatione in pochis.mo spatio di tempo. La inventione non mi par male, nè men la spiegatura; è vero che la parte di Licori per essere molto varia non dovrà cadere in mano di donna che hor non si facci homo, et hor donna con vivi gesti et separate passioni, perchè la immitatione di tal finta pazzia dovendo havere la consideratione solo che nel presente et non nel passato et nel futuro, per conseguenza la immitatione dovendo havere il suo appoggiamento sopra alla parola et non sopra al senso de la clausola, quando donque parlerà di guerra bisognerà immitar di guerra, quando di pace, pace, quando di morte, di morte et va seguitando; et perchè le transformationi si faranno in brevissimo spatio et le immitationi, chi dunque haverà da dire tal principalis.ma parte che move al riso et alla compassione, sarà necessario che tal donna lassi da parte ogni altra immitatione che la presentanea che gli somministrerà la parola che haverà da dire; crederò non di meno che la Sig.ra Margherita sarà la excell.ma, ma per mostrar di più effetto, del mio interno affetto ancor che so di certo che l'opera sarebbe di maggior mia fatica. Mando il presente Narciso opera del Sig.r Ottavio Rinuccini non posto in stampa, non fatto in musica da alcuno, nè mai recitato in scena. Esso Sig.r quando era in vita, che hor sij in cielo, come glielo prego di core, me ne fece gratia de la copia non tanto ma di pregarmi che la pigliassi, amando egli molto tal sua opera sperando ch'io l'havessi a porre in musica. Holle dato più volte assalti et l'ho alquanto digesta nella mia mente, ma a confessar il vero a V. S. Ill.ma mi riuscisse al parer mio non di quella forza ch'io vorrei per gli molti soprani che gli bisognerebbero, per le tante Ninfe impiegate, et con molti tenori per gli tanti pastori et non altro di variatione, et più con tragico et mesto. Non ho però voluto mancare di mandarla a vedere a V. S. Ill.ma atiò gusti il suo fin giuditio. Nè dell'uno nè dell'altra non ho altra copia che la presente che invio a V. S. Ill.ma. Letto il tutto mi farà gratia rimandarmi gli detti originali per potermene valere secondo il mio interesse alle occasioni, et sappia che mi sono caris.me. Et qui facendo hum.a riverenza et aspettando gli bramati comandi, da Dio ogni felicità gli prego. Da Venetia gli 7 Maggio 1627.

Per aricordare a V. S. Ill.ma parte alcuna di basso che fosse a proposito secondo il gusto di S. A. S.ma et al bisogno de le parti eccellenti che si trova S. A. S.ma, in particolare per li soprani che sono quelle donne, io non saprei torno a dire che aricordare. Ho però inteso così di lontano che vi è un non so che di buono in Milano nel duomo. Qui per camera non habiamo di meglio che il Rapalino mantovano che ha nome D.n Jacomo qual è prete, ma è baritono et non basso, del resto fa intendere la oratione, ha un pocco di trillo et un poco di gorgia et canta ardito. Starò su l'avertito per aricordar di meglio, et qui torno a far riverenza a V. S. Ill.ma.

Di V. S. Ill.ma

Ser.re aff.mo et hum.mo
Claudio Monteverdi.

XLIII. Al Segretario ducale Ercole Marigliani.

Ill.mo mio Sig.re et padron Coll.mo

Ho ricevuto la carissima et cortesissima lettera di V. S. Ill.ma con insieme una obligata del Sig. Alessandro Consorte de la Sig.ra Settimia, nella quale altro non mi tratta che sicurezza di brevità di tempo in quello vogliono fare que Seren.mi Prencipi ne per anco si veggono versi ne alcun principio, assicurandomi di bel novo con la sua gentilezza che a niun altro consentirà che ubidischi nel cantare che alla persona mia la sua sig.ra Moglie, et che non mi stupischi che egli habbi risposto al sig.r Sigismondo non potendo patire che l'amico che egli ama sij da alcuno ne a torto ne a ragione laurato pregandomi se cosa alcuna sapessi glie ne voglia dar motto et nella fine di essa lettera mi fa sapere che egli non e musico di S. A. S. et che di gratia non gli dij più quel titolo di musico di S. A. S., il che non sapendolo io non è statta meraviglia ch'io habbi errato, et scrivendo a sua Signoria come farò per lo venturo ordinario cercherò di non cadere in tal errore passato; ma quello che mi ha fatto errare e statto il vedere le formate parole nella sua lettera; se niuno (fuori che la persona di V. S. ha da pretendere la carica di tali musiche la deve pretendere io più di niun altro si perchè non cedo in qual si voglia cosa dell'arte alli detti (che mi scrive) quanto maggiormente per li particolari meriti de la sua sig.ra Consorte, et de la sua servitu di molti anni fatta a quella Seren.ma casa; Et io dico tal carica convenendo al musico et non al medico, per tali fondamenti l'ho adimandato tale. Ma scrivendole saperò emendar l'errore et me ne perdoni, lettera sua però piena di moltissimo amore et gentilezza; sono invitato ad andar sino a Mantova dall'Ill. Signor Conte Alessandro Striggio molto mio Signore per desiderio che tiene di voler parlar meco passato il Rosario, et tornato S. A. S. da Maderno, sarà facil cosa che giunghi fino a Mantova et mi sarà carissimo si per godere di quella patria da molto da me amata come per ralegrarmi con il Signor Marigliani molto mio Signore godendo sempre come sempre anco goderò d'ogni sua compita felicita che N. S. glie la concedi sempre mentre con ogni riverenza a S. S. Ill.ma bacio le mani. Da Venetia gli 10 settembre 1627.

D. V. S. Ill.

Ser.re Obblig.mo
Claudio Monteverdi.

XLIV. Al Marchese Bentivoglio, Parma.

Ill.mo et Ecc.mo mio Sig, et pron. Coll.

Heri che fu alli 9 del presente dal curriere ricevei un plicco di V. E. Ill.ma nel quale vi era un Intermedio et una lettera di V. E. Ill.ma piena d'infinita humanita et honore verso la persona mia, et insieme una copia d'un capitolo di una lettera della Sire.ma Sig.ra Duchessa di Parma scritta a V. E. Ill.ma nel quale si degna honorarmi di comandarmi con il mezzo di V. E. Ill.ma ch'io ponga in musica quello che da V.E.Ill.ma mi sarà comandato. Appena ho potuto leggiere due volte il detto Intermedio p. l'occasione del scrivere hauta essendo giorno che si parte il curriere, ho però visto tanto di bello che in verita son rimasto dedicatissimo con l'affetto a così bell'opera. Et si ben è statto poco il tempo, non per questo son statto indarno in tutto, perchè di già gli ho datto principio come ben ne faro vedere qualche poco d'effetto p. mercore venturo a V. E. Ill.ma, havendo di già visto che quattro generi di armonie saranno quelli che anderanno adoperati p. servitio del detto intermedio; l'uno che incomincia dal principio, et seguita sino al principio delle ire, tra Venere et Diana, et tra le loro discordie, l'altro dal principio delle ire sino finite le discordie, l'altro quando entra Plutone a metter ordine et quiete, durante sino dove Diana s'incomincia ad innamorare d'Endimione, et il quarto et ultimo dal principio di detto innamoramento sino alla fine. Ma mi credda V. E. Ill.ma che senza il delicato suo aiuto vedera che ci saranno lochi che mi porterebbero non poca dificoltà, dei quali mercore ne daro più minuto ragualio a V. E. Ill.ma. Altro per hora non intendero fare che rendere prima gratie a Dio che mi habbi fatto degno di poter ricevere così alti comandi da così alti signori et padroni, pregandolo insieme che mi facci degno così de li effetti come del affetto qual siccurmente cerchera di servire a padroni con ogni maggior potere che sapera rendendo infinite gratie a V. E. Ill.ma di cotanto favore, pregando insieme Dio che sempre in bona gratia di V. E. Ill.ma operi supplicandola a rendere p. me quelle gratie maggiori che si può alle bone gratie di quelle A. Se. me alle quali faccio humill.ma et profonda riverenza obligandomili p. suo umill.mo ser.re et a V. E. Ill.ma me l'inchino et gli bacio la mano. Da Venetia gli 10 sett.re 1627.

Di V. E. Ill.ma

Se.re Devotiss.mo et obblig.mo
Claudio Monteverdi.

XLV. Al Medesimo.

Ill.mo et Ecc.mo mio Sig. et padron Coll.mo

Supplico V. E. Ill.ma non si meravigliare si per l'ordinario di mercore passato non ho datto risposta alla humaniss.ma lettera di V. E. Ill.ma che la causa è statta, che l'ecc.mo Sig. Procuratore Foscarini mio singolar signore havendo un suo sig. filiolo podesta a Chioggia et quel Sig.r volendosi prevalere de la persona mia in una certa funtione di musica, mi trattenne in Chioggia un giorno di più di quel mi credevo che fu lo stesso giorno de la partenza del curriere, et ricevuto il plicco di V. E. Ill.ma con dentro un Intermedio bellis.mo et la comissione insieme ch'io dovessi trovarmi in Ferrara heri che fu alli 24 del pre-

sente, et havendo visto tal mio mancamento, mi creddı. V. E. Ill.ma che ne ho sentito particolare afflitione al anima, come tutta via sentirò per sino che non si sia degnata. V. E. Ill.ma di novo aviso di la sua sodisfatione; essendo dunq. scorso questo poco di tempo contro il mio volere, vorrei supplicar V. E. Ill.ma che si degnasse farmi gratia ch'io potessi restare in Venetia sino alle 7 del venturo mese, posciache il signor doge in tal giorno pos... mente se ne va a Santa Justina per rendere gratie a Dio N. S. de la felice vittoria navale et ci va con tutto il senato insieme et ivi si canta solenne musica; che subbito fatta tal funtione, mi porro in barca con il curriere et vero ad ubidire alli comandi di V. E. Ill.ma et sarà cosa santa, l'andare a vedere il Teatro a Parma, per poterle applicare più che sia possibile le proprie armonie decente al gran sito, che non sara così facil cosa (secundo me) il concertar le molte et variate orationi che veggo in tali bell.mi intermedii, fra tanto andero facendo et scrivendo per poter mostrar a V. E. Ill.ma altra cosa et maggiore che mi ritrovo; et qui facendo humilis ma riverenza a V. E. Ill.ma Da Dio N. S. gli prego con tutto il core il colmo d'ogni maggior felicita; Da Venetia gli 25 sett.bre 1627.
D. V. E. Ill.ma

S.e Humil.mo et Oblig.mo
Claudio Monteverdi.

XLVI. AL CONTE ALESSANDRO STRIGGIO.

Ill.mo mio Sig.re et Pad.ne mio Coll.mo

Ho ricevuto due lettere di V. S. Ill.ma a Parma, nel una mi comandava che io gli facessi havere l'Armida, che così era di gusto del Ser.mo Sig. duca mio Signore, et insieme ch'io arivassi sino a Mantova; nell'altra V. S. Ill.ma mi ha comandato ch'io mi adoperi per haver un castrato soprano de' migliori, nè al una nè al altra diedi risposta perchè procuravo di giorno in giorno essere a Venetia et di la servirla. Hora ch'io mi trovo in Venetia che sono tre giorni, subbito ho dato da ricopiare l'Armida, qual manderò a V. S. Ill.ma per lo venturo ordinario, ragguagliandola del Castrato, che in Parma si trova il migliore essere il Sig.r Gregorio, che serve il Sig.r Ill.mo Cardinale Borghese, qual con fatica grand.ma a mio credere si potria rimovere; vi è anco il Sig. Antonio Grimano, et questo manco si potria sperare di havere. Ve ne sono duoi altri pervenuti da Roma che sono un tal castrato che canta in S. Pietro, ma non mi par cosa troppo buona poichè ha voce che tira al catarro non troppo chiara et gorgia duretta, et poco trillo; vi è ancora un putto di qualche 11 anni, ne questo mi par haver voce grata, ha qualche gorgietta et qualche trillo, ma il tutto pronuntiato con una certa voce alquanto ottusa. Intorno a questi duoi, se gusterà V. S. Ill.ma farò qualche passata, ma de gli altri io credo nulla farei. Ho però lasciato ch, gli sij parlato, et come ritorno (piacendo a Dio) che sarà agli duoi o trei de l'altro mese, meglio informerò V. S. Ill.ma perchè tardi son stato a ricevere le humanissime di V. S. Ill. Della mia venuta a Mantova mi havera per iscusato così al presente perchè per l'amor mio non mi è concesso il venirci per ritrovarsi nelle carceri del Santo Ufficio Massimigliano mio figlio già passati sono tre mesi, la causa per haver letto un libro non conosciuto da mio figlio per proibito ma acusato dal possessor del libro qual medesimamente sta carcerato essendo statto ingannato dal possessore che esso libro conteneva solo medicina ed astrologia subbito carcerato il sig.r padre Inquisitore me scrisse, s'io gli davo una sicurtà di cento ducati di rapresentarmi sino espedita la causa che subbito l'haverebbe rilasciato. Il Sig.r Ercole Marigliani consigliere con una sua spontaneamente mi si esibi a favorir mio figlio per il qual suo affetto conosciuto lo supplicai di passare ufficio di accettar la mia sicurtà con il Sig.r Padre d'inquisitione sopra la mia annua rendita pagatami da cotesto Ser.mo prencipe mio signore et essendo passato duoi mesi ch'io non ho riceuto alcuna risposta ne dal Sig.r Padre Inquisitore ne dal Sig.r Marigliani.

Ricorro con ogni maggior riverenza alla protetione de la V. S. Ill.ma a passar ufficio con il Sig.r Marigliani di questo particolare in favore di Massimigliano et come stanno gli suoi interessi, che non volendo accettar detta sicurtà, io sarò sempre pronto a depositare cento ducati atiò sij rilassato. Et questo haveria già fatto se havessi hauto risposta dal Sig.r Marigliani; In tanto che V. S. Ill. favorira mio figlio come son sicurissimo gli pregherò da N. S. la salute in queste sante feste di Natale et bon capo d'anno facendole humilissima riverenza con baciarle la mano. Da Venetia gli 18 dicembre 1627.

D. V. S. Ill.ma

Ser.re obblig.mo
Claudio Monteverdi.

[Anno 1628]

XLVII. Al Segretario ducale Ercole Marigliani.

Ill.mo mio Sig.re et padron Coll.mo

Mi fara gratia V. S. Ill. perdonarmi se per la passata posta non diedi subbita risposta alla humanissima et cortessima lettera di V. S. Ill.ma che causa ne fu quello che dispensa le lettere, qual stette sino partita la posta a consegnarmi le mie; Vengo pertanto hora non havendo potuto prima a rendere infinite gratie a V. S. Ill.ma del cotanto favore che si è spontaneamente esibita farmi per servitio di quel povero disgratiato di Massimigliano mio filiolo atiò uscischi fuori di quelle carceri, favore così grande ch'io non so mai di poterlo in una minima parte canzellare, qual mi terra così obligato che sempre sarò tenuto almeno pregar Dio per la continua conservatione et esaltatione di se et di tutta la sua Ill.ma

*casa. Il favore però del quale supplico con ogni affetto la molta autorita di V.
S. Ill. e questo che si degni solamente operare con il Sig.r padre inquisitore, che
lassi andare a casa sua Massimigliano, con il mezzo della sicurtà che egli stesso
mi ha richiesto, che altro non bramo da la gratia di V. S. Ill.ma poichè ho
portato una collana di cento ducati in mano al Sig.r Barbieri mercante di gioie
ricco che sta qui in Venetia et mio paesano et amico stretto de molti anni atiò
scrivi per questa presente posta al Sig.r Zavarella che tiene gli datij dell'Altezza
Seren.ma di Manto in mano, qual'è strettissimo amico del detto Sig. Barbieri,
che venghi da V. S. Ill.ma ad offerirsi per far la detta sicurta lui. Altro non
intendo discomodarla ne supplicarla che nel disporre il Sig. Padre Inquisitore
al lasciar andar a casa Massimigliano. Se ardisco troppo appresso la gratia di
V. S. Ill. incolpi il molto bisogno ch'io tengo del suo favore et incolpi la sua
molta humanita et gentilezza che mi ha datto animo al ardire. Ho poi inteso con
estremo dolore la morte del Sereniss.mo Sig.r Duca Vincenzo che Dio l'habbi in
cielo si per il particolar affetto che portavo a tutti quei Sereniss.mi padroni in
particolare a questo Seren.mo Sig.re per quel spontaneo affetto con il quale s'era
mosso ad aricordarsi della debole persona mia con mostrar di haver gusto et di
vedermi et de la deboli compositioni mie si anco perchè speravo da la sua benignita
poter havere il fondo di quella mia pensione o corispontione de li cento scudi ;
et per ottener con maggior facilità tal gratia, m'ingegnavo mettermi da banda
qualche pochi denaretti, che perciò per causa di agiongere qualche cosa di più
andai come feci ad affaticarmi per gli Seren.mi di Parma ; ma la mia sorte
che mi e statta sempre più tosto contraria che altro nel più bello mi ha voluto
dar questa gran mortificatione ; piacia a Dio ch'io non habbi perso et il padrone
et quel poco di bene che con tanto stento di sangue Dio mi ha concesso, qual
prego et supplico con tutto il core atiò il presente Sereniss.mo Signore vivi con
felice tranquillità che come giustissimo che son sicurissimo che è essendo di quella
Sereniss.ma casa non creddo mai ne crederò che mi levasse il mio, tanto più
appoggiato sopra la gratia di V. S. Ill.ma io la quale spero di certo mi sara
favore volissima in aintarmi se bisognasse. Caro Sig.re mi consoli con una parola
sopra a tal capo che mi darà la vita ; et qui humilmente facendole riverenza
da Dio gli prego con tutto il core ogni continuata felicità. Da Venetia il primo
gennario 1628.*

D. V. S. Ill.ma

Ser. humiliss.mo et obblig.mo

Claudio Monteverdi.

*Ho detto di sopra che il Sig.r Zanarelli verà da V. S. Ill. ad offerirsi
per la sicurtà, ma hora ritorno a dire che non sarà quello ma bensi il Sig.r Gio.
Ambrogio Spiga Gioiogliere di S. A. S., questo sarà che vera ad offerirsi, per la
sicurtà, et per l'amor di Dio mi perdoni del tanto incomodo ; et di bel novo torno
a farle humiliss.ma riverenza.*

XLVIII. Al Medesimo.

Ill.mo mio Sig.re et padron Coll.mo

Ho riceuto favore da V. S. Ill.ma in tempo che quasi non era possibile chi aricordasse de li stessi suoi ; argomento certo che col benigno affetto di V. S. Ill.ma si è degnata farmi una gratia de le più singolari et de le più intime che potessi mai sperare da la mia miglior fortuna, non ho merito perchè son il più debole sogetto che sij al mondo, ho però questo da Dio che conosco un estremo debito che devo, et questo non mi sarà negato da sua Divina Maesta del che lo supplico et prego, che almeno lo possa confessare, se non lo posso pagare ; offerisco però ala gran bonta di V. S. Ill.ma et quella poca di robba che mi trovo et il lostesso sangue, a questo mondo ; et le orationi benche dibolissime apresso Dio. Il Sig.r Spiga verrà a rilevare V. S. Ill.ma di sicurtate, poichè così havera per lo presente ordinario espressa comissione di farlo, in altra maniera vi sentirei adolorato non bramando altro da la sua innatta gentilezza che la sua prottezione che è pur troppo, ho inteso come che è fuori de le carceri Massimigliano starò aspettando sue lettere per darle un tema con le mie assai differente da quello s'immagina ; resto poi doppiamente consolato havendo inteso che così vero nella medesima mia correspontione, tanto maggiormente appoggiato sopra la bona gratia di V. S. Ill. della quale prego Dio che si degni conservarmela, desiderando di cercar sempre con ogni mia diligenza di mantenermela et conservarmela. Tra duoi giorni spero tornero a Parma, per metterle a quelle Altezze Ser.me all'ordine musiche per torneo et per intermedij di comedia che si havera a recitare ; da di la se così gustera darolle nova de la riuscita de le cose ; da Venetia per bocca del Sig.r Ecc.mo procuratore Contarino mio Sig.re per essere procuratore di Santo Marco ho heri inteso che teme non solamente credde sua Ecc.za che tali nozze non si faranno per questo carnevale ne per questo maggio come mi aveva scritta da Ferrara chis faranno all'hora ; ma neanche forse più, tuttavia anderò a mettere al ordine quelle musiche che mi sono statte datte da fare, più oltre non posso ne devo. Dio feliciti V. S. Ill.ma mentre con tutto l'affetto del core gli bacio le mani et gli prego ogni maggior felicità. Da Venetia gli 9 Gennaio 1628.

D. V. S. Ill.ma

Ser.re Obblig.mo
Claudio Monteverdi.

XLIX. Al Marchese Alessandro Striggio.

Ill.mo mio Sig.re et padron Coll.mo

La nova che mi ha datta il Sig.r Ill.mo Marchese Entio hora passato per Mantoa et gionto a Parma, qual è statta che V. S. Ill. e statta fatta Marchese

1a questo Sereniss.mo novo Sig.re quanto mi sij statta cara et grata al core, l'obligo infinito, che devo, et che deverò sino che haverò vita, et il lungo et continuato amore che sempre si è degnata farmene degno usando meco continuati effetti di gratie particolari et straordinarie et lunga servitu ch'ho sempre professata mantener con bramar sempre d'essere fatto degno d'essere conosciuto da la sua gratia per suo vero et real servitore dichino per me et parlino, et faccino fede a V. S. Ill.ma de la mia consolatione; supplicola con ogni instante affetto che si voglia degnare anco per l'avvenire mantenermi nel medesimo stato di gratia, assicurando V. S. Ill.ma che se non potrò in altro servirla per essere debolissimo sogetto non mancherò sempre nelle mie deboli orationi di pregar il Sig.re che la continui et prosperi in questa et maggior felicità nella sua santa gratia.

Quanto poi mi sij spiaciuto l'haver riceuto il comando da V. S. Ill.ma che di novo l'invij l'Armida per trovarmi come mi trovo in Parma, et essa Armida havendola a Venetia Dio lo dichi per me. Restai di mandarla a V. S. Ill.ma questo Natale per la causa de la morte del Ser.mo Sig.r Ducca Vincenzo che sia in gloria; che mai haverei pensato che lei se ne havesse voluto compiacere per questo carnevale; Tal mancamento mio se V. S. Ill.ma mi vedesse nel core mi credda certo che estremamente mi affligge; Tal Armida si trova però nelle mani del Sig.r Ill. Mozenigo mio affezionatissimo et particolarissimo Sig.re; hora per lo presente ordinario qual hoggi si parte per Venetia scrivo con estrema instanza al detto Ill. Sig.re che me ne honori di una copia et che la dij al Sig. D. Giacomo Rapallini mantoano et molto servitore a V. S. Ill. cantore in Santo Marco et mio carissimo amico al quale hora gli scrivo caldamente atiò procuri di haverla dal detto Sig.r Ill.mo Mozenigo suo molto Sig.re et da esso molto amato, et che senza intervallo di tempo se si puo la invij a nome mio a V. S. Ill.ma et conoscendo il Cavagliere essere compitissimo et il detto Sig.r Rapallini desiderando estremamente di farsi conoscere Servitore a V. S. Ill.ma io non dubito ponto che V. S. Ill. quanto più presto si puo gli sarà mandata. Qui in Parma si provano le musiche da me composte in pressa credendo queste Seren.me Altezze che le loro Seren.me Nozze si havessero a fare di gran lunga un pezzo prima di quello si tiene anderano et tali prove si fanno per trovarsi in Parma cantori Romani et Modenesi, et sonatori piacentini et altri; che havendo visto queste Ser.me Altezze come rieschino per li loro bisogni et la riuscita che fanno et la sicura speranza al occasione che in breve giorni si metteranno al ordine, si tiene che tutti se ne anderemo alle case nostre, sino il sicuro aviso del effetto qual si dice potrebbe essere a questo Maggio, et altri tengono di questo Settembre, saranno due bellisime feste l'una comedia recitata con gli intermedi apparenti in musica et non vi è intermedio che non sij longo almeno trecento versi, et tutti variati d'affetto le parole de quali le ha fatte il Sig. Ill. D. Ascanio pel Genero del Sig. Marchese Entio, Cavalier dignissimo et virtuosissimo, l'altra sarà un Torneo nel quale interveranno quattro squadriglie di Cavaglieri, et il Mantenitore sarà il Sereniss.mo stesso. Le parole di esso Torneo le ha fatte il Sig.r Aquilini et sono più di mille versi, belle si per il Torneo, ma per musica assai lontane, mi hanno dato estremo da fare; hora si provano le dette musiche d'esso

Torneo; et dove non ho potuto trovar variationi nelli affetti, ho cercato di variare nel modo di concertarle, et spero che piaceranno. Comisi al Sig.r Barbieri mercante ricco di Venetia che procurasse di far levare V. S. Ill.ma di sicurta per Massimigliano fatta; et a questo effetto gli lassia una collana in mano di cento ducati, ne sto aspettando la risposta et V. S. Ill.ma mi perdoni della tardanza. Et qui facendole humilissima riverenza gli bacio la mano et gli prego ogni felicità. Da Parma gli 4 febbraio 1628.

    D. V. S. Ill.ma

                  Ser. re obblig.mo et sempre humiliss.mo

                  Claudio Monteverdi.

L. AL MEDESIMO.

        Ill.mo mio Sig.re et padron Coll.mo

Sforzato dal acidente che mi preme all'hanima et confidato nella infinita bonta di V. S. Ill.ma venga a supplicarla che mi honori di leggere queste quattro parole, et con giovarmi con la sua gratia la supplico con le viscere del core; l'accidente è questo che credendo che Massimigliano mio filiolo fosse affatto libero de la sua disgratia, et per conseguenza de la sicurta et d'ogni altro pensamento gia 15 giorni fa mi scrive il filiolo che per non essere ancora espedita la causa di quel tristo che gli portò da leggere quel libro proibito teme di bel nuovo andar in prigione, et non sa perchè poichè di già ha fatto vedere che la colpa non è sua. Hora per tal tema, io ne pregai il Sig.r Consiglier Marigliani mio Signore atiò provocasse che il filiolo si transferisse sino da me, la qual gratia havendola ottenuta et informatomi bene del fatto et discorerne con Sig.r padri inquisitori da Padoa, mi hanno certificato che il filiolo non ha alcuna colpa con che meritava star in prigione per alcun tempo; Hor temendo che non lo torni ad imprigionare, ancora che certificato dal Sig.r Consigliere Marigliani, Vengo a supplicar V. S. Ill.ma degnarsi di trattar di tal negotio con esso Sig.r Consigliere Marigliani, et pregarla per l'amor di Dio che inciò mi voglia congiovare atteso che pur il filiolo non tanto non ha errato ma è mantovano et è entrato nel collegio de Sig. Medici, et e tanto servitore a V. S. Ill.ma la supplico a la bramata gratia mentre di vero core gli faccio humilissima riverenza et da Dio gli prego ogni vera felicità. Da Venetia il primo di luglio 1628.

    D. V. S. Ill.ma

                  Ser.re obblig.mo

                  Claudio Monteverdi.

LI. Al Medesimo.

Ill.mo mio Sig.re et padron Coll.mo

La necessità in che mi ritrovo de la bona gratia di V. S. Ill.ma essendo tale che gli supremi favori ch'io ricevo mi fa temere effetti ordinarii così è piaciuto a Dio per mia estrema mortificatione pormi poichè l'accidente troppo mi fa temere non puo però tanto ch'io non conosca che troppo V. S. Ill.ma mi merita et mi honora, Dio mio non tantosto holla supplicata di favore come di lungo senza aspettar tempo mi ha favorito et d'effetti et di estrema bonta d'animo. Conosco et conoscerò sin ch'io vivo il gran debito mio et non havendo altro modo di pagarlo supplicherò Dio che mi aiuti con la bona gratia sua verso a V. S. Ill. con felicitarla et crescerla a que supremi gradi che ella possa mai desiderare et la sua Ill. casa tutta insieme. Ho inteso da la sua humaniss.ma lettera come che di presenza è statto a parlare al Rever.mo Sig.r Padre Inquisitore favore tale che assende al troppo così che mi fa arossire, il quale ha riposto a V. S. Ill.ma che solamente duoi giorni che Massimigliano stii prigione basterà a liberarlo affatto; Io sospetto Ill.mo Sig.re et mi perdoni se parlo così chiaro verso alla cotanta confidanza di V. S. Ill. Io sospetto et esso insieme cioè il filiolo sospetta che non venghi corda et che non venghi a qualche condanna de denari non ordinaria, et a qualche prigionia assai, assai più lunga de duoi giorni per voler esaminarlo in quello che mai habbi pensato non che fatto, si che questa dubitatione ancora riuscisse l'effetto tutto al contrario nulla dimeno tal timore concentrato nell'animo molto lo spaventa et mi credda V. S. Ill.ma che quasi non passa giorno che non pianga et non si affligga per tal concentrato pensiero. Mi ha scritto il Sig.r Padre Reverend.mo Inquisitore per lo presente passato ordinario le formate parole, che si contenta lasciarmi il filiolo quanto voglio; quanto voglio lo voglio per sempre rispondo a V. S. Ill.ma. Se ha dunque questa bona intentione, et che ha provato la vita di filiolo per sei mesi in donzina, perchè non si degni liberarmelo et levarmelo da questa tribulatione et me insieme et lassiarmelo esercitar la medicina in sua et mia sodisfatione et se bisognasse che pagassi ne venti ne venticinque ducati per memoria de la pena atiò mai più non havesse da tornar a leggere cose varie et impertinenti così fatte ancora che so di certo che mai più senz'altro non ci tornerà volontieri, gli pagheria caro Sig.re se si potesse ricevere così segnalata gratia la prego con tutto il core et con tutta l'anima farmi gratia che la possa ricevere; che l'assicuro che et al putto et a me dara la vita perchè certamente per tal pensiero mi sento tormentar l'affetto, mi consoli la supplico se è mai possibile che maggior gratia non mi sarà di questa, mi è carissimo l'utile in questo mondo, ma molto più la quiete de l'animo et l'honor proprio; mi perdoni la supplico di cotanto incomodo mentre con tutto l'affetto del core faccio humilissima riverenza et li bacio la mano. Da Venetia gli 8 luglio 1628.
D. V. S. Ill.ma

Ser.re humiliss.mo et obblig.mo
Claudio Monteverdi.

LII. AL SIGNOR G. B. DONI (?)

Molto Ill.mo et Rev.mo mio Sig.re et padron Coll.mo

Ad una lettera humanissima dell' Ill.mo Sig. Vescovo Cervaro mio singolar Sig.re et padron collendissimo inviatami da Padova era annessa una di V. S. R.ma, a me diretta, ricca de frutti di honore et di lode cotanta verso la debil persona mia, che ne restai quasi ammirato, ma considerato poscia che da una pianta virtuosissima et gentilissima come la persona di V. S. Rev.ma, non poteva nascere altro frutto che di simile natura, mi tacqui, non ricevendo però la raccolta come degno, ma bensi per conservarla alli singolari meriti di V. S. R.ma conoscendomi bensi esser pianta verde ma di quella natura che altro non produce che frondi et fiori di niun odore, si degnerà dunque ad accettar da me per risposta le degne lodi de la sua nobilissima lettera, tenendo per gran favore che mi honori d'essere da lei ricevuto per suo humilissimo servitore. Monsignor Vicario di Santo Marco havendomi favorito in trattar de le nobil qualita et singolari virtu di V. S. R.ma mi notificò come che ella scriveva un libro di Musica, nel qual accidente, soggiunsi che anch'io ne scriveva un altro, ma con tema de la mia debolezza per poter giungere al creduto fine; qual sig.re essendo molto servitore al Sig.re, Ill.mo Vescovo di Padova, vo credendo che per tal via sua Signoria Ill.ma habbi inteso del mio scrivere, che per altro non sò, non curandomi che si sappia. Ma poichè sua signoria Ill.ma, si e degnata honorarmi cotanto presso alla gentillezza di V. S. Ill.ma la supplico ad intendere di più anco il rimanente.

Sappia dunque come che è vero ch'io scrivo ma però sforzatamente; essendo che l'accidente che già anni mi spinse a così fare, fu di così fatta natura che mi tirò non accorgendomi a promettere al mondo quello che dopo avedutomene non potevano le debil forze mie, promisi dicco in istampa di far conoscere ad un certo Theorico di prima pratica, che ve ne era un altra da considerare intorno al armonia, non conosciuta da lui, da me adimandata seconda; et la causa fu perchè si pigliò per gusto di far contro purre in istampa ad un mio Madrigale cioè in alcuni passi armonici suoi fondato sopra alle ragioni di prima pratica cioè sopra alle regole ordinarie come che se fossero state solfe, fatte da un fanciullo che incominciasse ad imparar notta contra notta, et non in ordine alla cognition melodica, ma udito egli una certa divisione mandata in istampa in mia diffesa da mio fratello, si quetò in maniera che per l'avenire non solamente si firmò di passar più oltre ma volgendo la penna in lode, comincio ad amarmi et a stimarmi; la promessa publica però non volle che mancassi alla promessa, perloche sforzatamente tendo a pagar il debito, la supplico dunque a tenermi per iscusato del ardire.

Il titolo del libro sara questo : Melodia, overo seconda pratica musicale. Seconda (intendendo io) considerata in ordine alla moderna, prima in ordine all'antica; divido il libro in tre parti rispondenti alle tre parti della Melodia nella prima discorro intorno al oratione, nella seconda intorno all'armonia, nella terza intorno alla parte Rithmica; Vado credendo che non sarà discaro al mondo posciache ho provato in pratica che quando fui per scrivere il pianto del Arianna, non trovando libro che mi aprisse la via naturale alla imitatione ne meno che mi illuminasse che dovessi essere imitatore, altri che Platone per via di un suo lume rinchiuso così che appena potevo di lontano con la mia debil vista quel poco che mi mostrasse; ho provato dicco la gran fatica che sia bisogno fare in far quel poco ch'io feci d'immitatione, et perciò spero sij per non dispiacere ma rieschi come si voglia alla fine son per contentarmi d'essere più tosto poco lodato nel novo, che molto nel ordinario scrivere; et di questa altra parte d'ardire ne chieggio novo perdono.

Quanta consolatione poi habbi sentito in haver inteso che a nostri tempi si sia ritrovato, un novo istromento, Dio lo dichi per me qual prego con ogni affetto mantenghi et feliciti la virtuosissima persona del Sig. inventore che è statta la persona di V. S. R.ma. In verita ho molto et molte volte fra me pensato sopra la causa per ritrovarla, sopra la quale dicco ove si fondavano gli antichi per ritrovarne di cotante differenze come hanno fatto che non solamente sono molte quelle che usiamo ma molte quelle che si sono perse ne vi è statto per un theorico di nostri tempi, et pur hanno fatto professione di saper il tutto del arte che pur uno ne habbino mostrato al mondo, spero però dir qualche cosa nel mio libro intorno a tal capo che forse non spiacera.

Dala consolatione mia narata, ben puotrà argomentare V. S. R.ma se mi sarà caro il favore promessomi dala sua gentillezza a suo tempo cioè in essere favorito di una copia di così degna lettura aportante cose recondite et nove, perciò la supplico de la promessa gratia, si come a supplico a tenermi per suo humill.mo servitore et obligatissimo, et qui facendole humill.ma riverenza con tutto l'affetto gli bacio le honoratiss.me mani. Da Venetia gli 22 ott.re 1633.

Di V. S. Molto Ill.ma et Rev.ma.

Servitore Devotiss.mo et obligat.mo

Claudio Monteverdi.

[ANNO 1634]

LIII. AL MEDESIMO.

Molto Ill.mo et Rev.mo mio Sig.re et padron Coll.mo

Due lettere di V. S. R.ma ho ricevuto, l'una avanti Natale, in tempo che mi trovavo tutto occupato nel scrivere la messa per la notte di Natale, messa aspettata dal uso de la cita nova dal Maestro di Capella, l'altra quindici giorni fa dal coriere, quale mi ritrovò in stato non ben guarito da una discesa catarale che poco dopo Natale mi comminciò a sopravenire sopra al occhio sinistro la quale

*mi ha tenuto lunghi giorni lontano non solamente dal scrivere ma dal leggere;
ne per anco mi trovo libero affatto che ancora mi va alquanto travagliando,
per gli quali dui veri impedimenti, vengo a supplicar V. S. R.ma a perdonarmi
l'errore de la tardanza mia nel scrivere, lessi quindici giorni fa et non prima
la cortessima et virtuossissima prima lettera di V. S. R.ma da la quale ne cavai
affettuosissimi avisi et degni tutti da essere molto considerati da me; perloche
gliene vengo a rendere infinite gratie, ho però visto non prima, d'ora anzi venti
anni fa il Galilei che ove nota quella poca pratica antica, mi fu caro all'hora
l'haverla vista, per haver visto in questa parte come che adoperavano gli antichi
gli loro segni praticali a differenza de nostri, non cercando di avanzarmi più
oltre ne lo intenderli, essendo sicuro che mi sarebbero riusciti come oscurissime
zifere et peggio, essendo perso in tutto quel modo praticale antico; perloche
rivoltai gli miei studi per altra via appogandoli sopra a fondamenti de migliori
filosofi scrutatori de la natura, et perchè secondo ch'io leggo, veggo che s'in-
contrano gli affetti con le dette ragioni et con la sodisfatione de la natura mentre
scrivo cose praticali con le dette osservationi, et provo realmente che non ha che
fare queste presenti regole, con le dette sodisfationi, per tal fondamento ho posto
quel nome di seconda pratica in fronte al mio libro et spero di farla veder così
chiara che non sarà biasimata ma bensi considerata dal mondo, lascio lontano
nel mio scrivere quel modo tenuto da Greci con parole et segni loro, adoperando
le voci et gli carateri che usiamo ne la nostra pratica; perchè la mia intentione
è di mostrare con il mezzo de la nostra pratica quanto ho potuto trarre da la
mente de què' filosofi a servitio de la bona arte, et non a principii de la prima
pratica, armonica solamente.*

*Piacesse a Dio che mi trovassi vicino alla singolar amorevolezza et singolar
prudenza et avisi di V. S. R.ma, come che il tutto a bocca supplicandola ad
udirmi il tutto dicco gli direi, così intorno all'ordine come alli principii et alle
divisioni de le parti del mio libro, ma questo essere lontano me lo vieta; per gratia
spetiale riceuta da la somma bonta de la Santissima Vergine l'anno contagioso
di Venetia son in obligo d'andar alla santissima casa di Loreto di voto; spero
nel Signore presto scioglierlo, con la qual occasione son per giungere sino a Roma
che piacea al Signore mene facci la gratia per potermi constituir di presenza
servitore a V. S. R. ma et godere et de la vista et del nobillissimo suono del suo
nobillissimo istromento et ricever l'honore de suoi virtuosissimi discorsi.*

*L'ho visto in dissegno sopra ad una carticella da lei mandatami la quale in
guisa di se marmi la volonta per lo contrario me l'ha fatto più crescere, et perchè
nella detta seconda lettera mi comanda ch'io mi adoperi con Scapino acio
possi io mandare a V. S. R.ma gli dissegni de suoi molti istromenti stravaganti
che egli tocca, per il desiderio grande ch'io tengo d'incontrar occasione di servirla in questo non havendo potuto per recitar egli in Modena et non in Venetia;
perciò ne ho sentito molto disgusto; ho però usato questa poca di diligenza con certi
amici che almeno mi discrivano quelli che loro si ponno ricordare; così mi hanno
datto la presente cartina che hora qui invio à V. S. R.ma non ho mancato di
scrivere ad amico che veggea deessi di haverne de più differenti dal uso gli*

dissegni. Jo non gli ho mai visti, ma da la detta poca informatione ch'io mando mi pare che siano novi di forma ma non d'armonia, poi che tutti cadono ne le armonie de gli istrumenti che usiamo. Quello che ho visto io già trenta anni fa in Mantova, tocco e fatto da un tal Arabo che all'hora veneva da Turchia et questo era loggiato in corte di quella Altezza di Mantova mio Signore era una cettera de la grandezza de le nostre, cordata con le stesse corde, et parimente sonata, la quale havera questa differenza che il coperto di essa era mezzo di legno da la parte verso il manico, et mezza di carta pecora da la parte di sotto ben tirata et incolata intorno ad esso cerchio de la cettera le corde de la quale erano arracate bensi al cerchio di sotto di essa et si appoggiavano sopra al scanello quale era posto nel mezzo di essa carta pecora, et il dito picciolo de la mano de la persona fascendo ballare la detta carta pecora mentre toccava le armonie, esse armonie uscivano con il moto del tremolo che rendevano un gratissimo effetto altro di più novo non ho udito al mio gusto ; staro ne l'haviso et se mi sarà acennato cosa che possa portarle gusto non mancherò di subbito mandarliene un dissegnetto; supplicola a conservarmi servitore nelle sua bona gratia mentre con tutto l'affetto et riverente gli baccio la mano et da N. S. gli prego ogni più compita felicità. Di Venetia gli 2 feb.ro 1634.

Di V. S. Molto Ill.mo et Rev.mo

Servitore devotiss.mo

Claudio Monteverdi.

BIBLIOGRAPHY

ADLER, GUIDO. *Handbuch der Musikgeschichte.* Frankfurt, 1924, 4to.
ADEMOLLO. *La Bella Adriana.* Città di castello, 1888, in 12mo.
ALLACCI. *Dramaturgia.* 1755, Venise, in 4to.
AMBROS-LEICHTENTRITT. *Geschichte der Musik.* T. IV. Leipzig, 1909.
ANCONA ALESS. D'. *Origini del Teatro italiaro.* Turin, 1891, 2 vols.
ARTUSI. GIO-MARIA. *L'Artusi overo delle Imperfettioni della musica moderna.*
    Venetia, 1600. *Seconda parte,* 1603, in 4to. *Discorso secondo musicale
    . . . di Antonio Braccino da Todi.* Venetia, 1608. *(Liceo Musicale
    Bologna.)*
BASCHET. *P. P. Rubens à la Cour de Mantoue (Gazette des Beaux-Arts,* 1866).
BERTOLOTTI. *Musici alla corte dei Gonzaga in Mantova del sec. XV al XVIII.*
    Ricordi, 1891, in 4to.
BORREN, CH. VANDEN. Preface to the Tiraboschi edition of the *Missa a 4 da
    cappella.*
BONAVENTURA ARNOLDO. *Teatro Musicale Italiano.* Livorno, 1913, in 12mo.
BURNEY. *A General History of Music.* London, 1789, vols. III and IV.
CAFFI. *Storia della Musica sacra nella già cappella ducale di San Marco in
    Venezia.* Venice, 1858, 2 vols. in 8vo.
CANAL, PIETRO. *Della musica in Mantova* (Memorie del R. Instituto Veneto di
    Scienze, Lettere ed Arti), 1858.
CESARI, GAETANO. *Die Entstehung des Madrigals im 16 Jahr.* Cremona, 1906,
    in 8vo.
COURVILLE XAVIER DE. *L'Arianne de Monteverdi. Revue Musicale,* November
    1921.
DASSORI. *Dizionario-Lirico.* Genoa, 1903, 8vo.
DAVARI STEFANO. *Notizie biografiche del distinto Maestro di Musica Claudio
    Monteverdi.* Mantova, 1885, in 8vo.
    La Musica a Mantova (Rivista Storica Mantovana, 11/21/884).
DONI, G. B. *Lyra Barberina* Florence, 1763, 2 vols. in fol.
EITNER. *Quellenlexicon.* Leipzig, 1900 (10 vols.).
FETIS. *Biographie Universelle des Musiciens* (2ème édit.).
FLORIMO. *La scuola Musicale di Napoli.* Napoli, 1880.
GANDOLFI RICARDO. *La Riforma Melodrammatica.* Firenze, 1895, in fol.
GASPARI GAETANO. *Catalogo della Biblioteca del Liceo Musicale di Bologna.*
    Bologna, 1905, 4 vols. in 8vo.
GALVANI, LIVIO. *I Teatri Musicali di Venezia nel sec. XVII.* Ricordi, 1878,
    in 4to.
GOLDSCHMIDT. *Studien zur Geschichte der Italienischen Oper in 17 jahr.*
    Leipzig, 1901–4, 2 vols. in 8vo.

HAAS, DR. ROBERT. *Il Ritorno d'Ulisse*. Studien zur Musikwissenschaft, IX. Wien, 1922, in 8vo.

HEUSS, ALFRED. *Die Instrumental Stücke des Orfeo und die venezianischen Opern Sinfonien*. Leipzig, 1903, in 8vo.

HUYGHENS, CONSTANTIN. *Correspondance*. Leyden, 1882, in 4to.

KINSKY, GEORG. *Katalog des Musikhistorischen Museums von W. Heyer*, 2 vols., 4to.

KIRCHER, ATH. *Musurgia universalis*. Rome, 1650, 2 vols. in fol.

KRETZSCHMAR, HERMANN. *Die Venetianische Oper Und die Werke Cavallis und Cestis, Vierteljahrschrift*, 1892.
Beiträge zur Geschichte der Venetianischen Oper. Jahrbuch, Peters, 1907

LAFAGE, A. DE. *Essais de Diphtérographie Musicale*. Paris, 1844, 2 vols., 4to.

LAVIGNAC. *Encyclopédie de la Musique*. Paris, Delagrave, Part I, Vol. II.

LEICHTENTRITT, HUGO. *Claudio Monteverdi als Madrigalkomponist. Samm der I.M.G.* 1910.
Geschichte der Motette. 1908.

MANDOSIO. *Biblioteca Romana*. Roma, 1692 (Vatican Library).

MARTINI PADRE. *Esemplare o sia Saggio fondamentale*. Bologna, 2 vols. in fol.

MAUGARS. *Response à un curieux sur le sentiment de la musique d'Italie*. Edit. Thoinan, 1865, in 8vo.

MERSENNE, P. MARIN. *Harmonie Universelle*. Paris, 1836, 2 vols. in fol.

MITJANA, RAFAELO. *Claudio Monteverdi y los origenes de la opera italiana*. Malaga 1911 (lecture).

PARRY, HUBERT. *The Music of the Seventeenth Century*. Oxford, 1902, in 4to.

PEREYRA, M. L. *Explication de la lettre qui est imprimée dans le cinquième livre de Madrigaux de Monteverdi*. Paris, Schola Cantorum, 1911, Plaquette in 4to.

PICENARDI, DR. GIORGIO SOMMI. *Claudio Monteverdi a Cremona*. Ricordi, 1895. 12mo.

PIRRO, ANDRO. *Schutz*. Alcan, 1913, in 12mo.
1895, in 12mo.
Descartes et la Musique, 1907.

PROD'HOMME. *Ecrits de Musiciens*. Mercure de France, 1912, 12mo.

PRUNIERES, HENRY. *L'Opéra Italien en France avant Lully*. Champion, 1913, in 8vo.
Le Ballet de Cour en France. Laurens, 1914, in 8vo.
Monteverdi and French Music. The Sackbut, Nov. 1922. (III, 4).

ROLLAND, ROMAIN. *Histoire de l'Opéra en Europe avant Lully et Scarlatti*. Paris, 1895, in 8vo.
L'Opéra Italien, Encyclopedie Lavignac, Tome II.

SANT DIDIER, DE. *La Ville et la Republique de Venise*. Paris, 1680.

SCHNEIDER, LOUIS. *Monteverdi*. Perrin, 1921, in 8vo.

SONNECK, TH. *Catalogue of Opera Librettos* (Library of Congress), 1911.

SOLERTI, ANGELO. *Gli albori del melodramma*. Sandron s.d., 3 vols. in 8vo.
*Origini del Melodramma.** Milan, Bocca, 1903, 1 vol. in 8vo.
Musica Ballo e Drammatica. Naples, Bemporad, 1915, in 8vo.
Un balletto musicato da Cl. Monteverdi. Rivista Musicale, 1914.

* As this little volume contains all the most important documents for the history of the *Riforma Melodrammatica*, they are not reproduced here.

Tassini. *Curiosità Veneziane.* V. ediz. Fuga. Venezia (no date).

Tessier, André. *Les deux styles de Monteverdi, Revue Musicale,* Juin 1922.

Vicentino Nicola. *L'antica Musica ridotta alla moderna pratica.* Roma, 1557, fol.

Vogel. *Claudio Monteverdi, Viertelj. für Musikwiss.* 1887.
Marco da Gagliano, Viertelj. für Musikwiss. 1889.
Bibliothek der gedrückten weltlichen Vokalmusik Italiens. Berlin, 1892, 2 vols. in 8vo.

Wellesz, Dr. Egon. *Cavalli und der Stil der Venetianischen Oper von 1640–1660.* (Studien zur Geschichte der Wiener Oper), in 8vo.

Wiel, Taddeo. *Codici contariniani del sec. XVII.* Venice, 1888, in 8vo.
Francesco Cavalli. Venezia, 1914, in 8vo.

Wotquenne. *Libretti d'opéras et d'oratorios italiens du XVII° siècle.* Bruxelles, 1901, in 4to.

Zacconi. *Prattica di Musica.* Venetia, 1596, in fol.
Seconda parte. Venetia, 1602, in fol.

INDEX

A CATALOGUE OF SELECTED DOVER BOOKS
IN ALL FIELDS OF INTEREST

AMERICA'S OLD MASTERS, James T. Flexner. Four men emerged unexpectedly from provincial 18th century America to leadership in European art: Benjamin West, J. S. Copley, C. R. Peale, Gilbert Stuart. Brilliant coverage of lives and contributions. Revised, 1967 edition. 69 plates. 365pp. of text.
21806-6 Paperbound $3.00

FIRST FLOWERS OF OUR WILDERNESS: AMERICAN PAINTING, THE COLONIAL PERIOD, James T. Flexner. Painters, and regional painting traditions from earliest Colonial times up to the emergence of Copley, West and Peale Sr., Foster, Gustavus Hesselius, Feke, John Smibert and many anonymous painters in the primitive manner. Engaging presentation, with 162 illustrations. xxii + 368pp.
22180-6 Paperbound $3.50

THE LIGHT OF DISTANT SKIES: AMERICAN PAINTING, 1760-1835, James T. Flexner. The great generation of early American painters goes to Europe to learn and to teach: West, Copley, Gilbert Stuart and others. Allston, Trumbull, Morse; also contemporary American painters—primitives, derivatives, academics—who remained in America. 102 illustrations. xiii + 306pp.
22179-2 Paperbound $3.00

A HISTORY OF THE RISE AND PROGRESS OF THE ARTS OF DESIGN IN THE UNITED STATES, William Dunlap. Much the richest mine of information on early American painters, sculptors, architects, engravers, miniaturists, etc. The only source of information for scores of artists, the major primary source for many others. Unabridged reprint of rare original 1834 edition, with new introduction by James T. Flexner, and 394 new illustrations. Edited by Rita Weiss. 6⅝ x 9⅝.
21695-0, 21696-9, 21697-7 Three volumes, Paperbound $13.50

EPOCHS OF CHINESE AND JAPANESE ART, Ernest F. Fenollosa. From primitive Chinese art to the 20th century, thorough history, explanation of every important art period and form, including Japanese woodcuts; main stress on China and Japan, but Tibet, Korea also included. Still unexcelled for its detailed, rich coverage of cultural background, aesthetic elements, diffusion studies, particularly of the historical period. 2nd, 1913 edition. 242 illustrations. lii + 439pp. of text.
20364-6, 20365-4 Two volumes, Paperbound $6.00

THE GENTLE ART OF MAKING ENEMIES, James A. M. Whistler. Greatest wit of his day deflates Oscar Wilde, Ruskin, Swinburne; strikes back at inane critics, exhibitions, art journalism; aesthetics of impressionist revolution in most striking form. Highly readable classic by great painter. Reproduction of edition designed by Whistler. Introduction by Alfred Werner. xxxvi + 334pp.
21875-9 Paperbound $2.50

CATALOGUE OF DOVER BOOKS

ALPHABETS AND ORNAMENTS, Ernst Lehner. Well-known pictorial source for decorative alphabets, script examples, cartouches, frames, decorative title pages, calligraphic initials, borders, similar material. 14th to 19th century, mostly European. Useful in almost any graphic arts designing, varied styles. 750 illustrations. 256pp. 7 x 10.   21905-4 Paperbound $4.00

PAINTING: A CREATIVE APPROACH, Norman Colquhoun. For the beginner simple guide provides an instructive approach to painting: major stumbling blocks for beginner; overcoming them, technical points; paints and pigments; oil painting; watercolor and other media and color. New section on "plastic" paints. Glossary. Formerly *Paint Your Own Pictures*. 221pp.   22000-1 Paperbound $1.75

THE ENJOYMENT AND USE OF COLOR, Walter Sargent. Explanation of the relations between colors themselves and between colors in nature and art, including hundreds of little-known facts about color values, intensities, effects of high and low illumination, complementary colors. Many practical hints for painters, references to great masters. 7 color plates, 29 illustrations. x + 274pp.
20944-X Paperbound $2.50

THE NOTEBOOKS OF LEONARDO DA VINCI, compiled and edited by Jean Paul Richter. 1566 extracts from original manuscripts reveal the full range of Leonardo's versatile genius: all his writings on painting, sculpture, architecture, anatomy, astronomy, geography, topography, physiology, mining, music, etc., in both Italian and English, with 186 plates of manuscript pages and more than 500 additional drawings. Includes studies for the Last Supper, the lost Sforza monument, and other works. Total of xlvii + 866pp. 7⅞ x 10¾.
22572-0, 22573-9 Two volumes, Paperbound $10.00

MONTGOMERY WARD CATALOGUE OF 1895. Tea gowns, yards of flannel and pillow-case lace, stereoscopes, books of gospel hymns, the New Improved Singer Sewing Machine, side saddles, milk skimmers, straight-edged razors, high-button shoes, spittoons, and on and on . . . listing some 25,000 items, practically all illustrated. Essential to the shoppers of the 1890's, it is our truest record of the spirit of the period. Unaltered reprint of Issue No. 57, Spring and Summer 1895. Introduction by Boris Emmet. Innumerable illustrations. xiii + 624pp. 8½ x 11⅝.
22377-9 Paperbound $6.95

THE CRYSTAL PALACE EXHIBITION ILLUSTRATED CATALOGUE (LONDON, 1851). One of the wonders of the modern world—the Crystal Palace Exhibition in which all the nations of the civilized world exhibited their achievements in the arts and sciences—presented in an equally important illustrated catalogue. More than 1700 items pictured with accompanying text—ceramics, textiles, cast-iron work, carpets, pianos, sleds, razors, wall-papers, billiard tables, beehives, silverware and hundreds of other artifacts—represent the focal point of Victorian culture in the Western World. Probably the largest collection of Victorian decorative art ever assembled—indispensable for antiquarians and designers. Unabridged republication of the Art-Journal Catalogue of the Great Exhibition of 1851, with all terminal essays. New introduction by John Gloag, F.S.A. xxxiv + 426pp. 9 x 12.
22503-8 Paperbound $4.50

THE ARCHITECTURE OF COUNTRY HOUSES, Andrew J. Downing. Together with Vaux's *Villas and Cottages* this is the basic book for Hudson River Gothic architecture of the middle Victorian period. Full, sound discussions of general aspects of housing, architecture, style, decoration, furnishing, together with scores of detailed house plans, illustrations of specific buildings, accompanied by full text. Perhaps the most influential single American architectural book. 1850 edition. Introduction by J. Stewart Johnson. 321 figures, 34 architectural designs. xvi + 560pp.
22003-6 Paperbound $4.00

LOST EXAMPLES OF COLONIAL ARCHITECTURE, John Mead Howells. Full-page photographs of buildings that have disappeared or been so altered as to be denatured, including many designed by major early American architects. 245 plates. xvii + 248pp. 7⅞ x 10¾.
21143-6 Paperbound $3.00

DOMESTIC ARCHITECTURE OF THE AMERICAN COLONIES AND OF THE EARLY REPUBLIC, Fiske Kimball. Foremost architect and restorer of Williamsburg and Monticello covers nearly 200 homes between 1620-1825. Architectural details, construction, style features, special fixtures, floor plans, etc. Generally considered finest work in its area. 219 illustrations of houses, doorways, windows, capital mantels. xx + 314pp. 7⅞ x 10¾.
21743-4 Paperbound $3.50

EARLY AMERICAN ROOMS: 1650-1858, edited by Russell Hawes Kettell. Tour of 12 rooms, each representative of a different era in American history and each furnished, decorated, designed and occupied in the style of the era. 72 plans and elevations, 8-page color section, etc., show fabrics, wall papers, arrangements, etc. Full descriptive text. xvii + 200pp. of text. 8⅜ x 11¼.
21633-0 Paperbound $5.00

THE FITZWILLIAM VIRGINAL BOOK, edited by J. Fuller Maitland and W. B. Squire. Full modern printing of famous early 17th-century ms. volume of 300 works by Morley, Byrd, Bull, Gibbons, etc. For piano or other modern keyboard instrument; easy to read format. xxxvi + 938pp. 8⅜ x 11.
21068-5, 21069-3 Two volumes, Paperbound $8.00

HARPSICHORD MUSIC, Johann Sebastian Bach. Bach Gesellschaft edition. A rich selection of Bach's masterpieces for the harpsichord: the six English Suites, six French Suites, the six Partitas (Clavierübung part I), the Goldberg Variations (Clavierübung part IV), the fifteen Two-Part Inventions and the fifteen Three-Part Sinfonias. Clearly reproduced on large sheets with ample margins; eminently playable. vi + 312pp. 8⅛ x 11.
22360-4 Paperbound $5.00

THE MUSIC OF BACH: AN INTRODUCTION, Charles Sanford Terry. A fine, nontechnical introduction to Bach's music, both instrumental and vocal. Covers organ music, chamber music, passion music, other types. Analyzes themes, developments, innovations. x + 114pp.
21075-8 Paperbound $1.25

BEETHOVEN AND HIS NINE SYMPHONIES, Sir George Grove. Noted British musicologist provides best history, analysis, commentary on symphonies. Very thorough, rigorously accurate; necessary to both advanced student and amateur music lover. 436 musical passages. vii + 407 pp.
20334-4 Paperbound $2.25

JOHANN SEBASTIAN BACH, Philipp Spitta. One of the great classics of musicology, this definitive analysis of Bach's music (and life) has never been surpassed. Lucid, nontechnical analyses of hundreds of pieces (30 pages devoted to St. Matthew Passion, 26 to B Minor Mass). Also includes major analysis of 18th-century music. 450 musical examples. 40-page musical supplement. Total of xx + 1799pp.
(EUK) 22278-0, 22279-9 Two volumes, Clothbound $15.00

MOZART AND HIS PIANO CONCERTOS, Cuthbert Girdlestone. The only full-length study of an important area of Mozart's creativity. Provides detailed analyses of all 23 concertos, traces inspirational sources. 417 musical examples. Second edition. 509pp. (USO) 21271-8 Paperbound $3.50

THE PERFECT WAGNERITE: A COMMENTARY ON THE NIBLUNG'S RING, George Bernard Shaw. Brilliant and still relevant criticism in remarkable essays on Wagner's Ring cycle, Shaw's ideas on political and social ideology behind the plots, role of Leitmotifs, vocal requisites, etc. Prefaces. xxi + 136pp.
21707-8 Paperbound $1.50

DON GIOVANNI, W. A. Mozart. Complete libretto, modern English translation; biographies of composer and librettist; accounts of early performances and critical reaction. Lavishly illustrated. All the material you need to understand and appreciate this great work. Dover Opera Guide and Libretto Series; translated and introduced by Ellen Bleiler. 92 illustrations. 209pp.
21134-7 Paperbound $1.50

HIGH FIDELITY SYSTEMS: A LAYMAN'S GUIDE, Roy F. Allison. All the basic information you need for setting up your own audio system: high fidelity and stereo record players, tape records, F.M. Connections, adjusting tone arm, cartridge, checking needle alignment, positioning speakers, phasing speakers, adjusting hums, trouble-shooting, maintenance, and similar topics. Enlarged 1965 edition. More than 50 charts, diagrams, photos. iv + 91pp. 21514-8 Paperbound $1.25

REPRODUCTION OF SOUND, Edgar Villchur. Thorough coverage for laymen of high fidelity systems, reproducing systems in general, needles, amplifiers, preamps, loudspeakers, feedback, explaining physical background. "A rare talent for making technicalities vividly comprehensible," R. Darrell, *High Fidelity*. 69 figures. iv + 92pp. 21515-6 Paperbound $1.00

HEAR ME TALKIN' TO YA: THE STORY OF JAZZ AS TOLD BY THE MEN WHO MADE IT, Nat Shapiro and Nat Hentoff. Louis Armstrong, Fats Waller, Jo Jones, Clarence Williams, Billy Holiday, Duke Ellington, Jelly Roll Morton and dozens of other jazz greats tell how it was in Chicago's South Side, New Orleans, depression Harlem and the modern West Coast as jazz was born and grew. xvi + 429pp.
21726-4 Paperbound $2.50

FABLES OF AESOP, translated by Sir Roger L'Estrange. A reproduction of the very rare 1931 Paris edition; a selection of the most interesting fables, together with 50 imaginative drawings by Alexander Calder. v + 128pp. 6½x9¼.
21780-9 Paperbound $1.25

POEMS OF ANNE BRADSTREET, edited with an introduction by Robert Hutchinson. A new selection of poems by America's first poet and perhaps the first significant woman poet in the English language. 48 poems display her development in works of considerable variety—love poems, domestic poems, religious meditations, formal elegies, "quaternions," etc. Notes, bibliography. viii + 222pp.
22160-1 Paperbound $2.00

THREE GOTHIC NOVELS: THE CASTLE OF OTRANTO BY HORACE WALPOLE; VATHEK BY WILLIAM BECKFORD; THE VAMPYRE BY JOHN POLIDORI, WITH FRAGMENT OF A NOVEL BY LORD BYRON, edited by E. F. Bleiler. The first Gothic novel, by Walpole; the finest Oriental tale in English, by Beckford; powerful Romantic supernatural story in versions by Polidori and Byron. All extremely important in history of literature; all still exciting, packed with supernatural thrills, ghosts, haunted castles, magic, etc. xl + 291pp.
21232-7 Paperbound $2.00

THE BEST TALES OF HOFFMANN, E. T. A. Hoffmann. 10 of Hoffmann's most important stories, in modern re-editings of standard translations: Nutcracker and the King of Mice, Signor Formica, Automata, The Sandman, Rath Krespel, The Golden Flowerpot, Master Martin the Cooper, The Mines of Falun, The King's Betrothed, A New Year's Eve Adventure. 7 illustrations by Hoffmann. Edited by E. F. Bleiler. xxxix + 419pp.
21793-0 Paperbound $2.50

GHOST AND HORROR STORIES OF AMBROSE BIERCE, Ambrose Bierce. 23 strikingly modern stories of the horrors latent in the human mind: The Eyes of the Panther, The Damned Thing, An Occurrence at Owl Creek Bridge, An Inhabitant of Carcosa, etc., plus the dream-essay, Visions of the Night. Edited by E. F. Bleiler. xxii + 199pp.
20767-6 Paperbound $1.50

BEST GHOST STORIES OF J. S. LEFANU, J. Sheridan LeFanu. Finest stories by Victorian master often considered greatest supernatural writer of all. Carmilla, Green Tea, The Haunted Baronet, The Familiar, and 12 others. Most never before available in the U. S. A. Edited by E. F. Bleiler. 8 illustrations from Victorian publications. xvii + 467pp.
20415-4 Paperbound $2.50

THE TIME STREAM, THE GREATEST ADVENTURE, AND THE PURPLE SAPPHIRE—THREE SCIENCE FICTION NOVELS, John Taine (Eric Temple Bell). Great American mathematician was also foremost science fiction novelist of the 1920's. The Time Stream, one of all-time classics, uses concepts of circular time; The Greatest Adventure, incredibly ancient biological experiments from Antarctica threaten to escape; The Purple Sapphire, superscience, lost races in Central Tibet, survivors of the Great Race. 4 illustrations by Frank R. Paul. v + 532pp.
21180-0 Paperbound $3.00

SEVEN SCIENCE FICTION NOVELS, H. G. Wells. The standard collection of the great novels. Complete, unabridged. First Men in the Moon, Island of Dr. Moreau, War of the Worlds, Food of the Gods, Invisible Man, Time Machine, In the Days of the Comet. Not only science fiction fans, but every educated person owes it to himself to read these novels. 1015pp.
20264-X Clothbound $5.00

How to Know the Wild Flowers, Mrs. William Starr Dana. This is the classical book of American wildflowers (of the Eastern and Central United States), used by hundreds of thousands. Covers over 500 species, arranged in extremely easy to use color and season groups. Full descriptions, much plant lore. This Dover edition is the fullest ever compiled, with tables of nomenclature changes. 174 full-page plates by M. Satterlee. xii + 418pp. 20332-8 Paperbound $2.75

Our Plant Friends and Foes, William Atherton DuPuy. History, economic importance, essential botanical information and peculiarities of 25 common forms of plant life are provided in this book in an entertaining and charming style. Covers food plants (potatoes, apples, beans, wheat, almonds, bananas, etc.), flowers (lily, tulip, etc.), trees (pine, oak, elm, etc.), weeds, poisonous mushrooms and vines, gourds, citrus fruits, cotton, the cactus family, and much more. 108 illustrations. xiv + 290pp. 22272-1 Paperbound $2.50

How to Know the Ferns, Frances T. Parsons. Classic survey of Eastern and Central ferns, arranged according to clear, simple identification key. Excellent introduction to greatly neglected nature area. 57 illustrations and 42 plates. xvi + 215pp. 20740-4 Paperbound $1.75

Manual of the Trees of North America, Charles S. Sargent. America's foremost dendrologist provides the definitive coverage of North American trees and tree-like shrubs. 717 species fully described and illustrated: exact distribution, down to township; full botanical description; economic importance; description of subspecies and races; habitat, growth data; similar material. Necessary to every serious student of tree-life. Nomenclature revised to present. Over 100 locating keys. 783 illustrations. lii + 934pp. 20277-1, 20278-X Two volumes, Paperbound $6.00

Our Northern Shrubs, Harriet L. Keeler. Fine non-technical reference work identifying more than 225 important shrubs of Eastern and Central United States and Canada. Full text covering botanical description, habitat, plant lore, is paralleled with 205 full-page photographs of flowering or fruiting plants. Nomenclature revised by Edward G. Voss. One of few works concerned with shrubs. 205 plates, 35 drawings. xxviii + 521pp. 21989-5 Paperbound $3.75

The Mushroom Handbook, Louis C. C. Krieger. Still the best popular handbook: full descriptions of 259 species, cross references to another 200. Extremely thorough text enables you to identify, know all about any mushroom you are likely to meet in eastern and central U. S. A.: habitat, luminescence, poisonous qualities, use, folklore, etc. 32 color plates show over 50 mushrooms, also 126 other illustrations. Finding keys. vii + 560pp. 21861-9 Paperbound $3.95

Handbook of Birds of Eastern North America, Frank M. Chapman. Still much the best single-volume guide to the birds of Eastern and Central United States. Very full coverage of 675 species, with descriptions, life habits, distribution, similar data. All descriptions keyed to two-page color chart. With this single volume the average birdwatcher needs no other books. 1931 revised edition. 195 illustrations. xxxvi + 581pp. 21489-3 Paperbound $3.25

AMERICAN FOOD AND GAME FISHES, David S. Jordan and Barton W. Evermann. Definitive source of information, detailed and accurate enough to enable the sportsman and nature lover to identify conclusively some 1,000 species and sub-species of North American fish, sought for food or sport. Coverage of range, physiology, habits, life history, food value. Best methods of capture, interest to the angler, advice on bait, fly-fishing, etc. 338 drawings and photographs. 1 + 574pp. 6⅝ x 9⅜.
22383-1 Paperbound $4.50

THE FROG BOOK, Mary C. Dickerson. Complete with extensive finding keys, over 300 photographs, and an introduction to the general biology of frogs and toads, this is the classic non-technical study of Northeastern and Central species. 58 species; 290 photographs and 16 color plates. xvii + 253pp.
21973-9 Paperbound $4.00

THE MOTH BOOK: A GUIDE TO THE MOTHS OF NORTH AMERICA, William J. Holland. Classical study, eagerly sought after and used for the past 60 years. Clear identification manual to more than 2,000 different moths, largest manual in existence. General information about moths, capturing, mounting, classifying, etc., followed by species by species descriptions. 263 illustrations plus 48 color plates show almost every species, full size. 1968 edition, preface, nomenclature changes by A. E. Brower. xxiv + 479pp. of text. 6½ x 9¼.
21948-8 Paperbound $5.00

THE SEA-BEACH AT EBB-TIDE, Augusta Foote Arnold. Interested amateur can identify hundreds of marine plants and animals on coasts of North America; marine algae; seaweeds; squids; hermit crabs; horse shoe crabs; shrimps; corals; sea anemones; etc. Species descriptions cover: structure; food; reproductive cycle; size; shape; color; habitat; etc. Over 600 drawings. 85 plates. xii + 490pp.
21949-6 Paperbound $3.50

COMMON BIRD SONGS, Donald J. Borror. 33⅓ 12-inch record presents songs of 60 important birds of the eastern United States. A thorough, serious record which provides several examples for each bird, showing different types of song, individual variations, etc. Inestimable identification aid for birdwatcher. 32-page booklet gives text about birds and songs, with illustration for each bird.
21829-5 Record, book, album. Monaural. $2.75

FADS AND FALLACIES IN THE NAME OF SCIENCE, Martin Gardner. Fair, witty appraisal of cranks and quacks of science: Atlantis, Lemuria, hollow earth, flat earth, Velikovsky, orgone energy, Dianetics, flying saucers, Bridey Murphy, food fads, medical fads, perpetual motion, etc. Formerly "In the Name of Science." x + 363pp.
20394-8 Paperbound $2.00

HOAXES, Curtis D. MacDougall. Exhaustive, unbelievably rich account of great hoaxes: Locke's moon hoax, Shakespearean forgeries, sea serpents, Loch Ness monster, Cardiff giant, John Wilkes Booth's mummy, Disumbrationist school of art, dozens more; also journalism, psychology of hoaxing. 54 illustrations. xi + 338pp.
20465-0 Paperbound $2.75

CATALOGUE OF DOVER BOOKS

THE PRINCIPLES OF PSYCHOLOGY, William James. The famous long course, complete and unabridged. Stream of thought, time perception, memory, experimental methods—these are only some of the concerns of a work that was years ahead of its time and still valid, interesting, useful. 94 figures. Total of xviii + 1391pp.
20381-6, 20382-4 Two volumes, Paperbound $6.00

THE STRANGE STORY OF THE QUANTUM, Banesh Hoffmann. Non-mathematical but thorough explanation of work of Planck, Einstein, Bohr, Pauli, de Broglie, Schrödinger, Heisenberg, Dirac, Feynman, etc. No technical background needed. "Of books attempting such an account, this is the best," Henry Margenau, Yale. 40-page "Postscript 1959." xii + 285pp.   20518-5 Paperbound $2.00

THE RISE OF THE NEW PHYSICS, A. d'Abro. Most thorough explanation in print of central core of mathematical physics, both classical and modern; from Newton to Dirac and Heisenberg. Both history and exposition; philosophy of science, causality, explanations of higher mathematics, analytical mechanics, electromagnetism, thermodynamics, phase rule, special and general relativity, matrices. No higher mathematics needed to follow exposition, though treatment is elementary to intermediate in level. Recommended to serious student who wishes verbal understanding. 97 illustrations. xvii + 982pp.   20003-5, 20004-3 Two volumes, Paperbound $5.50

GREAT IDEAS OF OPERATIONS RESEARCH, Jagjit Singh. Easily followed non-technical explanation of mathematical tools, aims, results: statistics, linear programming, game theory, queueing theory, Monte Carlo simulation, etc. Uses only elementary mathematics. Many case studies, several analyzed in detail. Clarity, breadth make this excellent for specialist in another field who wishes background. 41 figures. x + 228pp.   21886-4 Paperbound $2.25

GREAT IDEAS OF MODERN MATHEMATICS: THEIR NATURE AND USE, Jagjit Singh. Internationally famous expositor, winner of Unesco's Kalinga Award for science popularization explains verbally such topics as differential equations, matrices, groups, sets, transformations, mathematical logic and other important modern mathematics, as well as use in physics, astrophysics, and similar fields. Superb exposition for layman, scientist in other areas. viii + 312pp.
20587-8 Paperbound $2.25

GREAT IDEAS IN INFORMATION THEORY, LANGUAGE AND CYBERNETICS, Jagjit Singh. The analog and digital computers, how they work, how they are like and unlike the human brain, the men who developed them, their future applications, computer terminology. An essential book for today, even for readers with little math. Some mathematical demonstrations included for more advanced readers. 118 figures. Tables. ix + 338pp.   21694-2 Paperbound $2.25

CHANCE, LUCK AND STATISTICS, Horace C. Levinson. Non-mathematical presentation of fundamentals of probability theory and science of statistics and their applications. Games of chance, betting odds, misuse of statistics, normal and skew distributions, birth rates, stock speculation, insurance. Enlarged edition. Formerly "The Science of Chance." xiii + 357pp.   21007-3 Paperbound $2.00

PLANETS, STARS AND GALAXIES: DESCRIPTIVE ASTRONOMY FOR BEGINNERS, A. E. Fanning. Comprehensive introductory survey of astronomy: the sun, solar system, stars, galaxies, universe, cosmology; up-to-date, including quasars, radio stars, etc. Preface by Prof. Donald Menzel. 24pp. of photographs. 189pp. 5¼ x 8¼.
21680-2 Paperbound $1.50

TEACH YOURSELF CALCULUS, P. Abbott. With a good background in algebra and trig, you can teach yourself calculus with this book. Simple, straightforward introduction to functions of all kinds, integration, differentiation, series, etc. "Students who are beginning to study calculus method will derive great help from this book." Faraday House Journal. 308pp.
20683-1 Clothbound $2.00

TEACH YOURSELF TRIGONOMETRY, P. Abbott. Geometrical foundations, indices and logarithms, ratios, angles, circular measure, etc. are presented in this sound, easy-to-use text. Excellent for the beginner or as a brush up, this text carries the student through the solution of triangles. 204pp.
20682-3 Clothbound $2.00

TEACH YOURSELF ANATOMY, David LeVay. Accurate, inclusive, profusely illustrated account of structure, skeleton, abdomen, muscles, nervous system, glands, brain, reproductive organs, evolution. "Quite the best and most readable account,' Medical Officer. 12 color plates. 164 figures. 311pp. 4¾ x 7.
21651-9 Clothbound $2.50

TEACH YOURSELF PHYSIOLOGY, David LeVay. Anatomical, biochemical bases; digestive, nervous, endocrine systems; metabolism; respiration; muscle; excretion; temperature control; reproduction. "Good elementary exposition," The Lancet. 6 color plates. 44 illustrations. 208pp. 4¼ x 7. 21658-6 Clothbound $2.50

THE FRIENDLY STARS, Martha Evans Martin. Classic has taught naked-eye observation of stars, planets to hundreds of thousands, still not surpassed for charm, lucidity, adequacy. Completely updated by Professor Donald H. Menzel, Harvard Observatory. 25 illustrations. 16 x 30 chart. x + 147pp. 21099-5 Paperbound $1.25

MUSIC OF THE SPHERES: THE MATERIAL UNIVERSE FROM ATOM TO QUASAR, SIMPLY EXPLAINED, Guy Murchie. Extremely broad, brilliantly written popular account begins with the solar system and reaches to dividing line between matter and nonmatter; latest understandings presented with exceptional clarity. Volume One: Planets, stars, galaxies, cosmology, geology, celestial mechanics, latest astronomical discoveries; Volume Two: Matter, atoms, waves, radiation, relativity, chemical action, heat, nuclear energy, quantum theory, music, light, color, probability, antimatter, antigravity, and similar topics. 319 figures. 1967 (second) edition. Total of xx + 644pp. 21809-0, 21810-4 Two volumes, Paperbound $5.00

OLD-TIME SCHOOLS AND SCHOOL BOOKS, Clifton Johnson. Illustrations and rhymes from early primers, abundant quotations from early textbooks, many anecdotes of school life enliven this study of elementary schools from Puritans to middle 19th century. Introduction by Carl Withers. 234 illustrations. xxxiii + 381pp.
21031-6 Paperbound $2.50

CATALOGUE OF DOVER BOOKS

THE PHILOSOPHY OF THE UPANISHADS, Paul Deussen. Clear, detailed statement of upanishadic system of thought, generally considered among best available. History of these works, full exposition of system emergent from them, parallel concepts in the West. Translated by A. S. Geden. xiv + 429pp.
21616-0 Paperbound $3.00

LANGUAGE, TRUTH AND LOGIC, Alfred J. Ayer. Famous, remarkably clear introduction to the Vienna and Cambridge schools of Logical Positivism; function of philosophy, elimination of metaphysical thought, nature of analysis, similar topics. "Wish I had written it myself," Bertrand Russell. 2nd, 1946 edition. 160pp.
20010-8 Paperbound $1.35

THE GUIDE FOR THE PERPLEXED, Moses Maimonides. Great classic of medieval Judaism, major attempt to reconcile revealed religion (Pentateuch, commentaries) and Aristotelian philosophy. Enormously important in all Western thought. Unabridged Friedländer translation. 50-page introduction. lix + 414pp.
(USO) 20351-4 Paperbound $2.50

OCCULT AND SUPERNATURAL PHENOMENA, D. H. Rawcliffe. Full, serious study of the most persistent delusions of mankind: crystal gazing, mediumistic trance, stigmata, lycanthropy, fire walking, dowsing, telepathy, ghosts, ESP, etc., and their relation to common forms of abnormal psychology. Formerly *Illusions and Delusions of the Supernatural and the Occult.* iii + 551pp.   20503-7 Paperbound $3.50

THE EGYPTIAN BOOK OF THE DEAD: THE PAPYRUS OF ANI, E. A. Wallis Budge. Full hieroglyphic text, interlinear transliteration of sounds, word for word translation, then smooth, connected translation; Theban recension. Basic work in Ancient Egyptian civilization; now even more significant than ever for historical importance, dilation of consciousness, etc. clvi + 377pp. 6½ x 9¼.
21866-X Paperbound $3.95

PSYCHOLOGY OF MUSIC, Carl E. Seashore. Basic, thorough survey of everything known about psychology of music up to 1940's; essential reading for psychologists, musicologists. Physical acoustics; auditory apparatus; relationship of physical sound to perceived sound; role of the mind in sorting, altering, suppressing, creating sound sensations; musical learning, testing for ability, absolute pitch, other topics. Records of Caruso, Menuhin analyzed. 88 figures. xix + 408pp.
21851-1 Paperbound $2.75

THE I CHING (THE BOOK OF CHANGES), translated by James Legge. Complete translated text plus appendices by Confucius, of perhaps the most penetrating divination book ever compiled. Indispensable to all study of early Oriental civilizations. 3 plates. xxiii + 448pp.   21062-6 Paperbound $3.00

THE UPANISHADS, translated by Max Müller. Twelve classical upanishads: Chandogya, Kena, Aitareya, Kaushitaki, Isa, Katha, Mundaka, Taittiriyaka, Brhadaranyaka, Svetasvatara, Prasna, Maitriyana. 160-page introduction, analysis by Prof. Müller. Total of 826pp.   20398-0, 20399-9 Two volumes, Paperbound $5.00

CATALOGUE OF DOVER BOOKS

JIM WHITEWOLF: THE LIFE OF A KIOWA APACHE INDIAN, Charles S. Brant, editor. Spans transition between native life and acculturation period, 1880 on. Kiowa culture, personal life pattern, religion and the supernatural, the Ghost Dance, breakdown in the White Man's world, similar material. 1 map. xii + 144pp.
22015-X Paperbound $1.75

THE NATIVE TRIBES OF CENTRAL AUSTRALIA, Baldwin Spencer and F. J. Gillen. Basic book in anthropology, devoted to full coverage of the Arunta and Warramunga tribes; the source for knowledge about kinship systems, material and social culture, religion, etc. Still unsurpassed. 121 photographs, 89 drawings. xviii + 669pp.
21775-2 Paperbound $5.00

MALAY MAGIC, Walter W. Skeat. Classic (1900) ; still the definitive work on the folklore and popular religion of the Malay peninsula. Describes marriage rites, birth spirits and ceremonies, medicine, dances, games, war and weapons, etc. Extensive quotes from original sources, many magic charms translated into English. 35 illustrations. Preface by Charles Otto Blagden. xxiv + 685pp.
21760-4 Paperbound $4.00

HEAVENS ON EARTH: UTOPIAN COMMUNITIES IN AMERICA, 1680-1880, Mark Holloway. The finest nontechnical account of American utopias, from the early Woman in the Wilderness, Ephrata, Rappites to the enormous mid 19th-century efflorescence; Shakers, New Harmony, Equity Stores, Fourier's Phalanxes, Oneida, Amana, Fruitlands, etc. "Entertaining and very instructive." *Times Literary Supplement*. 15 illustrations. 246pp.
21593-8 Paperbound $2.00

LONDON LABOUR AND THE LONDON POOR, Henry Mayhew. Earliest (c. 1850) sociological study in English, describing myriad subcultures of London poor. Particularly remarkable for the thousands of pages of direct testimony taken from the lips of London prostitutes, thieves, beggars, street sellers, chimney-sweepers, street-musicians, "mudlarks," "pure-finders," rag-gatherers, "running-patterers," dock laborers, cab-men, and hundreds of others, quoted directly in this massive work. An extraordinarily vital picture of London emerges. 110 illustrations. Total of lxxvi + 1951pp. 6⅝ x 10.
21934-8, 21935-6, 21936-4, 21937-2 Four volumes, Paperbound $14.00

HISTORY OF THE LATER ROMAN EMPIRE, J. B. Bury. Eloquent, detailed reconstruction of Western and Byzantine Roman Empire by a major historian, from the death of Theodosius I (395 A.D.) to the death of Justinian (565). Extensive quotations from contemporary sources; full coverage of important Roman and foreign figures of the time. xxxiv + 965pp. 21829-5 Record, book, album. Monaural. $3.50

AN INTELLECTUAL AND CULTURAL HISTORY OF THE WESTERN WORLD, Harry Elmer Barnes. Monumental study, tracing the development of the accomplishments that make up human culture. Every aspect of man's achievement surveyed from its origins in the Paleolithic to the present day (1964) ; social structures, ideas, economic systems, art, literature, technology, mathematics, the sciences, medicine, religion, jurisprudence, etc. Evaluations of the contributions of scores of great men. 1964 edition, revised and edited by scholars in the many fields represented. Total of xxix + 1381pp. 21275-0, 21276-9, 21277-7 Three volumes, Paperbound $7.75

ADVENTURES OF AN AFRICAN SLAVER, Theodore Canot. Edited by Brantz Mayer. A detailed portrayal of slavery and the slave trade, 1820-1840. Canot, an established trader along the African coast, describes the slave economy of the African kingdoms, the treatment of captured negroes, the extensive journeys in the interior to gather slaves, slave revolts and their suppression, harems, bribes, and much more. Full and unabridged republication of 1854 edition. Introduction by Malcom Cowley. 16 illustrations. xvii + 448pp. 22456-2 Paperbound $3.50

MY BONDAGE AND MY FREEDOM, Frederick Douglass. Born and brought up in slavery, Douglass witnessed its horrors and experienced its cruelties, but went on to become one of the most outspoken forces in the American anti-slavery movement. Considered the best of his autobiographies, this book graphically describes the in-human treatment of slaves, its effects on slave owners and slave families, and how Douglass's determination led him to a new life. Unaltered reprint of 1st (1855) edition. xxxii + 464pp. 22457-0 Paperbound $2.50

THE INDIANS' BOOK, recorded and edited by Natalie Curtis. Lore, music, narratives, dozens of drawings by Indians themselves from an authoritative and important survey of native culture among Plains, Southwestern, Lake and Pueblo Indians. Standard work in popular ethnomusicology. 149 songs in full notation. 23 drawings, 23 photos. xxxi + 584pp. 6⅝ x 9⅜. 21939-9 Paperbound $4.50

DICTIONARY OF AMERICAN PORTRAITS, edited by Hayward and Blanche Cirker. 4024 portraits of 4000 most important Americans, colonial days to 1905 (with a few important categories, like Presidents, to present). Pioneers, explorers, colonial figures, U. S. officials, politicians, writers, military and naval men, scientists, inventors, manufacturers, jurists, actors, historians, educators, notorious figures, Indian chiefs, etc. All authentic contemporary likenesses. The only work of its kind in existence; supplements all biographical sources for libraries. Indispensable to anyone working with American history. 8,000-item classified index, finding lists, other aids. xiv + 756pp. 9¼ x 12¾. 21823-6 Clothbound $30.00

TRITTON'S GUIDE TO BETTER WINE AND BEER MAKING FOR BEGINNERS, S. M. Tritton. All you need to know to make family-sized quantities of over 100 types of grape, fruit, herb and vegetable wines; as well as beers, mead, cider, etc. Complete recipes, advice as to equipment, procedures such as fermenting, bottling, and storing wines. Recipes given in British, U. S., and metric measures. Accompanying booklet lists sources in U. S. A. where ingredients may be bought, and additional information. 11 illustrations. 157pp. 5⅝ x 8⅛.
(USO) 22090-7 Clothbound $3.50

GARDENING WITH HERBS FOR FLAVOR AND FRAGRANCE, Helen M. Fox. How to grow herbs in your own garden, how to use them in your cooking (over 55 recipes included), legends and myths associated with each species, uses in medicine, perfumes, etc.—these are elements of one of the few books written especially for American herb fanciers. Guides you step-by-step from soil preparation to harvesting and storage for each type of herb. 12 drawings by Louise Mansfield. xiv + 334pp. 22540-2 Paperbound $2.50

INCIDENTS OF TRAVEL IN YUCATAN, John L. Stephens. Classic (1843) exploration of jungles of Yucatan, looking for evidences of Maya civilization. Stephens found many ruins; comments on travel adventures, Mexican and Indian culture. 127 striking illustrations by F. Catherwood. Total of 669 pp.
20926-1, 20927-X Two volumes, Paperbound $5.00

INCIDENTS OF TRAVEL IN CENTRAL AMERICA, CHIAPAS, AND YUCATAN, John L. Stephens. An exciting travel journal and an important classic of archeology. Narrative relates his almost single-handed discovery of the Mayan culture, and exploration of the ruined cities of Copan, Palenque, Utatlan and others; the monuments they dug from the earth, the temples buried in the jungle, the customs of poverty-stricken Indians living a stone's throw from the ruined palaces. 115 drawings by F. Catherwood. Portrait of Stephens. xii + 812pp.
22404-X, 22405-8 Two volumes, Paperbound $6.00

A NEW VOYAGE ROUND THE WORLD, William Dampier. Late 17-century naturalist joined the pirates of the Spanish Main to gather information; remarkably vivid account of buccaneers, pirates; detailed, accurate account of botany, zoology, ethnography of lands visited. Probably the most important early English voyage, enormous implications for British exploration, trade, colonial policy. Also most interesting reading. Argonaut edition, introduction by Sir Albert Gray. New introduction by Percy Adams. 6 plates, 7 illustrations. xlvii + 376pp. 6½ x 9¼.
21900-3 Paperbound $3.00

INTERNATIONAL AIRLINE PHRASE BOOK IN SIX LANGUAGES, Joseph W. Bátor. Important phrases and sentences in English paralleled with French, German, Portuguese, Italian, Spanish equivalents, covering all possible airport-travel situations; created for airline personnel as well as tourist by Language Chief, Pan American Airlines. xiv + 204pp.
22017-6 Paperbound $2.00

STAGE COACH AND TAVERN DAYS, Alice Morse Earle. Detailed, lively account of the early days of taverns; their uses and importance in the social, political and military life; furnishings and decorations; locations; food and drink; tavern signs, etc. Second half covers every aspect of early travel; the roads, coaches, drivers, etc. Nostalgic, charming, packed with fascinating material. 157 illustrations, mostly photographs. xiv + 449pp.
22518-6 Paperbound $4.00

NORSE DISCOVERIES AND EXPLORATIONS IN NORTH AMERICA, Hjalmar R. Holand. The perplexing Kensington Stone, found in Minnesota at the end of the 19th century. Is it a record of a Scandinavian expedition to North America in the 14th century? Or is it one of the most successful hoaxes in history. A scientific detective investigation. Formerly *Westward from Vinland*. 31 photographs, 17 figures. x + 354pp.
22014-1 Paperbound $2.75

A BOOK OF OLD MAPS, compiled and edited by Emerson D. Fite and Archibald Freeman. 74 old maps offer an unusual survey of the discovery, settlement and growth of America down to the close of the Revolutionary war: maps showing Norse settlements in Greenland, the explorations of Columbus, Verrazano, Cabot, Champlain, Joliet, Drake, Hudson, etc., campaigns of Revolutionary war battles, and much more. Each map is accompanied by a brief historical essay. xvi + 299pp. 11 x 13¾.
22084-2 Paperbound $6.00

CATALOGUE OF DOVER BOOKS

MATHEMATICAL PUZZLES FOR BEGINNERS AND ENTHUSIASTS, Geoffrey Mott-Smith. 189 puzzles from easy to difficult—involving arithmetic, logic, algebra, properties of digits, probability, etc.—for enjoyment and mental stimulus. Explanation of mathematical principles behind the puzzles. 135 illustrations. viii + 248pp.
20198-8 Paperbound $1.25

PAPER FOLDING FOR BEGINNERS, William D. Murray and Francis J. Rigney. Easiest book on the market, clearest instructions on making interesting, beautiful origami. Sail boats, cups, roosters, frogs that move legs, bonbon boxes, standing birds, etc. 40 projects; more than 275 diagrams and photographs. 94pp.
20713-7 Paperbound $1.00

TRICKS AND GAMES ON THE POOL TABLE, Fred Herrmann. 79 tricks and games—some solitaires, some for two or more players, some competitive games—to entertain you between formal games. Mystifying shots and throws, unusual caroms, tricks involving such props as cork, coins, a hat, etc. Formerly *Fun on the Pool Table*. 77 figures. 95pp.
21814-7 Paperbound $1.00

HAND SHADOWS TO BE THROWN UPON THE WALL: A SERIES OF NOVEL AND AMUSING FIGURES FORMED BY THE HAND, Henry Bursill. Delightful picturebook from great-grandfather's day shows how to make 18 different hand shadows: a bird that flies, duck that quacks, dog that wags his tail, camel, goose, deer, boy, turtle, etc. Only book of its sort. vi + 33pp. 6½ x 9¼. 21779-5 Paperbound $1.00

WHITTLING AND WOODCARVING, E. J. Tangerman. 18th printing of best book on market. "If you can cut a potato you can carve" toys and puzzles, chains, chessmen, caricatures, masks, frames, woodcut blocks, surface patterns, much more. Information on tools, woods, techniques. Also goes into serious wood sculpture from Middle Ages to present, East and West. 464 photos, figures. x + 293pp.
20965-2 Paperbound $2.00

HISTORY OF PHILOSOPHY, Julián Marias. Possibly the clearest, most easily followed, best planned, most useful one-volume history of philosophy on the market; neither skimpy n[...] system of every major philosopher and dozens of less im[...] thinkers from pre-Socratics up to Existentialism and later. Strong on many European figures usually om[...] Has gone through dozens of editions in Europe. 1966 edition, translated by Stan[...] Appelbaum and Clarence Strowbridge. xviii + 505pp. 217[...] Paperbound $3.00

YOGA: A SCIENTIFIC EVALUA[...] Kovoor T. Beha[...] [...]c but non-technical study of physiological results o[...] yoga exercises[...] done un[...] auspices of [...] Relations to Indian thought, to [...] analys[...] 16 ph[...] iii + [...]
20[...] Paperbo[...] $2.00

Prices subject t[...] without notice.
Available at you[...] write for free catalog[...]
Publications, Inc., 180 V[...]
150 book[...] each year on science, elementary[...]
music, art, literary history, social sciences and othe[...]